IFLA

International Federation of Library Associations and Institutions
Fédération Internationale des Associations de Bibliothécaires et des Bibliothèques
Internationaler Verband der bibliothekarischen Vereine und Institutionen
Международная Федерация Библиотечных Ассоциаций и Учреждений
Federación Internacional de Asociaciones de Bibliotecarios y Bibliotecas

About IFLA **www.ifla.org**

IFLA (The International Federation of Library Associations and Institutions) is the leading international body representing the interests of library and information services and their users. It is the global voice of the library and information profession.

IFLA provides information specialists throughout the world with a forum for exchanging ideas and promoting international cooperation, research, and development in all fields of library activity and information service. IFLA is one of the means through which libraries, information centres, and information professionals worldwide can formulate their goals, exert their influence as a group, protect their interests, and find solutions to global problems.

IFLA's aims, objectives, and professional programme can only be fulfilled with the cooperation and active involvement of its members and affiliates. Currently, over 1,700 associations, institutions and individuals, from widely divergent cultural backgrounds, are working together to further the goals of the Federation and to promote librarianship on a global level. Through its formal membership, IFLA directly or indirectly represents some 500,000 library and information professionals worldwide.

IFLA pursues its aims through a variety of channels, including the publication of a major journal, as well as guidelines, reports and monographs on a wide range of topics. IFLA organizes workshops and seminars around the world to enhance professional practice and increase awareness of the growing importance of libraries in the digital age. All this is done in collaboration with a number of other non-governmental organizations, funding bodies and international agencies such as UNESCO and WIPO. IFLANET, the Federation's website, is a prime source of information about IFLA, its policies and activities: www.ifla.org

Library and information professionals gather annually at the IFLA World Library and Information Congress, held in August each year in cities around the world.

IFLA was founded in Edinburgh, Scotland, in 1927 at an international conference of national library directors. IFLA was registered in the Netherlands in 1971. The Koninklijke Bibliotheek (Royal Library), the national library of the Netherlands, in The Hague, generously provides the facilities for our headquarters. Regional offices are located in Rio de Janeiro, Brazil; Dakar, Senegal; and Singapore.

IFLA Publications 124

Librarianship as a Bridge to an Information and Knowledge Society in Africa

Edited by

Alli Mcharazo and Sjoerd Koopman

K · G · Saur München 2007

IFLA Publications
edited by Sjoerd Koopman

Recommended catalogue entry:
Librarianship as a Bridge to an Information and Knowledge Society in Africa / edited by Alli Mcharazo and Sjoerd Koopman ; [International Federation of Library Associations and Institutions]. – München : K.G. Saur, 2007. – 248 p. : ill. ; 21 cm.
– (IFLA Publications ; 124).

ISBN 978-3-598-22031-9

Bibliographic information published by the Deutsche Nationalibliothek
The Deutsche Nationalbibliothek lists this publication in the Deutsche Nationalbibliografie; detailed bibliographic data is available in the Internet at http://dnb.d-nb.de.

∞

Printed on permanent paper
The paper used in this publication meets the minimum requirements of
American National Standard – Permanence of Paper
for Publications and Documents in Libraries and Archives
ANSI/NISO Z39.48-1992 (R1997)

Cover illustrations: PhotoCase.com / aboutpixel.de

Printed in the Federal Republic of Germany by Strauss GmbH, Mörlenbach

ISBN 978-3-598-22031-9
ISSN 0344-6891 (IFLA Publications)

Contents

Preface

Over the last three decades, library and information science professionals in the East, Central and Southern African region have been pre-occupied with the process of re-evaluating the new roles of libraries and information centres in addressing challenges in the continent. Specifically, they have debated modalities of making our libraries and information centres more Afro-centric, people centred institutions, geared towards stimulating the region's socio-economic and cultural development processes and national transformation. The recent XVII Standing Conference of Eastern, Central and Southern Africa Library and Information Associations (SCECSAL XVII) that took place in Dar es Salaam, Tanzania from 10 to 14 July 2006 has served as a useful platform for leading librarians and information science specialists from the sub-region and beyond to grapple with issues of the role of information and knowledge in social change. The volume of proceedings was distributed to all participants at the conference. This selection of papers chosen by an editorial committee is intended for wider audience.

This endeavour to influence social change and regional development through information sharing has encountered a series of challenges including inadequate communications infrastructures, lack of rural electrification, illiteracy, HIV/AIDS-pandemic, gaps in the government policy and regulatory framework, and above all, poverty which, often, derailed the process and efforts of making the people of the region have better access to information and knowledge to satisfy the need for human development and dignity.

The essays presented in this publication explore the complex dynamics of addressing these issues of information and development of the people in the region. They are insightful in that they take a cross disciplinary approach to the complex interaction between knowledge, information and development and how the three can together mould a new and more informed society. The papers are also exploratory and interpretative because they look into new challenges, which our libraries and information units in the region ought to address. At the forefront is the issue of making them people centered and Afro-centric. For many years, libraries have served the interest of the elite, and quite often totally ignored the plight of the rural and urban poor. This perception has to change. Libraries in the region should be more inclusive and serve the needs of all users in society.

Many of the authors who wrote these papers are however querying the readiness of our governments to help these key institutions to transform themselves into this new thinking. Will the governments afford the costs involved? Are the societies ready to cope with the changes? Will librarians and information specialists willingly change a mindset that favours serving the elite and powerful at the expense of the marginalized majority communities? How does the new global challenge of moving towards an information and knowledge society influence these concerns? No doubt not only this book but future discussions will pick upon these issues and shed more light on the paradox of information being the most valuable development resource, yet in our underdeveloped subregion we are unprepared to fully harness this new resource for human development.

These papers are provocative in that they raise questions on all these issues but sometimes the answers are yet to fully emerge. Many of these issues will be with us for a long time. Nevertheless we are glad to submit these papers written by highly trained and experienced professionals in the region and beyond to a wider audience. It is hoped that you will find them useful as they provide a glimpse of the state of information services in the sub region and their struggle to be part of an emerging information and knowledge society.

I would like to express my sincere gratitude to all those who contributed articles to this book, Tanzania Library Association for organizing SCECSAL XVII that invited useful papers and discussions on the topic and the International Federation of Library Associations and Institutions (IFLA) for agreeing to publish this book.

Asanteni sana kwa kazi nzuri! / Thank you very much for the good work.

Alli A.S. Mcharazo
Editor in Chief

Abbreviations and Acronyms

ABCs	Abstinence Faithfulness and Condoms
AFRO	WHO Regional Office for Africa
AGOA	African Growth and Opportunity Act
AGORA	Access to Global Online Research in Agriculture
AGRIS	Information System on Agriculture Sciences and Technology
AIDS	Acquired Immune Deficiency Syndrome
AIMS	Agriculture Information Management Standards
AISI	African Information Society Initiatives
AL	Artificial Intelligence
ALM	Africa Index Medicine
AMREF	African Medical and Research Foundation
APNET	African Publishers Network
AVLIN	African Virtual Library and Information Network
BIC	Business Information Center
BRIC	Brazil, Russia, India and Cuba
CBD	Conversion on Biological Diversity
CBO	Community Based Organization
CCIR	Cross-Cultural Information Retrieval
CD-ROM	Compact Disk Read Only Memory
CFKMP	Conceptual framework of Knowledge Management Process
CKO	Chief Knowledge Officer
CLIR	Cross Long Information Retrieval
COSTECH	Tanzania Commission for Science and Technology
DFD	Data Flow Diagram
DFID	Department for International Development
DG	Discussion Group
DRC	Democratic Republic of Congo
DRD	Department of Rural Development
DVD	Digital Video Disc
EAC	East African Community
EC	European Commission
ECM	Electronic Content Management
EDM	Electronic Document Management
EMR	Electronic Medical Records
ERM	Electronic Records Management
FAO	Food Agriculture Organization
FBO	Faith Based Organization
GDP	Gross Domestic Product
GFAR	Global Forum on Agriculture Resource

GNP	Gross National Product
HDI	Human development Index
HINARI	Health Inter-Network Access to Research Initiative
HIV	Human Immune Deficiency Virus
I&D	Information and Development
IAALD	International Association of Agricultural Information Specialists
IBM	International Business Machine Cooperation
ICA	International Council of Archive
ICESCR	International Covenant on Economic Social Cultural Rights
ICNBS	International Conference on National Bibliographic Service
ICT	Information Communication Technology
IDRC	International Development Research Centers
IEC	Information Education and Communication
IFLA	International Federation of Library Associations and Institutions
IK	Indigenous Knowledge
IKM	Information Knowledge Management Strategy
IKS	Information Knowledge System
ILO	International Labor Organization
IM	Information Management
IMARK	Information Management Resource Kit
IMF	International Monetary Fund
INASP	International Network for the Availability of Scientific Publications
IPR	Intellectual Property Right
IRMT	International Records Management Trust
ISAP	Index for South African Periodicals
ISI	Institute for Scientific Information
ISRM	International Standards on Records Management
IT	Information Technology
ITSA	Information Technology Standards Association
ITU	International Telecommunication Union
JWD	Journal Web Database
KEMRI	Kenya Medical research Institute
KIDMS	Kilifi Integrated data Management System
KM	Knowledge Management
KMTC	Kenya Medical Training College
KVL	Kilifi Virtual Library
LAN	Local Area Network
LIC's	Libraries and Information Centres
LIS	Library Information Science
MARECIK	Maasae Resource Center for Indigenous Knowledge
MCT	Multipurpose Community Telecentres

MDG	Millennium Development Goals
NARC	National Agricultural Research Center
NGO's	Non-Governmental Organization
OPAC	Online Public Access Catalogue
OSS	One Stop Shop
OVC	Orphans and Vulnerable Children
PALIAct	Progressive African Library and Information Activist
PDF	Portable Document Format
QLP	Quality Leaders Project
RM	Records Management
SABINET	South African Bibliographic Network
SADC	Southern African Development Commission
SCANUL ECS	Standing Conference of National University Libraries of Eastern, Central and Southern Africa
SCECSAL	Standing Conference of Eastern, Central and South African Librarians and Information Science
SCI	Science Citation Index
SES	Social Economic Status
SMME	Small Medium and Micro Enterprise
SSCI	Social Science Citation Index
SUA	Sokoine University of Agriculture
SWOT	Strength Weakness Opportunities and Threats
TAFORI	Tanzania Forest Research Institute
TB	Tuberculosis
TC's	Telecentres
TEEAL	The Essential electronic Agriculture Library
TLA	Tanzania Library Association
TM	Traditional Medicine
TPRI	Tropical Pesticide Research Institute
TRIPS	Trade Related Aspects of Intellectual Property Rights
TV	Television
UAC	Uganda Aids Commission
UDHR	Universal Declaration of Human Rights
UN	United Nations
UNCED	United Nations Conference Environment
UNDP	United Nations Development Programme
UNESCO	United Nations Educational Scientific and Cultural Organization
UNIDO	United Nations Industrial Development Organization
USA	United States of America
USAID	United States Agency for International Development

USAID	United States Agency for International Development
USDL	Uganda Science Digital Libraries
USIA	United States Information Agency
USSR	Union of Soviet Socialist Republic
VETA	Vocational Educational Training
WAICENT	World Agriculture Information Center
WCED	World Commission in Environment and Development
WHO	World Health Organization
WIPO	World Intellectual Property Organization
WKS	World Knowledge Society
WSF	World Social Forum
WSIS	World Information Summit on the Information Society
WSIS	World Summit on Information Society
WTO	World Trade Organization
WTRL	Welcome Trust Research Laboratory
WWII	World War II
ZCC	Zonal Communication Center

Authors' Contact Details

Kendra S. Albright
University of Sheffield, UK, k.albright@sheffield.ac.uk

Mohamed M. Aman
University of Wisconsin-Milwaukee, US, aman@sois.uwm.edu

Theo Bothma
University of Pretoria, South Africa, tbothma@postino.up.ac.za

Justin Chisenga
Food and Agriculture Organisation, Ghana, justin.chisenga@fao.org

Erica Cosijn
University of Pretoria, South Africa, ecosijn@postino.up.ac.za

Shiraz Durrani
City Metropolitan University, UK, shiraz.durrani@blueyonder.co.uk

Sara Harrity
Book Aid International, UK, sara.harrity@bookaid.org

Thore Hem
Knowledge Management, NORAD, Norway, tgh@norad.no

Judy Hoff
University of Tennessee, US, jhoff1@utk.edu

Kalervo Järvelin
University of Tampere, Finland, likaja@uta.fi

J. O. Kaduda
Kenya Medical Research Institute, Kenya, jkaduda@kilifi.mimcom.net

Dick Kawooya
University of Tennessee, U.S, dkawooya@utk.edu

Paul Kihwelo
Open University of Tanzania, Tanzania, paulkih@yahoo.com

Paul Manda
University of Dar es Salaam, Tanzania, pmanda@hotmail.com

Alli A.S. Mcharazo
Muhimbili University College of Health Sciences, Tanzania,
amcharazo@muchs.ac.tz

Kingo Mchombu
Department of Information and Communication, University of Namibia, Namibia, kmchombu@unam.na

Nathan Mnjama
Department of Library and Information Studies University of Botswana, Botswana, mnjamanm@mopipi.ub.bw

D.M. Mwazi
Kenya Medical Research Institute, Kenya

Nathan Ole Lengisugi
Maasae Resource Centre for Indigenous Knowledge, Tanzania, olelengisugi@yahoo.co.uk

C.H.O. Olola
Kenya Medical Research Institute, Kenya

T.O. Oluochi
Kenya Medical Research Institute, Kenya

Ari Pirkola
University of Tampere, Finland, pirkola@tukki.jyi.fi

Stephen Roberts
Thames Valley University, UK, strbrts@aol.com

HARNESSING KNOWLEDGE MANAGEMENT FOR AFRICA'S TRANSITION TO THE 21ST CENTURY

Kingo J. Mchombu

1 INTRODUCTION

The purpose of this paper is to analyse the factors which make knowledge management (KM) an important resource for accelerating the development of Africa as we move towards the 21st Century. As African information specialists we are faced with the urgent challenge of making our full contribution to ongoing efforts, in our respective countries, to end poverty and underdevelopment on our continent. The key objective of this paper is thus to answer the question: what are the methods that information and knowledge management can use to address poverty and underdevelopment in Africa? In addressing this topic, the paper raises the following sub-questions:

i) What are the basic concepts underlying the information and KM revolution?

ii) How best can Africa manage the transition process to an information and knowledge based economy?

iii) What role does KM play in national development?

iv) What challenges face information specialists in the knowledge revolution era?

In addition to this introduction, this paper has five other sections. The second section provides basic concepts and definitions of knowledge management. Section three explores the management of the transition process from an agricultural societies to an information and knowledge based society. Section four focuses on the role information and knowledge plays in human development. Section five continues the exploration by analysing specific sectors of national development, and section six looks at the challenges for information specialists in the knowledge revolution era.

2 CONCEPTUAL FRAMEWORK OF KM AND SHARING

2.1 The Knowledge Pyramid

This section starts with a discussion of the concepts of data, information and knowledge to establish their meanings in the context of knowledge as a strategic resource for economic development. Davenport and Prusak (1998) asserts that data is not information, and the latter is not knowledge. The conceptual relationship (data, information and knowledge) can be visualized as a pyramid of interdependent layers on top of each other, sometimes called the information pyramid (Marco, 2003). The bottom layer of the pyramid is data defined as symbols, facts and figures which are the raw materials to be processed to information. When data has been processed into a meaningful form it becomes information (Feather and Sturges, 2003). It has also been noted that knowledge is information which has been evaluated and organized in the human mind so that it can be used purposefully (Feather and Sturges, 2003).

Knowledge can be subdivided into two sub-categories – tacit and explicit knowledge. According to Nonaka (1998:28) explicit knowledge is formal and written, tacit knowledge is personal knowledge based on an individuals experience, insights and intuition. He asserts: "tacit knowledge consists partly of technical skills – the kind of informal, hard-to-pin-down skills captured in the term 'know how'. A master craftsman after years of experience develops a wealth of expertise at his fingertips but he is often unable to articulate the scientific or technical principles behind what he knows. It is recognized that such tacit knowledge has a cognitive dimension, made up of mental models, beliefs, and perspectives so ingrained that they are taken for granted and cannot be easily articulated. The popularization of the concept of tacit knowledge by Nonaka (1998) has profound implications on the production of knowledge in society as we shall attempt to show in a later section of this paper.

Embedded within tacit knowledge, is the concept of creativity (among others), which includes use of figurative language and symbolism to articulate and share insights and intuitions. Nonaka (1998) explains how creativity (and lateral thinking) has been used by Japanese companies to spur the creation of new products such as cars, electronic products, and others because it enables the sharing of complex insights among the workforce.

The recognition of the high value of experiential knowledge (tacit knowledge) has led to a new awareness about the need to reassess how human resources are managed in organizations, and the need to revisit the cultural content of knowledge. Joseph Stiglitz (1999) the renown former world Bank Chief Economist, has noted that the shift towards a knowledge based economy involves a shift in organization structures away from top-down hierarchical systems to horizontal structures such as networks, and semiautonomous teams, and other forms of matrix organizations. Stiglitz (1999) emphasizes the need for giving employees/citizens incentives to develop their own capacities, and confidence in using their own intelligence to empower change and learning activities. He makes a call for countries to shun external agencies which impose "best practices" imported from elsewhere because this only reinforces impotence. For countries to succeed in applying knowledge management to development, according to Stiglitz, they have to rely on their own internal understanding, wisdom and culture. As Stiglitz (1999) would have it, Africans are the best suited to change their own culture in order to transform the continent into a viable, knowledge based economy.

Relating libraries to KM, Vaagan (2004) claims that library and information sciences find it difficult to accommodate knowledge management because knowledge is more difficult to control/manage compared to information which can be treated as a measurable units onto which one may apply the classical skills of cataloguing, classification and indexing and bibliography. However it is my contention that libraries and information centres, can operate in both the domains of information management as well as knowledge management. Data management is more suited to computer centers. However it is important to recognize and plan for operating in the different domains, as they require different approaches, skills and roles.

2.2 Defining KM

There are many definitions of KM, each of which has a different context and aim in mind. For the purpose of this paper, however, knowledge management can be defined as:

> "... a disciplined approach to managing all the knowledge processes found in human collectives (a set of people with common goals). KM is what we do to accomplish our goals faster and more effectively by delivering the right knowledge to the right person at the right time and in the right context. By engineering human environments for optimal production, transfer, and usage of knowledge, we increase our ability to take effective action, compete, and survive. Knowledge management will ensure the survival of an organization by leveraging collective wisdom to increase responsiveness and innovation" (Drucker, 1993)

The same website describes KM as a cross disciplinary practice that enables organizations to improve the way they create, adopt, validate, diffuse, store and use knowledge in order to attain their goals faster and more effectively.

2.3 Branches of KM

It has been claimed that KM has a long history although it has only recently become a fashionable discipline (Davenport and Prusak 1998) and is both a science and an applied science and is multidisciplinary in nature. As a science KM asks questions on how individuals and human collectives work naturally with knowledge processes such as production, acquisition, transfer, and use of knowledge. On the other hand KM applied these studies to improve knowledge processes and their products by developing management techniques and tools for improving knowledge processes (Drucker, 1993)).

Several writers have also claimed that KM falls into two theoretical models. McAdam and McGreedy (1999) for example, have noted that one model focuses on theories that concentrate on the knowledge of people and knowledge construction. The second model involves theories that focus on information technology, which is more interested in the creation of databases for storing information, making information available, in general handling of explicit knowledge (Steyn, 2004)

Commenting on these two KM models, Kidwell et al (2000:30) notes that the early tendency was to focus on one type at the expense of the other which caused fierce debate between the experts advocating a techno-centric approach to KM and those advocating a learning-centric approach. It is concluded by these writers, however, that it is of little use to have robust technology solutions if the existing culture prevents knowledge sharing, and there is little benefit in having robust knowledge sharing without some technological means of making knowledge widely accessible.

However there is a much more comprehensive classification of knowledge management. KM can be classified into three branches: KM of organizations, KM of Science and KM of Society. Each of these branches addresses similar questions but has different problem domains, and often has different tools and techniques.

A comparison of the three branches shows that KM of Science is the oldest, over 100 years, and has the production of scientific knowledge as its main concern. It seeks to improve the management of knowledge within the scientific communities and laboratories. KM of Society is concerned with knowledge processes in society and culture. The concern of this branch of KM is with knowledge diffusion within society and cultures, for example how knowledge is transmitted in schools, and other groups in society. The youngest and fastest growing branch is KM of organizations. This branch is further divided into four sub branches: KM in Business, KM in Non-Profit Organizations, KM in Government, and KM in Educational Institutions. Of all these sub branches, KM of business is the most active as it seeks to improve a firm's competitiveness and profitability through knowledge application (Drucker, 1993).

There are overlaps in all these branches and many tools and techniques developed in one branch can be useful to other branches.

3 MAKING THE TRANSITION FROM AN AGRICULTURAL TO AN INFORMATION AND KNOWLEDGE ECONOMY

How a society transforms from an industrial economy to an information and knowledge society has not been clearly explained. The implied strategy is the increased use of computers in all spheres of society (Webster, 1996). The issue has been further complicated by the infusion of a heavy doze of ideology and contested terms such as globalisation, free flow of information, information superhighway, the information market place, deregulation, and privatization (Dick, 2002).

There has thus been a tendency to define an information society from an ICT perspective. This techno-centric approach to KM has received added force from some documents provided by the United Nations documents. The UN has set 2015 as a target date for attaining the Millennium Development Goals (MDG) of halving the number of people living in extreme poverty by building digital opportunities and putting ICT at the service of development. In his speech the Secretary General of the UN, Kofi Annan, urges African leaders to mould their economies to become active participants in the global economy by adopting ICT. He said "unless African countries become full actors in the global information revolution, the gap between the haves and have-nots will widen, opening the possibility of increased marginalization of the continent. On the other hand, participating in the information society offers tremendous opportunities for Africa to leapfrog … into the future" (Annan, 2001). Many other leaders in Africa, including Presidents Mbeki of South Africa, President Museveni of Uganda, former President Mkapa of Tanzania, and former President Nujoma of Namibia have spearheaded the expansion of ICT in their countries with the hope that this will accelerate development.

Vaagan (2004) and other social scientists have cautioned that "a country's high percentage of "online" inhabitants mean little when the sheer amount of information cannot be assimilated into knowledge". Vaagan calls this the "ICT trap" which highlights the danger of a one-sided ICT driven process where explicit or codified knowledge is made available through ICT but not optimally shared or used by others.

A case in point is when BP undertook to introduce its knowledge management programme; a decision was taken to put the programme under an independent group rather than the IT division because "it was believed that the program would be less likely to fall into familiar IT patterns if a group drawn from different parts of the company ran it. Also the intentional absence of IT control would make clear that the project was about communication, business change, and corporate behaviour, and not technology for its own sake." (Davenport and Prusak, 1998:20)

Several studies claim that the transition to an information society is a linear process, based on progression from an agrarian society to an industrial society and ultimately an information society. Several distinguished authors have pointed out that the information society represents an advanced form of industrial society but concede that information activities also played an important role in the industrial revolution process (Bell 1973, Drucker 1993). Supporting this viewpoint, is data from a study by Shifflet showing that although the majority of information workers are found in the tertiary sector, both the secondary and primary sectors also have relatively smaller numbers of information workers, with the primary sector having the smallest proportion of information workers (Shifflet, 2001).

The question which is still open to debate however is whether informatization of society represents a fundamental change in the pattern of society, specifically whether information has replaced industry as the major economic activity or whether it is an incremental process incorporating both new and old elements found in the earlier stage of development (Bell, 1973).

An African perspective to this debate concerns whether African countries can move from an agricultural economy to an information society without an established industrial base. A Ghanaian researcher on African information communication issues noted that:

> "A dream of transforming an agro-based economy into an information society must either be a flight of fancy or a thinking hardly informed by the industrial economic background of developed economies that are on transition to informational economies. For an economy with about half of its adult population engaged in food production sector, and about 70 per-

cent of its development budget sourced from donor support, any talk of transition into an information society sounds like a far-fetched dream." (Alhassan, 2004)

Arguing from a slightly different perspective, Kaariainen (2005) support the same view and argues that realism is called for in promoting information societies and ICTs. There is no leapfrogging into the information age as touted. Progress towards the information society is a gradual process and needs to be measured by social and intellectual development and not solely by technological advancement (Kaariainen, 2005)

The views of Alhassan, Kaariainen and others would seem to indicate the need for Africa to research carefully its own path towards the information and knowledge economy rather than simply copying what has happened in developed countries without much effort to look critically at alternative approaches. The conditions, culture and level of industrialization of developed countries differ from those of Africa and the outcomes from using technologies to achieve development might not bear the same results (Whyte, 2000, Menou and Mchombu 2004).

A compromise approach is to present the knowledge economy phenomenon as combining both the old and the new in one economy and the Internet being the platform for the economic fusion process, similar to Drucker's (1993) thinking. Proposing this view, Prime Minister Tony Blair (2000) noted that the knowledge economy and the old economy is really one economy. He asserts "there is no new economy, there is one economy, all of it being transformed by information technology … it is a profound economic revolution." He further notes that "in this new environment the most important commodities of a nation are information and knowledge."

This thesis would appear to suggest, among others, that libraries and information centers should work towards harnessing the power of the Internet for their communities, and train users in information/knowledge literacy and the use of ICT in order to facilitate the transformation of their nations. However it is to the broader issues of information and knowledge plays in development that the next section explores.

4 KNOWLEDGE FOR HUMAN DEVELOPMENT

This section looks at information and knowledge transfer as factors of production and ways African countries can use to address the deficit of development information in the continent.

4.1 Knowledge as a Factor of Production

It is now generally accepted that information and knowledge are a resource and commodity and key determinant in the progress of society. *The World Bank Development Report of 1998* subtitled Knowledge for Development points out that knowledge is needed to transform the resources we have into things we need, and to raise standards of living, improve health conditions, provide better education, and preserve the environment, and do all these in the most optimum way possible. All these value addition activities require knowledge. The report concludes that "for countries in the vanguard of the world economy, the balance between knowledge and resources has shifted. [and] … knowledge has become … the most important factor determining the standard of living – more than land, than tools than labour. Today's most technologically advanced economies are truly knowledge based" (World Bank 1998).

A critical dilemma for African (and other developing) countries is that the past 20 years have witnessed the most massive accumulation of explicit knowledge and information in human history. Digital information and communication technologies, and new ways of thinking on knowledge management, have revolutionized the ways in which knowledge and technical know how move around the world. According to Whyte (2000:4) among others, this proliferation of access to information has widened the gap between rich and poor countries. She gives the example of USA where it is claimed 75 percent of the population have access to the Internet, and Africa where the Internet penetration is below 1.2 per cent. This is a dilemma because amidst this world of plenty in terms of information and knowledge, the African local content is also very low, because of lack of capacity to produce, transfer, and disseminate information. It is concluded that African countries and their institutions such as universities, research centres, library and information centres, service organizations and private enterprises are at a major disadvantage in the current knowledge economy. She calls on countries to change how they think about training, organizational management, and interaction in order to take advantage of the soaring knowledge economy.

Despite of the examples cited above, the awareness of the central role knowledge plays in economic and social development is not new. One of the examples of this early awareness of the role of knowledge in human development, cited by Ramalingam, shows for example that former American President Truman had a clear focus on how the transfer and utilisation of knowledge could help in human development. President Truman noted in 1949 that:

> "... we must embark on a bold new program for making the benefits of our scientific advances and industrial progress available for the improvement and growth of underdeveloped areas. More than half the people of the world are living in conditions approaching misery. Their food is inadequate. They are victims of disease. Their economic life is primitive and stagnant. Their poverty is a handicap and a threat both to them and more prosperous areas. For the first time in history, humanity possesses the knowledge and the skill to relieve the suffering of these people ... The United States is pre-eminent among nations in the development of industrial and scientific techniques. The material resources which we can afford to use for the assistance of other peoples are limited. But our imponderable resources in technical knowledge are constantly growing and are inexhaustible. I believe that we should make available to peace-loving peoples the benefits of our store of technical knowledge in order to help them realize their aspirations for a better life ..." (Truman in Speech, 1949, cited by Ramalingam, 2005)

The transfer of knowledge for development has proven to be a more complex process than these early statements suggest. That is why transfer to knowledge is still regarded as a novel concept today. In the case of President Truman's address it was backed by the Marshall Plan for Western Europe for reconstruction after World War 2. It is said that the USA gave financial assistance and technical knowledge transfer worth 10 times what it gives for development aid today (Sachs 2005)

Preceding the World Bank Knowledge for Development report and its recommendations by some eight years, was a report from the Island state of Singapore titled *Library 2000: Investing in a Learning Nation* (Singapore Ministry of Information and the Arts 1994) noted that the future belongs to countries whose people makes the most productive use of information, knowledge and technology. Singapore had recognized that these were the key factors to economic success, not natural resources, which were very scarce.

In the information intensive society of today, knowledge production is taking place at a fast pace through out the world. Both knowledge and information are also becoming obsolete quicker – hence for African countries to compete internationally they need to have access to the latest knowledge and information similar to the countries African nations are competing with. Unfortunately many libraries are often known for their huge stock of out of date materials rather than the current information they possess. The reason for this situation might be lack of financial resources and lack of awareness of the critical and strategic importance of information and knowledge to a country's competitiveness and development.

4.2 Ways of Addressing the Knowledge Deficit in Africa

Addressing the knowledge deficit that separates them from technologically advanced countries is a crucial challenge for libraries and information centres. The World Bank (1998) report referred to above has proposed four steps to address the existing knowledge deficit. These steps are:

i) To acquire knowledge developed elsewhere rather than "reinvent the wheel" so as to save time and resources and adapt the imported knowledge to address information/knowledge deficits/gaps in a country

ii) Create knowledge locally through research and development (R & D) programmes. In fact the report proposes an investment of at least 1% of a country GDP in research and development activities. (South East Asian countries are investing at least 2–5% of their GDP in R & D. The creation of knowledge locally should include tapping into indigenous knowledge resources that the population has to assist in development activities.

iii) Build the capacity of the population to absorb and apply knowledge through universal basic education, adult literacy and life long learning, tertiary education and an emphasis on science and engineering education.

iv) Create a capacity to communicate knowledge throughout the country through the use of cheap telecommunications, mass media, and extension literature and services.

The World Bank's report is useful but its weakness is that it puts emphasis on explicit and external knowledge and largely ignores tacit knowledge.

We now turn attention to specific sectors of development which KM needs to address for African countries to accelerate their development towards the 21st Century.

5 KM AND THE KEY SECTORS OF NATIONAL DEVELOPMENT

Only if Knowledge Management can speedily be translated to action can we see social change on a large scale to ensure Africa claims her rightful place among other continents in the 21st Century. The six sectors which follow are vital areas to kick start the revival and reconstruction of respective countries in Africa. However, as already indicated elsewhere in this discussion, knowledge does not act alone, like a magic bullet, to bring about widespread and sustainable social change. There are other factors which must be in place for knowledge management to make an impact on national development, namely: i) a reasonably educated population to absorb and apply new knowledge ii) a financial system which can provide funding for the various social changes required iii) ICT (both old and new technologies) to be a vital tool to transfer and share information and knowledge iv) a policy framework which creates an enabling environment for sustainable social change.

In order to generate, transfer, share and apply information in an impact bearing manner, each one of the key sectors form an information and knowledge system (IKS) of its own. According to Solomon and Engels (1997) an IKS consists of a variety of different actors and stakeholders, including extension agents (or their equivalent), managers of various agencies, private and public sectors, research centres, education and training institutions, the NGOs and civil society, banks, and policy makers. In the tradition of knowledge management, all these actors possess both tacit and explicit knowledge which they manage, generate, transform, transmit, store, retrieve, integrate, and diffuse and use within the six sectors identified.

A big challenge for information specialists, in the area of explicit knowledge, to map out who the stakeholders of the respective sectors are, identify the existing information and knowledge resources and repositories, the gaps which exist in these repositories, knowledge sharing and communication capabilities, and recommend how the existing IKS can be strengthened and improved to support social change and the transformation of the respective sectors. Each one of the sectors below would benefit from such an approach.

5.1 Poverty Eradication and Wealth Generation

Poverty is a problem that requires deep reflection because poverty affects many people in Africa and most of the previous policies have not worked well. It is estimated that 45% of people in Sub-Saharan Africa live in extreme poverty while 30 percent live in moderate poverty thus making it an average of 75% of the population who are poor. Further recent data show that poverty has grown since the 1980s. The vision of MDG is to end extreme poverty by 2015 (UNDP website). There is a real possibility that by applying knowledge management, Africa could make a major impact on combating both extreme poverty and moderate poverty.

To reduce poverty one needs to address the causes of poverty, hence success of KM would be measured in terms of how it impacts on reducing the causes of poverty. The key causes of poverty are (Sachs 2005; Mkandawire and Saludo, 1999):

i) Low savings and capital formation. KM should provide ideas on alternative ways of generating savings from poor communities.

ii) Low growth in trade for example through agricultural surplus sales to nearby markets to generate more income. KM would have the goal of creating higher production and the introduction of high value crops to replace low value crops.

iii) Capacity building through literacy, improved education for children including girls. KM intervention would include information support for education and takes measure to increase flow of technological know how in the community. KM would have the goal of addressing all the human capital issues required in capacity building, literacy acquisition and improved education for all.

iv) Poor health caused by infectious diseases such as HIV/AIDS, malaria, TB and malnutrition. This calls for KM interventions directed towards behavior change. This is important to prevent such diseases from decimating the most productive members of the community and thus increasing poverty by creating child headed households and many orphans.

v) Lack of innovation which may become common because of poverty restricting the flow of innovations from outside and within the community thus robbing the community new ideas to increase production, start small business and commercialize their agriculture to a higher level of production. KM should provide support and diffusion of innovations and transfer of technologies from both outside and better sharing of technology and innovations within the community.

vi) Population explosion because the poor select to have many children as a form of old age insurance. Such children will not get good education and will in turn want to have many children, ultimately use of resources, overcrowding in cities, etc. Thus high population leads to deeper poverty and deeper poverty leads to high population and social conflict. The KM intervention would have the goal of family planning and cultural attitude change in favour of smaller families and women's position in society.

The importance of knowledge to development has already been raised by the World Bank (1998), UNDP (2003), international NGOs (Ramalingam, 2004) and various other agencies. In the context of urban and rural poverty, we can look at information and knowledge as two distinct components which dovetail into each other. Information refers to the poverty reduction ideas which are disseminated by agencies, the mass media, posters, video, interpersonal sources, and social networks. Knowledge is the information coming from different sources which has been consolidated, processed and internalized by individuals, a community or society in the context of what they know already, and can either add it to their knowledge base or reject it. Thus knowledge is filtered and contextualized information which can be used to take action against poverty.

Poverty reduction in Africa has been very disappointing – in spite of the continuing development of new programmes targeted at the poor, such as Poverty Reduction Strategies (PRSP) of the World Bank, Human Development Index (HDI) of the United Nations Development Programme (UNDP), The Millennium Development Goals (MDG) of the United Nations. Part of the failure of these development programmes comes from a KM failure of the knowledge support structures for the urban and rural poor.

The link of KM to poverty eradication is very weak because of a number of reasons: the first one is the focus on information transfer activities without monitoring and evaluating how effective the information disseminated has been. In most cases the information needs of the urban and rural poor are seldom taken into account when they are supplied with information to solve their problem of poverty. The assumption being that because they know very little they are poor, thus the information and knowledge system of the urban and rural poor is totally ignored when supplying them with external information. Indeed often their very way of life and culture are held responsible for the lack of development. We also have very few information centres which are dedicated to poverty eradication either as part of larger information systems, or stand alone information agencies.

5.2 KM and Diffusion of Innovations and Technologies

Diffusion of innovations can be defined as a process by which a new idea is communicated through certain channels over time among the members of a social system (Rogers, 1995). Both Rogers and other innovation researchers have pointed out that although the new idea (technical knowledge) is a central matter, social change is brought about as a result of a collective capacity to learn, involving a large number of semi-autonomous actors – individuals, groups, and institutions. Innovativeness can therefore be seen as a social competence based on social interaction among many stakeholders, rather than individual ability (Salomon and Engel, 1997). Innovativeness is the key driver of economic growth and productivity of any economy and at the centre of transition to an information and knowledge society. "Without innovation there is no forward movement which means lagging behind, since standing still is neither possible nor an option in a time bound universe, that is in constant motion" (Kaariainen, 2005)

A national innovation system needs several things to be in place: an educated population, a functioning financial system and a culture of innovation (Kaariainen, 2005). One should add to this list an information and knowledge system to support the process of innovation and knowledge production. Partly out of this realization, most advanced countries invest between 2 and 4 percent of the GDP into the research and development process (Sachs 2005) Governments should invest heavily into both the early stages of research and the later stages of development (Sachs 2005) It has been noted that the research needs of the Third World countries are not likely to be on top of the research agenda of developed countries thus they need to prioritise their own research and technology needs and devote resources towards meeting developing new knowledge in these areas. Priority needs for research have been identified in the following areas: (Sachs, 2005; Brouwers and Khoapa, 2005)

i) Health – new preventive and diagnostic measures for diseases specific to tropical countries including TB, HIV/AIDS, and malaria and other tropical diseases.

ii) Tropical agriculture – new seed varieties (green revolution model), water management techniques, and soil management techniques.

iii) Energy systems – special technologies for off grid power, renewable energy sources (for example solar energy, wind energy), improved batteries, and low watt illumination.

iv) Climatic changes research – researching and coping with climatic changes, forecasting and seasonal variations, with a view to more accurate predictions and adjustments.

v) Water conservation – improved technologies for water harvesting, desalination, small scale irrigation, and improved management of underground water resources. The importance of water management will increase because of increasing population and climatic changes.

vi) Sustainable management of ecosystems: fragile ecosystems around the world (coral reefs, mangrove swamps, fisheries, rain forests, river sources, desertification, biodiversity etc) are being destroyed with dire consequences. Poor communities do not have the technical capacity to monitor changes or to respond in an effective and sustainable manner.

vii) New approaches to socio economic development and the quality of life.

viii) Poverty alleviation – an assessment of effectiveness of various strategies to address poverty, and participation of various groups in society in poverty eradication programmes.

ix) Health and behaviour change – monitoring of factors which support behaviour change in relation to health and development issues in society.

x) Education, knowledge management and development – improvement of education in relation to development, evaluating and strengthening education systems, knowledge management, and innovative strategies to create employment.

However most developing countries find it difficult to invest in research and development , at times this means many of their scientists migrate to follow the better opportunities abroad (Sachs, 2005). At present poor countries have 37 per cent of the world's population and 11 percent of the world's GDP but contribute less than 1 percent of the US registered patents taken out by inventors in 2000. The top 20 countries accounted for 98 per cent of all the patents. This has created the innovation gap which allows the rich countries to move forward to more innovation, while the poor cannot get a foothold on the innovation ladder (World Bank, 1998, Sachs, 2005).

Even when countries are not inventors of technology, they can benefit through importation of technology and its diffusion through better knowledge sharing strategies within the country (World Bank 1998). Importation of innovations through: consumer goods, capital imports, FDI, textbooks, reverse engineering, conferences, and of course theft. However if a country is too poor such purchases may be difficult if not impossible. South Asia development was kick started by success in attracting foreign investment of high technology enterprises who served to introduce innovations into the region.

There are other forms of knowledge and innovation transfer which are mainly concerned with organization matters to allow society to better confront problems it faces. Examples of knowledge transfer which fall into this category include: Setting up NGOs which drive the development process forward modeled on those found in other countries which have worked very well e.g. Bangladesh Rural Advancement Committee (BRAC) an NGO which has done wonders in that country to uplift the state of the urban and rural poor. Bangladesh also offers another interesting innovation which could be adapted in Africa in the form of a micro-finance system for the poor in the form of the Grameen Bank, which has successfully addressed the capital formation for the rural and urban poor so that they can start small scale commercial activities and other micro businesses. The system works by lending a group rather than individuals so that repayment is the responsibility of the group. The Grameen Telecom program is another interesting innovation where a woman or man borrows to buy a cell phone which is used by the whole village and charges a small amount to customers. The Grameen Telecom program has been able to build a customer base of over a million in Rural Bangladesh and introduced good communication to the rural poor. There are many more innovations such as these described here – they need to be written in the local language so that individuals and communities can have access to such information to start similar innovations in their own communities to bring about development.

One aspect of innovation which is not always visible is creativity in society. Creativity based on opportunities provided by knowledge management and technology and new ways of thinking pave the way for an information and knowledge based society (Nonaka, 1998). Kaariainen (2005) maintains that the creation of a creative information and knowledge economy requires:

> "The creative economy needs investment in education and training. The means, that the quality of basic education must be improved and creative learning environments must be developed at all levels of education and training. In an information society, learning continues through out life,

> schools should, therefore, not only distribute information but build self-confidence and social skills, and help students to identify their talents and creative passions. The challenge of life long learning in the information society is that people must learn to learn (and unlearn). More attention needs to be paid to matters related to entrepreneurship at all levels of education."

Building inclusive societies should be the aim of an innovation system which has roots in different parts of the country. One of the agenda of the recent World Information Society conference was the digital divide, thus it would be terribly hypocritical if developing countries were to move towards an information society at the same time perpetuating digital divides within the borders of their own states. What is required are explicit policies which include equal access to knowledge and technologies for the whole nation so that the whole population and different parts of the population are part of the transition to a knowledge driven economy.

One source of innovation should be the cultural identity of people and their indigenous knowledge (tacit knowledge). The experience of Finland shows that a strong national cultural identity provides a platform to build technological capacity and develop social experimentation. She concludes that "national and cultural identities are important sources of meaning and value, but only on condition that people and countries are engaged in multicultural dialogue" (Kaariainen, 2005).

5.3 Knowledge and the Education Sector

KM is quite important to the education sector partly because there are several points of intersection between the two. The strengthening of knowledge management and sharing is dependent on learning at organization and national levels in order to meet the goals of the institutions or the nation. As noted in this website:

> "knowledge and learning also embodies a value system – an orientation of undertaking work that carries a democratic principle that all humans should be valued on their own terms, as should the knowledge they carry and they all should be given the opportunity to realize their potential as individual and as a member of a team or organization (KIT Website, 2004)

When reviewing knowledge management in the context of education, we can categorise the education sector in terms of two levels i.e. the formal education sector, and the non formal/life long learning education sector. The formal education sector operates at both lower and higher levels. Primary and secondary school, for example, requires access to adequate information resources (school libraries, teacher resource centres, and public libraries) for both the pupils and their teachers. Adequate access to information resources help to ensure that learning is done in a way that is not dominated by rote learning but offers opportunities for genuine independent and creative learning. To be able to cope with the demands of a knowledge society countries need to reform education curriculums, so that there is a balance between science and technological studies and the social and human sciences studies. These two branches of education should be given equal importance on a 50–50% basis. Such an education system ensures that lopsided systems of education are avoided, and there will be enough technicians and engineers in future. Access to ICT and the Internet can ensure that knowledge sharing takes place between teachers, pupils and education authorities irregardless of where they are, or time of day or night. Dedicated websites can be created which provide content mirroring the curriculum, examples of exercises, syllabi, and text book summaries. Given the digital divide, poorly supported school and public libraries, there is still a lot that needs to be done to make education interesting and exciting for the population of pupils, teachers, life long learners and education administrators.

The problems that affect education at the lower levels are also found in the higher education sector of most African countries. There is a need for educational innovations which are now being practiced in the fast developing countries of East Asia and other continents if Africa is not to be left behind.

As shown in the preceding discussions, countries look towards advancements in technology and science as the source of a breakthrough towards a knowledge economy and in most cases look towards their universities to produce new knowledge through research and development as well as consultancy projects sponsored through both public and private funding (Ryu, 1998). Apart from research and consultancy, universities are also active in teaching and curriculum delivery, as well as community service. Access to knowledge is vital for researchers and consultants in academic institutions to avoid "rediscovering the wheel" which happens when one has no access to the latest knowledge in their specialization.

In the context of knowledge management, some of the issues found in lower levels of education are also present in the higher education sector. Hsiao (2005) writing about Chinese higher education sector noted that it urgently required new teaching methods and reforms to overhaul the curriculum, to replace rote learning, and give students more responsibility for their own education. She calls for a system of education that allows students to put together their courses across the university to reflect their career aspirations rather than a rigid system where everything is prescribed for the student. She argues the focus of education must be creative and inquisitive based to replace rote learning. Rote learning leads to students cramming only to spit the information back on tests and exams. According to her this is the only way to move learning to life long learning mode and to make students learn to make critical decisions and open up to change.

Similar calls have come from India, for example, Josh and Murthy (2004) have called for a qualitative expansion of education and an end to the one way delivery of knowledge to make it more participatory and reciprocal. Both Josh and Murthy (2004) believe that education must consist of "exploratory processes that allow the learner to make full use of his or her own multiple cognitive maps. The students mutually construct their learning environments, which grow in the learning process"

While we can debate the relevance of the type of education advocated by the two authors there are few who will not agree that rote learning, and learning for the short term goal of passing examinations should be reviewed to include more life long and creative learning strategies. Similar problems face our education systems at both lower and higher levels. The role of knowledge management is vital for such education to succeed where the students have a responsibility to learn how to learn rather than cramming a set of facts. Equally important is the role of knowledge transfer for education to flourish so as to create the knowledge base required for countries to improve on the education process. Although there are strong academic libraries in the sub region, we have to be concerned that the state of school libraries and resource centres, and public libraries are not very strong in the delivery of educational information to the education sector and this is a vital building block for improving the education sectors performance ands life long learning

5.4 Knowledge for Improvement of the Agricultural Sector

Agriculture plays an important role in development of most African countries. In a country such as Tanzania, for example, according to recent report by the country's Prime Minister, the Government has set out to improve the agriculture sector because "the sector contributes between 45 and 50 per cent to the national gross domestic product (GDP). Tanzania has 94 million hectares of arable land, 44 million hectares of which are good for farming and 50 million hectares suitable for livestock rearing. However, only 10 million hectares are under cultivation. He was concerned; however, that even the 10 million hectares are not exploited fully (Lowassa, Daily News, 2006). The significance of the agriculture sector to development increases further because it also provides a livelihood to between 70 and 80 percent of the population of most African countries.

One Key weakness of the agriculture sector is the poor transfer of knowledge to farmers (and other stakeholders) by research and innovation centres. It is estimated for example that the productivity in agriculture in most of Africa, is 10 times higher for crop production in experimental research centres than the productivity of farmers just outside the gates of the centres. The problem is that the new knowledge being developed is inefficiently delivered because, often, the research centres act as silos for hoarding knowledge rather than sharing their agricultural knowledge with farmers. Mlaki (2005) states that because of the knowledge gap in Tanzania, is shown by high production of 8 tons of maize per hector in a research environment, while a peasant farmer produces only 2 tons of maize per hector. It is clear therefore that to turn around the productivity of the agriculture sector in a way that several African countries are planning to do, requires several KM strategies:

i) Transfer massive innovative knowledge to farmers using the Green Revolution model which was successfully adopted by Mexico and Asian countries e.g. India, Philippines, and China to promote high yield staple crop varieties. Such a strategy would ensure that the high yield varieties which grow faster, with the application of fertilizer and irrigation, if need be, can increase the income of farmers to 10 times the present level. The Green revolution provided Asian countries their first break through in economic development and Africa should adapt the same model (World Bank 1998). This strategy would require more funding of agricultural research to adapt knowledge from Asian countries, and a complete overhaul of the information and knowledge sharing system and strategies between farmers, research centres, infomediaries and other supporting institutions in a country to ensure better return to investments made in research and development.

ii) A useful suggestion made on knowledge management application to the agricultural sector is to use knowledge to process agricultural products rather than selling them in a raw or semi raw state. UNIDO has concluded that most developing countries do not pay sufficient attention to the value chain through which agricultural commodities and products reach the final consumers. This neglect leads to enormous losses of value through value added and employment opportunities. It is noted that 98 per cent of agricultural production in developed countries undergoes industrial processing, but barely 30 per cent is processed in developing countries (UNIDO, 2004). This is thus another area where the massive transfer of knowledge and technologies to develop an agro-industrial base would lead to employment creation and higher earning though the sale of processed agricultural products rather than the sale of raw materials to overseas and regional markets.

5.5 Knowledge Management in Small, Medium and Micro-Enterprises (SMMEs)

SMMEs are essential actors in the development process because they play a leading role in job creation, income generation, and value addition through processing local products in the agricultural and natural resources sector. UNIDO (2004) concludes that SMMEs provide a seedbed for developing and testing entrepreneurial talent. The later being an important cultural foundation for risk taking, technological and managerial innovations, and the adaptation and diffusion of available technologies. As with other sectors of development, knowledge is an important source of both competitive advantage and survival in SMMEs.

The importance of SMMEs in bringing about equitable development among different regions of country as each Local Government Authority can be charged with the responsibility to promote SMMEs development through the following actions:

i) Provision of information and direct assistance.

ii) Bringing local small business together for meetings to discuss the legal and regulatory environment.

iii) Acting as a catalyst and facilitator in identifying specific reform proposals and opportunities.

iv) Advocating for local entrepreneurs on specific reform proposals.

v) Improving reporting and other regulatory procedures that fall under the control of the Local Authority.

vi) Developing a local database on small business activity in the area.

vii) Introducing specific policies and regulations that promote local small businesses (e.g. local purchasing policies) (White 1997:7)

Many of these Regional and Local Authority responsibilities have a clear information and knowledge dimension to them.

Possibly because of the low levels of education among SMMEs operators, the use of information and knowledge as an economic resource is still at a low level in most African countries (Mchombu 2001). Thomas (1995) has elaborated on the need for information and knowledge among the existing SMMEs in Namibia by stating that:

> "The lack of knowledge by SMMEs about market opportunities, prices, quality needs, market trends, the nature of competition etc is at the root of much of what goes through as "lack of market access". One way to address this problem is to improve the dissemination of such information. This can happen through private sector sources, like better newspaper coverage of these issues, a wider network of marketing consultants, stronger emphasis on marketing related topics in training courses aimed as SMMEs, and … other ways"

Looking at the same issue information and knowledge needs for SMMEs from a different perspective, Levy et al (2003) have analysed the skills required by the SMMEs to be able to manage knowledge and information to gain success and become sustainable in a competitive and globalised world. According to the above mentioned authors, SMMEs are unable to obtain sustainable competitive advantage from knowledge and innovation and they need the following skills in knowledge management: i) they need to have skills in the use of both tacit and explicit knowledge for the purposes of day to day operations so they can invest in an information system rather than simply regard it as a cost ii) how to gather and use customer information for strategic purposes iii) use of information for efficiency and financial control iv) use of information to improve and coordinate on customer care v) to know how to use information to collaborate and exchange information with customers through use of systems such as email, postal mail marketing etc. vi) use of knowledge to manage business growth and identify new opportunities for the SMMEs thus to reposition the business into new areas of operation. Levy et al (2003) concludes that most of the skills that SMMEs have are in the area of using information and knowledge to achieve efficiency through basic record keeping but there are few internal databases to get information needed for their business strategies.

UNIDO (2004) diagnosis indicates that successful SMMEs are those which can apply new knowledge and innovation to improve productivity and facilitate market access. In most developing countries the sector suffers from failures in the provision of business information, which is often provided by stand alone institutions, and is difficult to access, limited in scope, and not provided in an integrated manner. SMMEs according to UNIDO, need tailor made information solutions, i.e. business information services that assess, verify and apply information to a specific business problem.

The recommendation of UNIDO (2004) and White (1997) and others is to set up business information services programme which bring together information from different sources and transform them into solutions including ICT, and e-business support, in integrated networks that link all relevant national and international sources into a "One Stop Shop (OSS)".

The experience of Asian countries, however, shows that success in SMMEs for the internal market is just the first step to creating SMMEs which can compete globally. Thus from the cheap assembly shop shoes, textiles, and lower end electronic products, countries such China and India have moved on towards higher end production in SMMEs based on the central role of knowledge based economies: (Hsiao 2005)

> "Now, it is laying the groundwork to become a global power in much more sophisticated, technology-intensive industries that also demand tons of capital. Billions of dollars are flowing into auto, steel, chemical, and high-tech electronics plants. Driving this massive spending push is voracious domestic demand for all manner of goods as well as a big shift by multinationals to manufacture in China. As a result, China is rapidly becoming more self-sufficient in key materials and components, and setting the stage to be a major exporter of high-end products"

These two countries have used other international programmes such as AGOA (the) ACP-EU programmes for developing countries strategically to take off in business development. These two programmes and others like them have produced vast information which needs to be packaged in a simple and integrated manner for the SMMEs to exploit fully.

Given the theme of our meeting, it is possible for public libraries and specialized information centres to work closely with local authorities and chambers of commerce to provide SMMEs information and knowledge support in the respective areas, and network closely with both the relevant Government Ministries and International Organizations to achieve this goal. This new business information services to cater for SMMEs would also include providing tourism information in the local authority area as well as district development information services based on the central government development plans of different ministries. Such a documentation centre at the district level would go some way to address the information gap at district level one finds in most African countries.

5.6 KM in the Health Sector

KM is as vital to the health sector as it is to other development sectors. Health care information and knowledge is needed to deliver the safest and most effective healthcare possible with available resources (Pakenham-Walsh, 2000). It has been pointed out by Powell (2003) that by applying knowledge management, a country can achieve the following goals: i) efficiency – which refers to helping people to quickly find the information they need, thus saving time and avoiding duplicating the efforts of others ii)effectiveness – refers to making people aware of lessons learned from research and experience and enabling them to adapt "best practices" iii) creativity – refers to exposing people to new ideas and approaches iv) empowerment – refers to giving workers and individuals at different levels knowledge and confidence to make well informed decisions on health issues.

When reviewing knowledge management in the context of the health sector we can categorise the sector into two broad target groups i.e. health workers (doctors, researchers, other medical staff, and health managers). Second category is members of the public who have to take responsibility for their health by preventing the spread of infectious and preventable diseases or following closely advice from health personnel.

After reviewing the health information situation in developing countries, Pakenham-Walsh (2000) conclude that health care workers have little or no access to practical information. She noted that access to health information support the generation of new knowledge and solutions based on the realities of the country, and help in the critical interpretation to new information accessed through ICTs and health information resource centres. Godlee et al (2004) argue that a knowledge based approach to health care among health workers is hampered by several factors: i) the poor state of ICT infrastructure to access the latest health information in most countries ii) lack of awareness of what information is available iii) lack of relevance of available information (in terms of scope, style, language, and format) iv) lack of time and incentives to use information v) lack of interpretation skills. One could add lack of a knowledge sharing culture among health workers as an important problem preventing a knowledge based approach to health care.

There have been several on going initiatives to address access to health information. The WHO has initiated the HINARI literature service, setting up of electronic and virtual libraries (http://www.bvsalud.org), publishing and distribution of health newsletters (http://www.healthlink.org.uk), and setting up of small scale health libraries, for example, WHOs Blue Trunk Library, for district hospitals and other frontline health workers. The Blue Trunk Library provides selected essential health information materials. Despite these initiatives, there is still a lot that needs to be done to ensure the knowledge based approach to health care in most of Africa.

Turning now to members of the public, health information is equally important to bring about sustainable behaviour change in preventable and infectious diseases. The outbreak of HIV/AIDS has highlighted the fact that members of the public need to also to have access to adequate information to change behaviour which is the best way to prevent the spread of HIV/AIDS which still has no cure. In the fight against HIV/AIDS, knowledge communication is required for improving the knowledge of sexually active members of the population to change attitudes, and develop the ability to protect themselves by adopting new practices e.g. condom use, abstinence, and being faithful to one partner (ABC model). In cases where infection has already taken place, information and knowledge play a key role to empower the infected and affected individuals to live positively through better nutrition, health regime, and how to take the anti-retroviral medication if available. Some of the information comes from health workers, the education system and NGOs. However, there is also considerable tacit knowledge from those who have experienced the pandemic (and other health problems) first hand and can share their experiences and insights through support groups. The fact that information on HIV/AIDS prevention does not flow freely because of stigmatization, cultural barriers to sharing sexual information across age groups, fear, and gender barriers means there is a lot of work still required to be done on how to create and design effective information and knowledge system to address the HIV/AIDS pandemic.

In addition to HIV/AIDS, there other preventable diseases such as malaria, tuberculosis, and various diseases which afflict children such as polio, whooping cough, tetanus, measles, diarrhea, smallpox and others. All these can be controlled or eradicated out right if the immunization plans are followed and the parents of a child use the knowledge that exists on how to bring up children. Sharing this information widely is done through campaigns in the media and interpersonal communication.

Access to basic health information can be improved by designing small scale health information resource centres at the workplace, public, school and other types of libraries. Facilitating knowledge sharing through public discussion forums is also very important to translate information into attitudinal change, action and new health practices. It is also vital to work closely with international, regional and national organizations such as WHO, Health Net, National AIDS Control Programmes, and organizations which represent the affected and infected.

6 CHALLENGES FOR AFRICAN INFORMATION SCIENCES SPECIALISTS IN THE ERA OF KNOWLEDGE MANAGEMENT

We have discussed Africa's need to harness information and knowledge management in order to make a successful transition to the 21st Century which is regarded as the knowledge revolution era. This section identifies six key challenges which information science specialists face if they are to reformulate their practices and become part of the transformation process. I believe it can be done if we become part of the change process rather than an obstacle to change.

1) Repositioning of information specialists in the knowledge pyramid. One of the challenge to information specialists lies in the concept of the knowledge pyramid which holds that data is processed to information from which people make their own sense to turn it into knowledge. Libraries, records and other information centers thus need to facilitate the process of converting information to knowledge. This process can be facilitated by providing access to adequate information resources but also by creating an environment which permit face to face forums and network formation to discuss and debate issues of concern to the population. The role of information specialists becomes that of infomediaries managing the process of turning information into knowledge for action. A key challenge is to train trainers in information centres who can train communities and organizations in the use and sharing of knowledge for development to build collective intelligence. The older concepts of information literacy and information retrieval now need to be revisited to include knowledge management literacy so as to keep up with the knowledge revolution. The new revolution calls for the use of knowledge as a strategic resource and behaviour change among people so that hoarding of information is replaced by sharing and communication of both tacit and explicit information to empower organizations and communities to meet development challenges.

2) Knowledge sharing, communication and information delivery. Information sharing is vital to ensure that information does not stay in silos isolated from the day to day problems facing society. Without an active communication programme in place information becomes static and stays in the same place and does not add value to the production processes in society. Thus the role of information centers must also include clear information delivery strategies to deliver information in appropriate formats, languages and subject matter. Delivery strategies should use multiple communication methods (including word of mouth, visual materials, drama, games and cultural interaction, and networks) to reach out to the whole community without excluding some groups in society such as women, youth, and minorities. An important challenge is to foster a culture of knowledge sharing among the community members to overcome information hoarding tendencies. This would also include addressing the problem of the organizations and communities not knowing what they know, and at other times, not knowing what they do not know. It is normal for disempowered communities (and third world organizations) to undervalue the vast resources of knowledge among its members. The belief among the poor is that those who come from outside the community have superior knowledge.

3) Assessing and mixing technology options. ICTs currently enable one to exchange and communicate information with anyone in the world any time. ICTs are also are developing very fast and every few months internet access, international telephone service (internet telephony or VOIP), wireless communications are becoming better and cheaper. However as stakeholders in technology use, we need to assess technologies, mix and match them to achieve the best results. Other technologies such as cell phones, CD ROM, DVD, radio, video, films, and posters in some cases might be more appropriate and more accessible than the latest technologies. Above all the information content use behaviour should drive the revolution and we should not fall to the trap of technology determinism.

4) Designing demand driven information systems. Most information centers were designed to build collections representing the subject profiles of the information collection developers. However the challenge now given scarcity of resources is to design information and knowledge systems that are demand driven and accurately reflect demand for information. Through a combination of user needs studies and national sectoral knowledge needs assessment we should be in much better position to design a national information and knowledge systems that reflects the vision and development aspirations of the country and its organizations. This should include investi-

gating the existing information and knowledge system (IKS) and what exists in the system so as to identify gaps and ways of strengthening the information and knowledge system that stakeholders already have in place rather than try to replace it with an externally driven system. Ultimately what are needed are also clear systems of monitoring and evaluation to be put in place to demonstrate the impact information and knowledge centers can make in social change.

5) Local content creation. In most cases information centres in Africa are known for the global content they offer rather than the local language content, which is more relevant to the local situation. Certainly one area that needs to be included in the information services reform is inclusion of indigenous knowledge of the community which is the knowledge that is part of the culture and heritage of the community and nation. The challenge here is for information centres to learn how to produce their own information products and repackage information which is rich in local content rather than perpetuating various forms of intellectual and cultural dependence. A related challenge concerns the need to step up digital content creation to offer online services to users 24 hours and seven days a week.

6) Lobbying to influence policy making. Library and Information Associations need to be better organized to influence policy and voice their opinions when policy issues related to information and knowledge management are being tabled in their country or international forums. The recent World Information Society was one such instance. It was dominated by computer and telecommunications specialists and only later did they realize that the driving force of what they were doing was information and knowledge not the ICT gadgets. Even the concept of WIS was a misconception it should have been the World Knowledge Society (WKS) conference. Most countries have formulated ICT policies which masquerade as information and knowledge management policies – such polices need to be challenged and modified and information specialists have a lot of lobbying ahead of them to achieve the goal of policy reformulation.

REFERENCES

Alhassan, Amin (2004). Development communication policy and economic fundamentalism in Ghana. Tampere (Finland): Tampere University Press (PhD Dissertation)

Annan, Kofi (2001). United Nations information technology task force. (Press Release SG/SM/8037/DEV/2354, 20 November 2001)

Bell, D. (1973) *The coming post-industrial society. A venture in social forecasting*. New York: Basic Books

Blair, Tony, Right Hon. (2000). Speech on knowledge economy, 11 September, (http://www.opengov.uk)

Brouwers, R and Khoapa, B (2005) *South African Netherlands research programme on alternatives in Development*. Zakari: Buitenlandse betrekkingen.

Davenport, T. and Prusak, L. (1998). *Working knowledge: how organizations manage what they know*. Boston: Harvard Business School Press

Dick, A (2002). *The philosophy, politics and economics of information*. Pretoria: UNISA

Drucker, Peter (1993). Post-capitalist society. New York: Harper and Collins eknowledgecenter.com website (2005). Introduction to Knowledge Management. (http://www.eknowledgecenter.com accessed 20/1/2006)

Feather, J and Sturges, P. (Eds.) (2003) *International encyclopedia of information and library science*, 2nd edition, London: Routledge

Hsiao, Julia (2005). Making waves in Guangdong. *Business Week Online*, August 2005. (http://www.businessweek.com/magazine/content/05_34/b3948489.htm) Accessed 30/3/2006

Josh, J and Murthy, I. (2004). Effect of ICT on modern education. KIT Website (2004) http://www.kit.nl/ (accessed 25/3/2006)

Levy, M. et. al. (2003) SMEs, competition and knowledge sharing: the role of information systems. In: European Journal of Information Systems, vol 12, pp. 3–17

Lowassa, Edward (2006). Motion to close the 3rd session of Parliament in Dodoma. Daily news, April 8

Kaariainen, M. (2005). The Making of an information society – The Finnish experience. Ottawa: IDRC (http://www.idrc.ca/en/ev-93069-201-1-DO_TOPIC.html accessed 27/1/2006)

Marco. D. (2003). A meta-data repository is the key to knowledge management. In: http://www.tdan.com/i024fe02.htm (access date 10.3.05)

Mbeki, Thabo (2002) *Africa Define yourself.* Cape Town: Tafelberg Publishers Ltd.

Mchombu, C. M. (2000). "Information needs of women in small businesses in Botswana. *Information and Library Review*, vol. 32, no.1

Menou, M. and Mchombu, K. J. (2004). *Os professionais da informacao em comunidades desfavorecidas. Atuacao professional na area de informacao.* Sao Paulo: Editora Polis Ltda.

Mkandawire, Thandika Saludo, Charles (1999) Our continent our future. Trenton, NJ and Asmara, Eriteria: Africa World Press

Mlaki, T. (2005). Personal communication. 31 December 2005 and 21 April 2006.

Mosimege, Mogege (2005). Indigenous knowledge systems. Presentation given at *"Information as a Strategic Resource for Africa's Development"*, Workshop for National Libraries in the Southern African Development Community (SADC), 16–18 March, 2005. Willow Park Conference Centre, Bredell, Johannesburg

Namibian Government *(2003). Namibia Vision (2030)* http://www.npc.gov/vision/vision2030.htm

Nonaka, Ikujiro (1998). *The knowledge creating company. In: Harvard Business Review on Knowledge Management.* Boson, MA: Harvard Business School Publishing

Powell, M (2003). *Information management for development organizations*, 2nd ed. Oxford: Oxfam, GB.

Prabhala, Achal (2005). Intellectual property, trade agreements, and WIPO: access to learning materials in Southern Africa. Presentation given at *"Information as a Strategic Resource for Africa's Development"*, Workshop for National Libraries in the Southern African Development Community (SADC), 16–18 March, 2005. Willow Park Conference Centre, Bredell, Johannesburg

Ramalingam, B. (2005). *Implementing knowledge strategies: Lessons from international agencies*. London: Overseas Development Institute

Rogers, E. (1995). *Diffusion of innovations*, 4th edition. New York: The Free Press

Ryu, Mikyung (1998) "A muted voice in academe: the Korean version of entrepreneurial scholarship". *Higher Education*, vol. 35, pp. 9–26

Sachs, J. (2005) *The End of Poverty: How can we make it happen in our lifetime*. London: Penguin

Salomon, l. M and Engel, P. (1997). *Networking for innovation: a participatory actor-oriented methodology*. Amsterdam: Royal Tropical Institute (KIT)

Shifflet, Mark (2001). "Information sector growth in market and non market economies: A comparative case study" *The Information Society*, vol. 17, pp. 165–177

Singapore Ministry of Information and the Arts (1994). Library 2000: Investing in a learning nation. Singapore: SNP Publishers (Report of the Library 2000 Review Committee)

Stiglitz, Joseph, (1999). Public policy for a knowledge economy, London, UK, 27 January, p.4

Thomas, Wolfgang (1995). Promoting business linkages to strengthen small business Thomas in Namibia: Lessons from South Africa Windhoek: Friedrich Ebert Stiftung – Namibia Office (SMME Development Discussion Paper no.2)

United Nations Development Programme. Millennium Development Goals. http://www.undo.org/mdg (accessed 23/5/2005)

United Nations Development Organization (2004). Services module 5: agro-industries – over view. http://www.unido.org/doc/5070 (accessed 26/3/2006

Vaagan, R. (2004) .Climbing the knowledge pyramid: R&D programs at Oslo University College. In: Nord I&D, Knowledge and Change

White, Simon (1997). *Strategies for small business development: a guide for regional and local authorities*. Windhoek: Namibia Chamber of Commerce and Industry and Friedrich Ebert Stiftung

Whyte, Anne (2000). Landscape Analysis of Donor Trends in International Development. Human and Institutional Capacity Building. A Rockfeller Foundation Series, Issue no 2, http://www.rockfound/Documents/707/hicb_whyte_donortrends.pdf (accessed 23/3/2005)

World Bank (1998). Knowledge for Development. Washington: World Bank http://www.org/wdr98/contents.htm (accessed 8/5/2005)

POLITICS OF INFORMATION AND KNOWLEDGE IN AFRICA: THE STRUGGLE FOR AN INFORMATION INCLUSIVE SOCIETY IN A GLOBALISED WORLD

Shiraz Durrani

ABSTRACT

The article looks at contradictions facing libraries in Africa where the information and developmental needs of workers and peasants remain largely unmet, while libraries tend to meet the needs of a minority. It maintains that the model of public libraries remains the same as the one introduced by the colonial powers and the opportunity at independence for bringing about a change to a people-orientated service was lost. The profession remains aloof from the political and social struggles of communities, thus alienating itself from the very people it seeks to serve. The article sees opportunities now for change in some positive aspects of globalisation and in developments in information and communications technology. The rise of China can create new possibilities for change. It calls for information professionals to be activists in information as well as in social and political struggles of people. They need to work with communities in partnership with other service providers. It makes the point that the profession is not neutral if it supports the status quo by remaining silent on social and political issues. The article calls for action to put ideas and new vision into practice and gives some details about the Progressive African Library and Information Activists' Group (PALIAct) proposal which aims to create an alternative vision, strategy and practice of a people-orientated service in active partnership with communities and service providers. The article calls upon countries which benefited from African slave trade to support initiatives such as PALIAct as a small way of acknowledging their debt to Africa. It ends by providing elements for an "African activist information programme", including suggestions for leadership development, collection building and "liberating the mind" collections.

1 INFORMATION IN AFRICA

"Silence in the library"

Perhaps the best way to understand the contradictions facing libraries in Africa today is through a story. It is only when social contradictions are accepted and understood that attempts can be made to resolve them. And resolve them we must, if libraries and information are to play their part in creating a new Africa where there is justice, democracy and development for all. The story is "silence in the library":

> Nyanjiru wakes up at 4 am; a water debe on her head, she walks for an hour and a half to the nearest stream. Then she climbs back from the river to her home, picking dry wood on the way for fire; she arrives home three hours later to start the day's other work: crying children to be calmed with bits of left over food, chicken to be fed and watered; then to start digging her half acre shamba in the hot, burning sun. This is the daily routine for a peasant.
>
> And then there is Kamau. Kamau pats his dogs fondly as they surround his new Volvo. This is his daily ritual. He realises that the gates are not open yet and hoots loudly. Where is Mutua? Does he not know that today is the library board meeting and he has to report early? They are to discuss library regulations. He has prepared a long list of "don'ts". As Mutua opens the gates, Kamau speeds out, the silent sound of the Volvo soothing his mind. He starts thinking about library rules. Yes, users must be controlled. Only last week he found a fellow eating mandazi in the library. How can that be allowed? Kamau had him thrown out. The first rule is going to be about eating in the library. And then of course "Silence: silence in the library"
>
> Kamau feels happy as he enters the library parking. "Silence Please, Silence in the Library"; "No eating in the library" ... In such an atmosphere of threats works the modern librarian. Inside the stone walls of the library, in total peace and calm among the well preserved volumes, he is oblivious to the ruin and chaos of hunger, starvation and mass exploitation outside.
>
> The contrasting lives of Nyanjiru and Kamau can be found anywhere in Africa. Their activities are taking place within miles of each other and on the same day. Yet the two are so removed from each other that they may easily be on different planets or in different historical ages.
>
> The library is a concrete structure inaccessible to Nyanjiru, and Nyanjiru as a library user is unacceptable to the librarians. For Nyanjiru there is no time to waste, no compromises to be made. All her labour and thoughts are to satisfy her family's basic needs: food, clothing and shelter. Anything that helps her in this work, she accepts with open arms and mind. Anything that prevents her from acquiring what she needs, she will fight.

> Her information needs are clear – she wants information which will help her to support and protect her family.
>
> On the other hand is the library service – set up during colonial days, with a colonial vision, through 'assistance' from a colonial, neo-colonial 'mother' country. A mother whose very touch brings death. "Silence please; please, silence in the library".
>
> Silence, in spite of Nyanjiru's dying children; silence, in spite of Nyanjiru's twenty hour working day; silence, even though Nyanjiru's hard labour fails to fill her family's stomachs.
>
> Nyanjiru knows no library. No library wants to know Nyanjiru.

The story of Nyanjiru and Kamau highlights the key need in Africa today: development – development of people, resources, industries, agriculture, art, culture ... But "development" does not take place in a vacuum. In order to develop, people and societies need relevant information and knowledge in a number of fields such as science, history, geography, history, technology. Yet, under capitalism, information and knowledge and the very process of learning and education have become commodities to be bought and sold on the "open" market. Those without resources to purchase information end up having no access to it. The irony is that even those who produce information often have no access to that information which is taken from them, copyrighted, patented, repackaged, and sold at prices which the original producers cannot afford.

Thus peoples, countries and societies have been forced into "un-development" and inequality by the economic policies and practices of international finance and transnational corporations using the mechanisms of international financial and political control, such as the IMF, WTO and the UN.

But are these issues that should concern the library profession? Some say it is not our "business" to get involved in "politics" as we are professional people, not politicians. But if we accept that Africa needs a second war of liberation – economic liberation this time – then we need to accept that no liberation can be successful without appropriate information vision, strategy and tactics as well as trained information activists. This is the lesson from the major revolutions in the world. This is also the lesson from Africa's long history of wars against colonialism and imperialism. And this is where we find a relevant social role for African librarians and information professionals and activists today.

The first requirement for liberation from an inequality imposed on Africa is access to information about the real reasons for poverty. Yet the information and communication systems created by the departing colonial powers were not expected or equipped to put this information before people. They were merely tools for a small, rich elite to impose its world outlook and culture on the poor and exploited majority of people. Post-independence systems and policies have made no fundamental change in this colonial-inspired information framework. We urgently need to seek a role for information profession that is relevant to the needs of Africa in the 21st century.

An important task for Africa is to document fully the achievements, successes and failures of the anti-colonial struggles in Africa. Information about these can arm us for current and future struggles. This has not been fully documented. But if the history of African struggle for political and economic liberation is poorly documented, the struggle for African information liberation is even less well documented and understood. It is not a matter of general knowledge, for example, that during the Mau Mau war of liberation in Kenya, the combatants controlled over 50 newspapers and many printing presses; they set up libraries in liberated territories in forests in cities, ran an efficient information collection system, and created their own distribution network, using "traditional" and modern methods available to them. This complex communications system was created and managed by activist librarians and information workers who were active not only in the information field, but in the larger political and social fields as well. Their experience, if fully documented, can help us find a relevant role for the information professional in Africa today.

And yet today, we tend to follow blindly the "Western" model of public library services which actively seeks to remove politics from information theories and practices. This model has not been successful in the "West" itself to provide information to all, particularly to those politely referred to as "socially excluded". Yet we in Africa have not fully challenged this situation. It is only by subjecting our current policies and practices to a vigorous challenge that new and relevant theories, policies and practices can emerge.

2 OPPORTUNITIES FOR INFORMATION LIBERATION

Just as in the political field, so in the information field, there are major developments when social contradictions are at their sharpest. It is at such key points in history that opportunities arise for making revolutionary changes in the way information and politics are organised. Colonial Africa has had a number of opportunities to change its societies for the better and serve the needs of the majority of people. One such opportunity was in late nineteen fifties and early sixties which saw achievement of political independence in many countries. It was a time when foundations of the old colonial world were being destroyed and those of new free societies were being laid. Many activists had the vision of a society where all would have free access to information and knowledge created by the work of all. It was a time of immense change and high hopes for a just, equitable future after decades of colonial oppression and exploitation. This was the time when people did influence events in a major way, underscoring what was said at the World Summit for Information Society (2003): it is "people who primarily form and shape societies, and information and communication societies are no exception".

But the opportunity at independence to challenge the very basis of social organisations such as libraries was lost. Library services continued to function on the same basis as under colonialism, targeting their services to the elite, although now this included some more people and became "multiracial". Class divisions, which formed the real divisions in the society, were deliberately played down, and racial, "tribal" and other "divisions" were brought into prominence. An information service operating in the real interest of people would have ensured that this "information blind-spot" was removed and the question of who the library actually serves would have been resolved in favour of the majority of working people. Thus an information service using resources from all but serving a few was developed. This situation has more or less continued until today.

Today, however, there is another possibility for change. Changes at a global level in the last 25 years now present Africa with another opportunity to make a fundamental shift in the way societies are organised – and in the way information services are organised. If managed correctly, we can make the transition to a people-orientated library service that did not take place at independence. Let us look at two major changes: globalisation and the rise of China.

3 GLOBALISATION

An intensified corporate globalisation is the current phase of capitalism and imperialism. This has been made possible by rapid changes in information technologies. The collapse of USSA has left only one imperialist world power (USA) with global imperialist ambitions and resources to impose its will on the world. This has major political as well as economic implications for countries around the world, as evidenced by the invasion of Iraq by USA in pursuit of oil and strategic advantage for profit-driven transnationals.

By its very definition, capitalism divides people along class lines. Working class people as a whole are historically excluded from enjoying wealth created by their labour. Hence capitalism creates a class that is automatically excluded from wealth, power, education and information. There has been a qualitative change in the process of social exclusion in the last quarter of this century on a global level. Castells (1998, p. 1) explains these changes as a "technological revolution, centered around information (which) has transformed the way we think, we produce, we consume, we trade, we manage, we communicate, we live, we die, we make war, and we make love: a dynamic global economy has been constituted around the planet, linking up valuable people and activities from all over the world, while switching off from the networks of the power and wealth, people and territories dubbed as irrelevant from the perspectives of dominant interests."

While this aggressive phase of capitalism resulted in increasing economic growth in some countries and regions, its own logic ensures that millions of people and large parts of the world remain excluded from growth. Many areas have thus experienced a decline in national product as capital moves out of less profitable countries and regions. The social and economic consequences of this global search for profit inevitably leads to marginalising and excluding millions of people around the world. Africa is a prime example of such exclusion. Castells (1999) explains the essence of corporate globalisation:

> "... this is a brand of capitalism that is at the same time very old and fundamentally new. It is old because it appeals to relentless competition in the pursuit of profit, and because individual satisfaction (deferred or immediate) is its driving engine. But it is fundamentally new because it is tooled by new information and communication technologies that are at the root of new productivity sources, new organizational forms, and the construction of a global economy."

Thus, while developments in technologies and science make it possible for rapid changes to be made, Africa lags behind. Yet possibilities exist in the world today, and within Africa, to bring about major changes in the way our societies – and information services – are organised. Possibilities exist in Africa today to put information at the service of people so that they help them meet their real needs, and not for a (mostly foreign) elite to enrich itself on African labour and resources.

There are other aspects of globalisation and development of information technologies which affect the development of Africa.

4 INFORMATION SOCIETY AND KNOWLEDGE ECONOMY IN AFRICA

The term "Information Society" can be used to describe a society in which the "creation, distribution, and manipulation of information has become the most significant economic and cultural activity" (IBM Community Development Foundation, 1997) which goes on to explain the terms further:

> An Information Society may be contrasted with societies in which the economic underpinning is primarily industrial or agricultural. The tools of the Information Society are computers and telecommunications. Progress in information technologies and communication is changing the way people lead their lives, how they work and do business, how they educate their children, study, carry out research, train themselves and how they are entertained.

Africa needs to make the shift from reliance on agricultural and industrial activities to a society based on knowledge. The term "Knowledge Economy" refers to using the generation and exploitation of knowledge as a predominant player in the creation of wealth. Matsuura (2005) gives a background of the emergence of the knowledge economy and looks at the process of turning information into knowledge:

> "The scientific upheavals of the 20th century have brought about a third industrial revolution. This revolution, which has been accompanied by Globalization, has laid down the bases of a knowledge economy. Yet information is not knowledge; and the world information society will only fulfil its potential if it facilitates the emergence of pluralistic knowledge societies that include rather than exclude … there is a clear awareness today that the development of societies predicated on the sharing of knowledge is the best way of waging effective war on poverty and forestalling major health risks such as pandemics, of reducing the terrible loss of life caused by tsunamis and tropical storms, and of promoting sustainable human development. For new modes of development are today within our grasp: these are no longer based, as in the past, on "blood, sweat and tears", but rather on intelligence, the scientific and technological capacity to address problems, intellectual added value, and the expansion of services in all sectors of the economy …"

These "new modes of development" appear to be far away from African shores. Yet it is possible to turn the new potential into reality by using existing visions and commitments as well experiences from other countries. The Vision of the

Information Society, as summed up in World Summit on Information Society, Civil Society (2003) is the one that best serves African interests:

> "We ... declare our common desire and commitment to build a people-centered, inclusive and development-oriented Information Society, where everyone can create, access, utilize and share information and knowledge, enabling individuals, communities and peoples to achieve their full potential in promoting their sustainable development and improving their quality of life, premised on the purposes and principles of the Charter of the United Nations and respecting fully and upholding the Universal Declaration of Human Rights.
>
> We are aware that ICTs should be regarded as tools and not as an end in themselves. Under favourable conditions, these technologies can be a powerful instrument, increasing productivity, generating economic growth, job creation and employability and improving the quality of life of all. They can also promote dialogue among people, nations and civilizations.
>
> We are also fully aware that the benefits of the information technology revolution are today unevenly distributed between the developed and developing countries and within societies. We are fully committed to turning this digital divide into a digital opportunity for all, particularly for those who risk being left behind and being further marginalized."

The above declaration surely provides a powerful weapon at an ideological level. Other developments at a political level can also support Africa's demand for an equal share in the new information and knowledge world. The political, economic and ethical developments in the "non-Western" world provide a more relevant experience and example for Africa. On the one hand is the rapid rise of the BRIC countries (Brazil, Russia, India and China). On the other hand is the experience from the principled stand taken in Cuba, Venezuela and Bolivia which provides a real chance for improvement in the lives of working people. Both these are relevant models that Africa can use for real development. Changes in the information level cannot take place in a vacuum. It is changes at the economic and political level in these examples that provides the possibilities for change in the information field.

5 THE RISE OF CHINA

The rise of China as a major international economic and political power is rapidly changing our world today. Already it has become the sixth largest economy in the world and is likely soon to become the fourth. It has enormous potential for the future. The significance of the rise of China is not only at economic and political level, it has the potential for developing an entirely different moral framework for development, international relations and world outlook. Unlike previous super-powers which resorted to occupation of land and subjugating people in order to satisfy their need for resources, China sets about developing mutually beneficial relations with countries such as Brazil, India and other "developing" countries so that there is mutual benefit. It seeks no colonies nor to enslave or colonise people. As Jacques (2005) explains:

> "The past two or three years have marked a new moment in the global perception of China. There is suddenly a new awareness that encompasses both a recognition of China's economic transformation and an understanding that, because of its huge size and cohesive character, it will have a profound impact on the rest of the world, albeit in ways still only dimly understood ... China has arrived and will increasingly shape our future, not just its own."

Africa has much to gain from developing relations with China in a way which benefits people of both continents. It will set a new standard of moral, economic and political relations between peoples and countries.

The rise of the BRIC countries (Brazil, Russia, India and China) as a whole provides a totally new global scene which can have tremendous impact on Africa. At an economic level, it challenges the monopoly of Western transnational companies to decide the terms of trade which have historically worked against Africa. Thus the objective condition for positive change has been set. It remains for Africa to take advantage of this positive development. But we do not have to look far for examples of how these global changes can be used in the interest of their people – there is an alternative way which increases social spending and turns away from free-market policies which have been imposed on Africa, causing increased poverty and stifling development.

6 THERE IS AN ALTERNATIVE

This alternative way of developing societies has been shown to work in Cuba, which, in spite of a USA-instigated blockade of over 40 years, is developing today at a highly enviable rate. Its GDP growth in 2005 was 11.8 percent – among the highest in the world. ("New Challenges and Victories Ahead", 2006). As an example in just one field, Cuba has become a major bio-medical power. Marx, Gary (2006) sums up Cuba's achievements:

> "Cuban scientists have produced a hepatitis B vaccine sold in more than 30 countries and streptokinase, a potent enzyme that dissolves blood clots and improves the survival rate of heart attack victims. The country also makes recombinant interferon that strengthens the immune system of cancer patients and a meningitis B vaccine.
>
> In the pipeline are products ranging from an injection that closes ulcers and improves circulation in diabetics to vaccines against cholera and hepatitis C, according to Cuban officials."

Similar changes are taking place in Venezuela which is also following an alternative economic and political path to development of its people, using oil revenues to set up Universities, literacy and health care programmes for working people, and other social projects. Similarly, in Bolivia, major changes are expected once the new President, Evo Morales take office in January, 2006. What is perhaps more significant is that not only are these three countries taking the alternative path, but they are also developing an alternative support and co-operation structure among themselves and with other progressive countries. As O'Keefe (2005) says, "there is an alternative". He sums up the new situation:

> "Today, global capitalism is being challenged most directly in Venezuela. Hugo Chavez's own discourse has sharpened dramatically against international capital in recent months and years. The Bolivarian leader has made repeated calls for the building of 'socialism for the 21st century'.
>
> The Bolivarian Revolution is carrying out a transformation of both the reality of Venezuela and of the global alignment of political forces. The gains of *el proceso* are preciously concrete, as seen in rising rates of literacy and education, mass expansion of health care services, land reform, new housing for the poor, and an explosion in cooperative worker co-managed enterprises. These reforms are part of a revolutionary process with a continental and global dynamic."

Such positive news about development can provide important examples to people of Africa, but our information services rarely provide such information to working people who need it the most. Such examples of development activities are highly relevant to Africa and perhaps the model of the "Community of South American Nations" may be a good one for Africa to follow.

A key requirement for development of Africa is a redrawing of the "information map" to reassess our information work. We need to assess the relevance of the sources of information we provide to the people and to review whose point of view such information reflects. We need to look afresh at the form and content of information in our libraries and look at what languages they cover. We need to see if the information is targeted correctly and review how outcomes are monitored. Our information needs to reflect Africa in a new perspective and reinterpret its history from the point of view of African working people. The world-view that people are daily presented by the Western media needs to be challenged for African people to see themselves as equal partners in a global context. An alternative vision and view of the world needs to be made available to *every* African. No people can develop under a situation of daily images of their own powerlessness and inadequacy, where facts about their exploitation are hidden and their suffering is shown as resulting from their own fault. In order to build our self-confidence we need to see the world from our own perspective in which the "other" is just that – the other.

Technological developments mentioned earlier already provide a basis for making this alternative position for Africa a reality. An example of this new way of thinking and doing is provided by the pioneering Pambazuka *News, Weekly* Forum for Social Justice for Africa.[1] This is "a tool for progressive social change in Africa" and is produced by Fahamu,[2] "an organisation that uses information and communication technologies to serve the needs of organisations and social movements that aspire to progressive social change".

It is in initiatives such as this that African librarians need to get involved. We need to form new alliance with global movements such as the World Social Forum. Another area in which librarians need to be active is initiatives such as the pan-Latin American TV channel, Telesur, which, as Bruce (2005) reports, aims to "counter cultural imperialism, which the Channel's president, Andres Izaara said had gone unchallenged in the region for 50 years".

But a key requirement for ensuring a meaningful information change is to reassess the social role of librarians and information workers. Too often we are satisfied with a very limited social role and have shied away from any active involvement in the political reality around us. But our so-called "neutrality" is not real neutral; it is, in effect, siding with the status quo which we reinforce if we do not challenge inequality and injustice.

---

1 Pambazuka News is available at: http://www.pambazuka.org/en/. "Pambazuka" means "arise" or "awaken" in Kiswahili).

2 Details about Fahamu are available at: http://www.fahamu.org/

7 SOCIAL AND POLITICAL ROLE OF LIBRARIANS

"The people's hour has arrived" said Bolivian President-elect Evo Morales while reiterating promises to recover Bolivia's natural resources, including natural gas, for all Bolivians (*Bolivia's Morales, Chavez Pledge to Strengthen Ties*, 2005). Such a programme for Africa is well overdue and needs active participation of information and community activists. Again, we need to work closely with progressive Pan African movements and activists, as the problems facing African can best be resolved on a continental-basis, and in partnership with others whose aims match ours. Blake (1989) examined the role of librarians in very clear terms:

> "There are those who, clinging to the idea that the library profession should be politically neutral, would contend that contributing to social projects is not an appropriate activity for librarians. However, without a clear and vital set of philosophical and political ideals acting as a guiding beacon, the library profession will not remain neutral, but will drift aimlessly with the currents of power and privilege.
>
> Librarians must forcefully articulate their commitment to serving the information needs of all segments of society. They must rededicate themselves to assuring the widest and most equitable access to information by opposing fees for services and the commercialization of knowledge. Furthermore, librarians must be willing to enter the political arena and advocate for these principles".

This call for involvement in the political arena is even more urgent in Africa today in view the changes taking place in the context of corporate globalisation and marketisation of services.

The rest of this paper looks at one attempt in the African information field to make a positive change in the way information services are managed and delivered.

8 PROGRESSIVE AFRICAN LIBRARY AND INFORMATION ACTIVISTS' GROUP (PALIACT)

It is perhaps time for information professionals to move away from lamenting the situation to turning their ideas into action. The Progressive African Library and Information Activists' Group (PALIAct) initiative is one such attempt. It was set up as a way of taking on board some of the issues raised above. It is being supported by the Department of Applied Social Sciences of the London Metropolitan University. It also has the potential to bring together the African Diaspora with progressive people in the "West" to create a powerful partnership with the information professionals in Africa to develop innovative information services which can help develop people and communities.

PALIAct seeks to develop people-oriented information services decided upon by workers, peasants, pastoralists, fisher people and other marginalized individuals and groups whose needs have not been met. It involves working in partnership with other professionals and service providers. PALIAct operates on principles of equality, democracy and social justice and encourages a Pan African world outlook among information and community activists.

PALIAct recognises the right to relevant information as a basic human right. The struggle for a relevant information service is intimately linked with the political struggles of the people to meet their material, social, cultural and political needs. PALIAct believes that the opportunity for creating a people-orientated information service at the time of political independence was lost. Instead of challenging the very basis on which library and information services were built, we allowed ourselves to be manipulated into making merely quantitative changes in library services, but failed to make any qualitative changes. The *classes* who were served by the colonial library service continued to be served and the needs of working people who had always remained outside the remit of such services remained unmet. Their experiences, their cultures, their very language remained outside the walls of impressive library buildings. Thus the advantage gained in the early period of struggle for a society and an information system which served the needs of *all* its people was lost. The struggle for such an information service continues to date.

The PALIAct programme is therefore an activist agenda to ensure that the information rights of African people are recognised in theory as well as in practice. PALIAct will set up pilot projects in a number of countries to develop ideas and practices to develop people-orientated information services.

PALIAct aims relate directly to meeting the Millennium goals for development. One of the challenges identified at the World Summit on the Information Society is to "harness the potential of information and communication technology to promote the development goals of the Millennium Declaration" (World Summit on Information Society, 2003b). PALIAct provides one very practical answer to this challenge.

8.1 PALIAct Principles[3]

In its commitment to developing a people-orientated information service, PALIAct is committed to:

- The principles of social justice, equality, equity, human welfare, and the development of cultural and social democracy; thus we shall actively address historical inequalities in the information field in Africa;
- Achieving equality of access to and inclusiveness of information services, especially extending such services to the workers, peasants and the poor, the marginalized and those who have been discriminated against;
- The provision of a relevant service to those active in the struggles for social justice and who are working towards the creation of a liberated Africa;
- Supporting the collection, organization, preservation and dissemination of the documents of people's struggles in all forms and languages;
- Making available alternative materials representing a wide range of progressive viewpoints from within Africa and overseas and which are often excluded by traditional libraries, mass media and educational and information systems;
- Encouraging the exploration of alternative models of services; promoting and disseminating critical analysis of information technology's impact on libraries and societies; and support the fundamental democratization of existing institutions of education, culture, communications;
- Undertaking joint, interdisciplinary research into fundamental library issues (e.g. into the political economy of information in the age of neo-liberalism and corporate globalization) in order to lay the basis for effective action in our spheres of work;
- Investigating and organizing efforts to make the library-as-workplace more democratic and encourage resistance to the managerialism of the present library culture;
- Promoting international solidarity among librarians and cooperation between libraries across borders on the basis of our commitment to the Uni-

[3] Based on the Ten program developed by Mark Rosenzweig for the groups which met at the Vienna Conference of progressive librarians sponsored by KRIBIBIE in 2000. Copyright Progressive Librarians Guild, 2000. http://www.libr.org/PLG/

versal Declaration of Human Rights and related covenants which create a democratic framework for constructive cooperative endeavours;

- Organizing in partnership with other activists in the cultural and educational fields, to help put issues of social responsibility on the agendas of international bodies such as IFLA and UNESCO;
- Opposing corporate globalization which, despite its claims, reinforces existing social, economic, cultural inequalities, and working towards the creation of a democratic globalism and internationalism which respects and cultivates cultural plurality, which recognizes the sovereignty of peoples, which acknowledges the obligations of society to the individual and communities, and which prioritizes human values and needs over profits.

PALIAct is discussing the possibilities of setting up pilot country centres in a number of countries. The experience gained in these pilots will help to develop further centres in other countries or regions of Africa. Such pilots require a committed group of local information professionals willing and able to work with local communities. Discussions are taking place for setting up the first pilots in Ghana and Kenya.

The Kenya chapter of PALIAct has now been registered and has already started making a mark on the information scene in Kenya. Further details about PALIAct and the work of the Kenya chapter are available in PALIAct's newsletter, *Information Equality, Africa.*[4]

The success of the PALIAct initiative will, in the end, be decided upon by how actively the information professionals in Africa support it. The ideas are ready to be implemented, but whether they will be taken up remains to be seen. They offer a possibility of reconciling the lives of Nyanjiru and Kamau in the story we heard earlier. I hope there will no longer be silence in the library.

9 AN AFRICAN ACTIVIST INFORMATION PROGRAMME

It is not within the scope of this presentation to discuss in detail what an activist information programme for Africa would or should look like. Such a programme will emerge when local information activists engage in the struggles of

---

[4] Details about PALIAct are available at http://www.seapn.org.uk/PALIAct-new.html. Information Equality, Africa, PALIAct's newsletter (formerly entitled PALIAct Ideas & Action) will also be available here when published in September 2006.

the people for their material and cultural rights. However, some possible direction for such a programme can be mentioned here:

9.1 Leadership development

No country, organisation or profession can expect to achieve its vision without developing its members in areas such as appropriate ideological awareness and orientation, an understanding of historical and current contradictions facing the country or organisation, a clarity about who and what their allies are in terms of achieving their goals, an understanding of organisational change brought about by innovation and creativity. The development of leadership requires that these theories are then reinforced by opportunities for practical work as a way of gaining experience which can give increased confidence to individuals as well as to organisations. It is only through such life-long learning programmes that there can be any hope of ensuring the sustainability required for long-term development.

These points were well understood in Kenya in the early 1960s when Pio Gama Pinto, Bildad Kaggia, Oginga Odinga and others set up the Lumumba Institute for developing political cadres. Those who killed the Institute (and Pinto) did a great disservice to the cause of African liberation. Today we can learn from this history and develop a thousand Lumumba Institutes as a way of developing our people to lead the war for African's second liberation which starts with liberating our minds.

The need for effective leadership in the profession is now well recognised. What African information sector needs are leaders who are not only good managers but provide a new vision, develop staff, create a new culture and appropriate organisational structures and remove habits that deaden, as Beckett's character Didi says in *Waiting for Godot*.[5] We need to pay attention to the warning sounded by Mao and stop working "half-heartedly without a definite plan or direction … work perfunctorily and muddle along". He goes on to warn of the danger of unthinking work: "So long as one remains a monk, one goes on tolling the bell."[6] We need to ensure that teaching institutes are delivering a learning

---

[5] In Samuel Beckett's Waiting for Godot, Didi, one of the two tramps, says to Gogo, the other tramp: "Habit is a great deadener".

[6] Mao Tse Tung: Correcting mistaken ideas. Available at: http://www.marxists.org/reference/archive/mao/works/red-book/ch24.htm. [Accessed 05 September, 2006].

programme to actively nurture and develop leadership, including all the attributes mentioned by various authors below:

- A leader needs to provide direction, it's the vision thing. To get a collective definition of success leaders must engage, motivate and animate people in their organisations. It isn't enough just to have the vision; they really have to engage with their people.[7]
- Leadership is a balancing act. It requires communicating a compelling vision, convincing others to buy into that vision, and marshalling resources and talent to make it happen.[8]
- Your ability to lead is only as good as your ability to motivate.[9]
- You earn leadership from those that you lead. You earn leadership from earning the respect of the people.[10]

A number of programmes being delivered or developed at the London Metropolitan University's Department of Applied Social Sciences are suitable for such a leadership programme. All of these are capable of being delivered in partnership with African Universities if there is interest. These include

- the Quality Leaders Project (QLP), "management development through service development" with its "combating racism, managing equality" and other project management modules
- various information management modules and short courses, including "leadership for innovation, equality and change", "society, information and policy", and "information and social exclusion". The new module "information for development" would be of particular relevance in Africa.

---

7 Bennis, Warren: Leading from the Top – An interview with Warren Bennis. EFMD. Available from http://www.efmd.org/html/Knowledge/cont_detail.asp?id=050209igbk&aid=050510mkfp&tid=1. Accessed 18 October, 2005.

8 Becoming an effective leader; the results-driven manager series (publicity). Harvard Business online. Available from Harvard_Business_Online@hbsp.ed10.net Accessed 31 August, 2005.

9 The right kind of leadership: how to motivate people to achieve their full potential (publicity). Harvard Business online. Available from Harvard_Business_Online@hbsp.ed10.net Accessed 31 August, 2005.

10 Mintzberg, Henry: Engaging Leadership; An interview with corporate strategist Henry Mintzberg. European Foundation for Management Development. Available from: http://www.efmd.org/html/Knowledge/cont_detail.asp?TID=1&AID=050209czte&ID=050209igbk. Accessed 18 October, 2005.

9.2 Collection building

An important area that needs to be addressed urgently is the collection policy and practice of African libraries. Again, this is not the forum to go into this in detail, but the following needs to be addressed:

- Material from African liberation struggle. The enormous amount of oral and written material generated during the long history of African struggle against colonialism needs to be collected, documented and made available. Developments in information and communications technologies make this task easier than it was some years back. Part of this process is the need to get back from colonial countries the vast amount of African documents, material culture, and archives stored in London, Paris and other colonial capitals.
- Documents of the Pan African movement need to be included in the above, as do material on slavery whose effects Africa has not recovered from even today.
- Documentation on the policies and activities of organisations and leaders active in the anti-colonial, anti-imperialist movements (before and after independence) need to be made available through every public and University library in Africa. These should include organisations and leaders in every African country. For example, films on Lumumba and other anti-imperialist activists need to be collected or commissioned.
- African libraries seems to be flooded by material from a Western, imperialist point of view. There is a need to actively collect material from an alternative, people's, point of view. This should include material on the World Social Forum (WSF) as well as on the people's anti-globalisation movements. The WSF has already included library events as part of its programme for its meetings in Bamako (2006) and in Nairobi in 2007. Two representatives of the PALIAct Kenya Centre have been sponsored by the Finnish Foreign Ministry to attend the Bamako event.[11] It is important for African library professional to be actively involved in this important initiative. A large number of East, Central, and Southern African librarians need to attend the Nairobi meeting in January 2007.
- Material from a Pan-African and internationalist perspective. African libraries need to collect material from other African countries, organise a transla-

[11] Details about these events are available from the WSF website mentioned in the Bibliography.

tion service to make material available to all, and promote major regional African languages throughout the continent (e.g. Kiswahili, Arabic, and Yoruba).

- Collections on social and economic development. Experiences on development in other parts of the world needs to be made available to African planners, teachers, lecturers, extension workers and others as a way of disseminating it to people. Thus experiences from China, Cuba, Venezuela and India should be actively collected.

9.3 The "liberating the mind"/"kuvunja minyororo"[12] collections

As a practical way of putting some of these ideas into action, I would like to suggest that a new information partnership be set up in interested countries, under the name "Liberating the mind"/"kuvunja minyororo" partnership. Key partners would include the local PALIAct country centre, a local University and the public library service. Other organisations such as Museums, Archives, and relevant Government ministries would also be able to join the partnership. International organisations such as the International Federation of Library Associations (IFLA), the African Union, and UNESCO etc could be invited as partners. The national partnerships would have representation in a continent-wide partnership.

The "liberating the mind" service would collect and disseminate the material mentioned above. It should include "audience development"[13] approach taken

---

[12] "Kuvunja minyororo" – Kiswahili for "to break the chains".

[13] The QLP approach identifies 2 aspects under the term "audience development":

The first aspect is to increase the reach of libraries and youth services to meet the needs of all young people, particularly refugees and asylum seekers and those who have not been reached before.

The second aspect expands on what has come to be known as "reader development". However, the term "audience development" is preferred to "reader development". "Audience development" is a more inclusive term: it includes people who may have visual impairment and meets the needs of disabled people generally. It includes people who may not be literate either in English or in their own languages. It also allows for connecting people to the "reading experience" through non print media, such as arts, cinema, music, drama and other cultural activities. It involves all the senses, rather than being restricted to the use of just one.

The "audience development" approach to library and youth work develops new areas of service provision which a "traditional" library may not have provided as mainstream activities. Over a period of time, this approach will help to develop a new model of joined-up library-youth service.

by the Quality Leaders project and develop activities in areas such as film, radio, music, drama all of which can be developed in partnership with other professionals. As a start, each country should have at least one library designated as a "liberating the mind" centre. A start can be made, for example, by making available material recommended by the World Social Forum as relevant for Africa. It would be in a language appropriate to the country and be in paper as well as electronic format.

This Conference can set up a working party to take these ideas forward, if there is sufficient interest. This proposed partnership can set the African librarian free from the colonial/imperialism shackle and can finally re-emerge with a new, socially-responsible role. The future is ours to make.

10 CONCLUSION

The year 2007 marks the bicentenary of the British Parliamentary abolition of the slave trade in the former British Empire. We hope to formally launch PALIAct at the IFLA Conference in South Africa in 2007. At the same time, it

---

Audience development workshops: These workshop sessions are perhaps the most innovative part of the programme. The sessions are programmed to reflect the specific aspects that the young people themselves decide meet their needs. They thus need to be flexible in order to be tailored to local requirements. They will also enable young people themselves to be the providers of such sessions, rather than being merely passive recipients of a service provided by an "outsider". At the same time, the programme will enable outside skills, ideas and expertise to be brought into the local youth communities, thereby injecting new and different ideas on the local scene.

The QLP-Y programme will provide regular workshop sessions in each of the 2 years of the life of the Project. This will enable activities such as:

presentations from writers, poets, film makers, media and other professionals

music workshops, book and newsletter production sessions, broadcast workshops, film making modules

various informal learning experiences

ICT-related activities

guest speakers from different fields as a way of enabling the young people to meet potential role models from diverse communities and from different fields.

Until the project requirements are worked out in some detail in consultation with the youth themselves, it is not possible to be any more specific than this. It is expected that these sessions will attract young people, who may never have used library or youth services, to be active participants in new service which they themselves help design and deliver.

The Workshops are incorporated in the QLP-Y on the basis that the learning and social needs of young people can be met more meaningfully as part of a cultural and social programme so as to avoid a feeling of "school out of school". The crucial element will be the empowerment of young people so that it is they who decide on the type of activity they are comfortable with.

would be appropriate for the library profession in Africa to make it a year of change to rededicate and reorient information services to meet the needs of the majority of its people. It would be appropriate for countries which have benefited from African slave trade to support initiatives such as PALIAct as a small way of acknowledging their debt to Africa.

But the prospects for a real new beginning for information services in Africa depend on whether African information professionals, activists and workers take up the challenge of development as part of their profession and work in active partnership with people they are supposed to serve. There is much interest among a younger generation of information professionals and activists to change the information scene. But they operate in an inappropriate environment that kills all initiatives and creativity, offering no chance for advancement to those proposing ideas and visions not liked by the "information establishment". What is required to ensure a meaningful change is a real desire for democracy in the workplace as well in the society as a whole, an environment that encourages risk taking and innovation, and a willingness to challenge status quo in the interest of developing services for people.

Perhaps the greatest challenge for information professionals is to develop a new model of an "activist" librarian. Information in Africa needs to be seen in its true political perspective and information professionals need to address their information role within the political context. Denying that information work has any connection with politics means denying development to people. As Durrani and Smallwood (2006) say:

> "It is important that those with conviction and commitment stand up for a new role of libraries in society – and actively practice this new role. In the world ruled by corporate globalisation, it is too easy to drift along with the tide of "neutral" librarianship and do nothing to make libraries play a central role in liberating people, their cultures, and their economies from the privatised future that globalisation has planned for them."

A new beginning for African librarians is possible only if the profession can take up this challenge.

REFERENCES

Henry, Blanke (1989). "Librarianship and political values: neutrality or commitment" *Library Journal*, July 1989, pp. 39–42.

Bruce, Iain (2005): "First broadcast for Latin channel". BBC News. 24 July. Retrieved 04 January, 2005 from: http://news.bbc.co.uk/1/hi/world/americas/4713361.stm.

Castells, Manuel (1998). The *power of identity.* Oxford, Blackwell.

Castells, Manuel (1999). Information Technology, Globalization and Social Development. UNRISD Discussion Paper No. 114, September 1999. The United Nations Research Institute for Social Development (UNRISD). Retrieved 26 October, 2005 from http://www.unrisd.org/80256B3C005BCCF9/(httpPublications)/F270E0C066F3DE7780256B67005B728C?OpenDocument&panel=seriespapers.

Durrani, Shiraz (1997). "The other Kenya: underground and alternative literature. *Collection Building* 16(2), pp. 80–87.

Durrani, Shiraz (1998): "Independence in Kenya and the lost opportunity to build a people-orientated Library Service". *Library Review*. 47: 388–394 (8) 1998; Link-*up* (1998); *Alternative Library Literature* (1998/99).

Durrani, Shiraz (2002). Kenyan libraries and information in times of social protest, 1960–1970. *Swedish Library Research (Svensk Biblioteks-forskning)* Vol. 14(3) 2002, pp. 20–32.

Durrani, Shiraz (2006). "Never be silent; publishing and imperialism in Kenya, 1884–1963". London: Vita Books.

Durrani, Shiraz and Smallwood, Elizabeth (2006). "The professional is political: redefining the social role of public libraries". *Progressive Librarian*. No. 27, July. (*Forthcoming*).

Ideas and Issues (2005), "an irregular current awareness service which alerts you to new ideas, experiences, reports and developments of relevance to the module". Ten issues were prepared as part of the "Information Policy" module (2005–06) at the Department of Applied Social Sciences Department of the London Metropolitan University. Copies available from the author.

IBM Community Development Foundation. (1997). *The Net Result: Report of the National Working Party for Social Inclusion*. London: Authors.

Jacques, Martin (2005): "China is well on its way to being the other superpower". The Guardian, December 8. Retrieved 02 January, 2006 from: http://www.guardian.co.uk/china/story/0,,1661736,00.html

Marx, Gary (2006): "Cuba cits [sic] 'world class' trail in biotech research". The Chicago Tribune. Retrieved 02 January, 2006 from www.thesouthern.com/articles/2006/01/01/business/doc43b6e887be9f4564996873.txt.

Matsuura, Koïchiro (2005). "Towards knowledge societies". Retrieved 13 November, 2005 from http://www.kantipuronline.com/kolnews.php?&nid=56661.

Bolivia's Morales, Chavez Pledge to Strengthen Ties (2005, update2). Retrieved 04 January, 2005 from http://www.bloomberg.com/apps/news?pid=10000086&sid=amUh3706gyHU&refer=latin_america.

"New Challenges and Victories Ahead" (2006). Havana, Prensa Latina. 1 Jan 2006 (Prensa Latina). Retrieved 02 January, 2006 from http://www.plenglish.com/article.asp?ID=%7B10EC2ABE-BE6D-486C-BF15-6728B96D2070%7D)&language=EN.

O'Keefe, Derrick (2005). "There is an alternative: Bolivia, Venezuela, and the struggle against neo-liberalism". December 27, 2005. Retrieved 29 December, 2005 from http://sevenoaksmag.com/commentary/91_comm3.html.

Open to all? The public library and social exclusion. (2000). Vol.1 *Overview and conclusions;* Vol. 2*: Survey, case studies and methods;* Vol. 3*: Working Papers.* London: Resource, the Council for Museum, Archives, and Libraries. ISBN 1-902394-49-6. ISSN 1466-2949. (See http://www.mla.gov.uk/documents/lic084.pdf for Vol. 1; and http://www.seapn.org.uk/publication.html for Vol. 3).

Pambazuka News, weekly forum for justice in Africa. Retrieved 03 January from: http://www.pambazuka.org/.

Quality Leaders Project. Details available from: http://www.seapn.org.uk/qlp.html.

UNESCO (2005). Towards knowledge societies. Paris: UNESCO Publishing. (UNESCO World Report). Retrieved 13 November, 2005 from http://unesdoc.unesco.org/images/0014/001418/141843e.pdf.

World Social Movement. Library events. See: http://www.nigd.org/libraries/bamako-nairobi.

World Summit on the Information Society (2003a). "Building the Information Society: a global challenge in the new Millennium". Retrieved 04 January, 2006 from: http://www.itu.int/wsis/index.html. More recent documents from the Tunic WSIS Conference (2005) are available from: http://www.itu.int/wsis/tunis/index.html.

World Summit on Information Society (2003b). "Declaration of principles; building the Information Society, a global challenge in the new Millennium". Document WSIS-03/GENEVA/DOC/4-E. Retrieved 17 November, 2005 from http://www.itu.int/wsis/docs/geneva/official/dop.html.

World Summit on Information Society (2003). "Shaping Information Societies for Human Needs; Civil Society Declaration to the World Summit on the Information Society". World Summit on the Information Society (WSIS) Plenary. Geneva, 8 December. Retrieved 21 December, 2005 from http://wsis.ecommons.ca/book/print/218.

LIBRARIES AND DEMOCRACY

Mohammed M. Aman

ABSTRACT

Africa and the African people are struggling for human decency, freedom, and dignity. Extremist ideas and ideologies thrive when millions of peoples are deprived of their basic rights and dignity and hope for a better future. The majority of Africans are young; millions are under age 20 years of age. These young people, are unlike their forefathers, are not fighting for independence from colonial and oppressive foreign powers. They are fighting unemployment, boredom, ignorance and health epidemic like AIDS and Malaria. They wish to have better lives than their fathers and they have dreams of becoming contributing members to their society. Libraries can play a role in the improvement of these young lives, through the promotion of reading, job training, access to the Internet and the promotion of e-government, e-commerce and Web centric education. This paper describes strategies that have developed in other countries to advance the standard of living for Africans, to promote freedom of expression, dialogue and a civil society. When we look back at the experiences of other countries, we find that public libraries, like those established by Carnegie, have promoted a free market economy, as well as freedom of expression and beliefs. In today's technological environment much can be done by libraries, media and other information outlets to promote the principles of free and democratic societies in Africa. Members of the international community have a deep-rooted interest to work with fellow African educators, information professionals and decision-makers to achieve genuine democracy and to ensure that libraries will play a major role in the process as they have done in Europe in recent and Asia in the recent history.

1 INTRODUCTION

Democracy has come to be acknowledged as the best way of respecting human rights and guaranteeing dignity and freedom for all.

Democracies are political systems characterized by popular participation, genuine competition for executive office, and institutional checks on power. Democracy recognizes that each citizen's vote is of equal value, that each citizen's voice has an equal right to be heard. This puts into practical effect the proclamation by the framers and signatories of the Universal Declaration of Human

Rights that "recognition of the inherent dignity and of the equal and inalienable rights of all members of the human family is the foundation of freedom, just and peace in the world." (United Nations, 1948). It adds that they have declared their "faith in fundamental human rights, in the dignity and worth of the human person and in the equal rights of men and women and have determined to promote social progress and better standards of life in larger freedoms."

Democracy is not a perfect system of government but it is the best available because it is based on the fundamental principle of human equity and operates via the mechanism of community decision making through individual choice. It seeks to balance the differing interests of individuals and, by extension, communal interests. Its growing acceptance internationally since the nineteenth century, especially since WWII, has demonstrated a broad international consensus that it offers the best available means of governing a state in order to ensure fair treatment for all of its members (Inglehart and Norris, 2003). In the present global environment, democracies are consistently outperforming autocracies and many of the latter know that they are standing on their last leg.

2 CIVIL SOCIETY AS THE FUEL FOR DEMOCRACY

The establishment of library associations or syndicates and the support of libraries to civil societies in their communities are part and parcel of the civil society movement that serves as the fuel for the engine of democracy. The civil society thesis presumes that through the collective force of its demands and interests, the associational sector can compel unwilling authoritarian governments to instigate periods of democratization. In most African and other developing societies, the absence of significant multiparty political competition, most anti-state political activity is routed through non-regime spaces and groups rather than the hopelessly outgunned opposition parties, where they exist. Yet, it does not follow that civil society can cure the autocratic ills of African societies.

The concept of civil society emerged in Western social science as the Cold War ended, when comparative social scientists borrowed the concept from European history in order to explain the ongoing wave of democratic transitions across the world. According to Tocqueville, civil society must maintain autonomy from the state and especially from "the control of the administration," whose influence could be seen in the state's monopoly of public instruction, health care, and provision of support for the unemployed" (Keane, 1988). In this sentiment, Tocqueville articulates a republican understanding of civil society that remains influential today. Keane summarizes Tocqueville vision of civil society as follows:

> Tocqueville never tired of repeating the point that "independent eye of society" … an eye comprising a popularity of interacting, self-organized and constantly vigilant civil associations-is necessary for consolidating the democratic revolution. In contrast to political forms of involvement (such as participation in elections or jury services, which are concerned with the wider, more general community interests, civil associations consist of combinations of citizens preoccupied with "small affairs."

A cadre of neo-Tocquevillian scholars has since repeated a simple casual claim: no civil society, no democratization. Most Western political scientists define civil society as the place where a mélange of groups, associations, clubs, guilds, syndicates, federations, unions, parties and groups come together to provide a buffer between state and citizen. Thus CSOs must be secular in ideology, civil in their behavior, legally recognized, and supportive of democratic reform.

Though the civil society thesis encapsulates several distinct hypotheses, the relevant one here entails that under conditions of authoritarian rule, an energetic associational life-comprising independent, voluntary organizations distinct from the state, economy, and family-can trigger democratic transitions by challenging autocratic leaders and forcing the state to accept liberal reforms.

In some African and North African countries, civil society facilitated democratization by restraining state coercion, inflating the overt cost of repression, and marshalling international support for reforms. By the mid-1990s, the Western academic and policy-making consensus was that the emergence of a dynamic civil society represented the sin qua non of democracy. According to one report, civil society resistance played a vital role in driving 50 out of 67 modern transitions from authoritarian rule. The United Nations Development Program (UNDP) portrays civil society as a vital pillar in sustaining human development and fostering transparent political governance. The World Bank and European Commission (EC) employ a broad portfolio of aid to support civil society. US foundations like the Ford Foundation and National Endowment for Democracy run numerous grant competitions for CSOs in developing countries, rewarding them with liquid funds, training workshops, and exchange programs. Between 1991 and 2001, the US Agency for International Development (USAID) allocated $150 million to projects classified as "civil society strengthening," Political donors, bilateral aid agencies, and multilateral financial institutions in the democracy promotion industry have clinched civil society as the magic bullet against African autocracy-empowering associational forces and stimulate would-be democratizes and impel authoritarian rulers to accept compromises regarding political rights, fair elections, and civil liberties.

3 THE ROLE OF LIBRARIES AND LIBRARIANS IN PROMOTING DEMOCRACY

Historically, librarians have been ranked among nations' intellectuals and wise men and women. Librarians were the guardians of knowledge and the heritage of mankind. Because of their status and stature as wise intellectuals, they were also victims of brutal authorities of kings and emperors. We have seen examples of persecution and prosecution of librarians in the China, the former Soviet Union, Cuba, and being the subject of ridicule by some of arch conservatives in the Bush administration, including the former Attorney General Ashcroft, when librarians and the American Library Association voiced their opposition to the Patriot Act and its infringement on intellectual freedom.

Libraries and librarians have also been used as forums for government propaganda as was the case during the Cold War when the Soviet Union and the West competed to establish libraries and distribute books in third world countries attacking each other and promoting their own policies, cultures and way of life as better than the others. I remember the years of my youth in Egyptian cities like Cairo and Alexandria where young people frequented the USIA Library, Goethe House, the British Council Library, the Russian and the Czech embassies in search of books to read and gifts of books to take home.

Throughout the past two centuries, libraries became essential institutions of democracies in countries which have been fortunate to enjoy this system of government. As early as 1815, Jesse Torrey spoke of "universal dissemination of knowledge and virtue by means of free public libraries" as a cause consecrated by religion and enjoined by patriotism." (Torrey 1815).

As "arsenal of democracy", the institution of libraries became the protectors of the written heritage of mankind and provided a gateway to the ideals of democracy. Writing at the onset of World War II, when book burning was a tradition in some European countries and a possibility in the United States, Archibald McLeish, then Librarian of Congress, spoke of the book as a "construction spirit" and librarians not only as 'keepers of the word" but also its partisans and advocates. He states that it is upon American libraries that the burden of his education must fall. He claims that education is not an altogether adequate answer to those who ask for a chance to work usefully and creatively.

The American President Franklin Delano Roosevelt best articulated the role of the library in a democratic society. During the darkest days of WWII, when the future of democracy was very much in question, he told the nation:

> Libraries are directly and immediately involved in the conflict which divides our world, and for two reasons; first because they are essential to the functioning of a democratic society; second, because the contemporary conflict touches the integrity of scholarship, the freedom of the mind, and even the survival of culture, and libraries are the great tools of scholarship, the great repositories of culture, and the great symbols of the freedom of the mind. (Ditzion)

The former Librarian of Congress Daniel Boorstin observed that today's libraries continue to function as "meccas of self-help ... the most open of open universities ... where there are no entrance examinations and no diplomas, and where one can enter at any age." For Boorstin, libraries are "full partners in a dynamic Learning Society." He added:

> As citizens of the world's longest-lasting democracy, we must have easy access to libraries more than ever before. How well we govern, how intelligently we think through on difficult issues after another, how rationally we perform at center stage on the planet, will depend on our taking advantage of those resources.

In today's information environment, the Internet, Cybercafés and television broadcasts directed at African, Asian, South American and Middle Eastern countries have surpassed libraries as sources of information, education as well as propaganda and misinformation by some.

Since libraries were not a European or American invention, people in the Third World countries should take pride in the fact that in their classic and ancient civilizations libraries flourished in such African countries as Egypt, Timbuktu, Mombassa, and as well as in China, Mesopotamia, Persia and other centers of ancient civilizations.

Just as libraries are not an American or Western invention neither is democracy. The Greeks gave it its new meaning; yet, it has been practiced in Africa at the tribal level where the councils of elders made the final decisions and were always consulted by the tribal chiefs.

It is these two institutions that we should emphasize today as we strive to push for a revival of two old traditions: democracy and libraries.

There is no doubt in my mind that that these two institutions, once forgotten under authoritarian regimes and the yoke of colonialism, will rise again and play a major role in the economic development of our African, Asian and Middle Eastern countries. However, we must be able to resist the arguments that advance the notion that without economic development there can be no democracy and freedom for the masses. The argument is colonial in its historic premise and condescending in its psychological impact. Does one have to wait to be a rich person to enjoy freedom and democracy in his own native land? Does one have to sacrifice his liberty for a decent living, employment, and health care? It is true that development can be measured by social indicators such as life expectancy, access to clean drinking water, literacy rates, agricultural yields, and the quality of public-health services. On nearly all of these quality of life measures, low-income democracies dramatically outdo their autocratic counterparts. (Siegle et. al,, 1994). The development-first thesis has persisted in the post-Cold War world, despite the abysmal economic record of Latin American military governments, the "strongman" rulers in Africa, and the communist states in Eastern Europe and the former Soviet Union. Countries often remain poor because they retain autocratic political structures and subscribe to the notion that development-first strategy perpetuates a deadly cycle of poverty, conflict, and oppression. (Siegle et. al., 1994). The development-first thesis rests on a commonsense notion, put forward by political sociologist Seymour Martin Lipset and others some 45 years ago, that economic growth creates the necessary preconditions for democracy by expanding literacy, creating a secure middle class, and nurturing cosmopolitan attitudes. Second, it fits comfortably with the demands of the era of its origin, the Cold War, when about a third of countries qualified as democracies and very few of them were poor.

I dare say that the majority of our African, Asian and Middle Eastern brothers and sisters would rather enjoy their freedom today rather than waiting for the unfulfilled promises of prosperity for tomorrow. Our people have been lied to for a long time and the prosperous tomorrow that was promised to them under British, French, Italian, or Portuguese occupation never came and their independence and freedom were never granted, but fought for with our ancestor's blood and sweat.

Today, libraries have proven themselves to be one of the basic corners of a democracy, in more ways than we can enumerate in the short time we have. Nonetheless, librarians can take pride in acknowledging the following facts:

- Libraries are frequently described as the "cornerstones of liberty"
- Libraries should continue to resist censorship and collection development
- The library is the center for community problem-solving
- Libraries, as educational institutions, and their managers who are also educators, can make a major contribution to the promotion and strengthening of democracy
- Public libraries should promote themselves as the "Peoples' University" and enlist independent learners in the ranks of politicians, business and industry, trade unions, places of worship, women's movement, and others
- Article 26 on the right to education, the Universal Declaration provides a powerful mission for those engaged in providing access to information, the libraries and information services of the world. It states the right to education "shall be directed to the full development of the human personality and to the strengthening of respect for human rights and fundamental freedoms ... [and] promote understanding, tolerance, and friendship among all nations, social or religious, and shall further the activities of the United Nations for the maintenance of peace." These principles have been elaborated in regard to library and information services through a variety of professional statements on intellectual freedom, ethics and guidelines for services, of which many examples have been gathered on the IFLA/FAIFE Web site (IFLA/FAIFE, 1998)
- The most influential international statement has been UNESCO *Public Library Manifesto*. Through that *Manifesto* and other statements, UNESCO and IFLA have expressed the strong relationship between good libraries and healthy democracies. It has built on a tradition which has gathered force since the ALA's adoption of the Library Bill of Rights on the eve of WWII. (ALA, 1939). It is of interest to us in this gathering to note that the release of the *Public Library Manifesto* by the UNESCO coincided with the South African shift to democracy. This timely document emphasized the principles of democracy and its relationship to public libraries. The *Manifesto* states:

  > "Freedom, prosperity and the development of society and individuals are fundamental human values. They will only be attained through the ability of well-informed citizens to exercise their democratic rights and to play an active role in society. Constructive participation and the development of democracy depend on satisfac-

tory education as well as on free and unlimited access to knowledge, thought, culture and information. (UNESCO 1994)"

- In this tradition, the 1973 IFLA Standards for Public libraries posits:
  - A democratic institution for education, culture and information;
  - The public library is a practical demonstration of democracy's faith in universal education as a continuing and life-long process in the appreciation of the achievement of humanity in knowledge and culture;
  - The public library is the principal means, whereby the record of man's thoughts and ideas and the expression of his creative imagination are made freely available to all (IFLA Section on Public Libraries, 1973, pp. 13–14).
  - Such statements give the public library an instrumental role in the strengthening of civil society through building social capital. The explicit inclusion of this role was one of the significant changes in the 1994 version of the *Public Library Manifesto* when compared to the 1972 revision and the 1949 original (Niegaard, 1994). It was later incorporated into the IFLA/UNESCO *School Library Manifesto* (IFLA Section on Libraries and Resource Centers and UNESCO, 2000).
  - Equally important to IFLA's *Manifesto* is Article 19 of the Declaration of Human Rights which states that everyone has the right to freedom of opinion and expression, this right includes freedom to hold opinions without interference and to seek, receive and impart information and ideas through any media.
  - Like the IFLA *Manifest I* and *Article 19, The Glasgow Declaration* declares that the role of libraries and information services as "democratic institutions" impose certain responsibilities starting from a professional commitment to intellectual freedom as a core responsibility. That commitment is expressed through codes of ethics and demonstrated through individual and organizational practices including the promotion of its principles.

4 LIBRARY ACTIVITIES IN SUPPORT OF DEMOCRACY

Among the activities that libraries can engage in their efforts to promote and sustain democracy are the following:

- Library resources should be presented in many formats including those accessible to the visually disabled and increasingly in digital forms. Collections, access arrangements, document delivery services-the whole interconnected network of library operations seek to respond to that right.
- Access to information can be inhibited by conditions such as lack of resources or the capacities to access them, or contractual or technological limitations, or it can also be limited by active measures such as censorship
- Library services should provide access to the widest variety of materials, reflecting the plurality and diversity of society
- The commitment to anticipating and meeting community needs flows from the right to be informed
- Access to information should include programs for the house-bound, children and teenagers, women and various ethnic and religious groups. It could include programs in a variety of languages and those meeting the needs of indigenous peoples.
- Protection of each user's right to privacy and confidentiality with respect to information sought or received and resources consulted, borrowed, acquired or transmitted. Democracy implies the right to free speech. Libraries can play an important role by encouraging debates and establishing and hosting debating clubs. Programs can center on issues affecting people's livelihood such as sex and sexually transmitted disease. The important thing is to encourage people to debate, respect each others' opinion, learn the facts about issues by reading, listening, encourage and assist people with the use of the Internet to debate with others beyond the library's borders.

5 OUR COMMITMENT

Our professional commitment to freedom of access to information puts us in direct opposition to restrictive measures. We might not demonstrate publicly against them or place our lives at risk by outright opposition but we should do all in our power to resist rate restrictions on responsible intellectual freedom and freedom of expression.

Intellectual repression is an inevitable result of censorship. It can be imposed by others or be the result of self censorship, which might be adopted for fear of the consequences of expressing one's thoughts, or in response to pernicious danger of political correctness. (Lessing, 2001). Either way, it stultifies the imagination and imprisons the human sprit. (Byrne, 2004). The responsibility of the library and its management is not to impose or allow political, moral, or religious views to dominate.

There should be no discrimination for any reason including race, national or ethnic region, gender or sexual preference age, disability, religious, or political beliefs. Librarians should protect each user's right to privacy and confidentiality with respect to information sought or received and resources consulted, borrowed, acquired or transmitted.

Libraries should involve themselves in civic literacy; formal and informal (independent) learning as well as being a reference, research and information center to the community and its citizens.

By fulfilling all of these responsibilities, managers not only "help safeguard democratic values and universal civil rights," but also are expected to offer "essential support for independent decision-making, cultural development, research and lifelong learning by both individuals and groups."

6 CONCLUSION

It has bee noted that democracy depends both on freedom and accessibility of information and on an informed public. To play this important role in Africa, libraries must have the financial resources to develop collections that are viable both in their quality and quantity. The print materials should be supplemented by electronic materials and by providing easy, free and unlimited access to the Internet. Libraries must also play a role with education to develop a public that is receptive, open, questioning, and discriminating. Reformed education and libraries can and must play a major part in developing such minds.

Libraries and librarians hold a key role in forming the lives of African children, the future citizens of a hopefully democratic society. Treat them with respect, trust them, and make them love books, knowledge, enrich their imagination, and help them live a dream.

International and NGOs should provide special technical and financial assistance to libraries and information systems in countries which have opted to democratic systems of government and civil societies. However, it is worth noting here that there are barriers to the flow of information. These include the following:

- Language difficulties

- Information pollution from within and without
- Legal and administrative barriers hindering the flow of information between the Arab countries and the West, and among themselves
- Lack of trust. Democracy and freedom rely on trusting people. Unfortunately, many libraries in Africa and Third World countries don't trust their own people with library books and other materials
- Library decision-makers must give effect to their commitment in the context of budgetary, staffing and resource limitations, legal and policy constraints and the daily exigencies of running service organizations.
- Too much emphasis on religious education
- Separation of the sexes results in duplication or restriction of services
- Too much decentralization at the macro levels
- Little or non-existent library cooperation
- Absence of formally established librarians societies or associations

REFERENCES

Block, Marylane (June/July 2001). "Keepers of the flame," *American Libraries*, vol. 32, no. 6, pp. 64–67.

Boorstin, Daniel J. (1986) *Alliance for Excellence, The Librarians Response to A Nation at Risk*, as quoted in Dickinson, Paul, *The Library in America: A Celebration in Words and Pictures*. New York: Facts on File Publications, p.236.

Byrne, Alex (2004)" Library management," *Bradford*, vol. 25, no. 1&2, p.11.

Brown, Nicole E. (2004). "The Shift from Apartheid to Democracy: Issues and Impacts on Public Libraries in Cape Tow, South Africa," *Libri*, vol. 54: pp. 169–178.

Ditzion, Sydney (1947). *Arsenals of a Democratic Culture*. Chicago: ALA.

Hafner, Arthur W., ed. (1993). *Democracy and the Public Library: essays on Fundamental Issues*. Westport, CT: Greenwood Press. (*Contributions in Librarianship and Information Science,* no. 78)

Keane, John (1988). "Despotism and Democracy: The Origins and Distinction Between Civil Society and the State 1750–1850." Pp. 35–71, in *Civil Society and the State: New European Perspectives*, edited by J. Keane. New York: Verso.

Kranich, Nancy (2001). *Libraries and Democracy: The Cornerstones of Liberty.* Chicago: American Library Association.

McLeish, Archibald (1991). "Libraries in the Contemporary Crisis," *Library Journal,* vol. 116, no. 11, pp. 10–13.

Mind Extension University (1991). *Equal Access for All: Democracy and the Public Library.* Englewood, CO: Mind Extension University.

Palm Beach Community College and Southeast Florida Library Information Network (1997). *Democracy in the Information Age, Who Should Govern the Web*. Lake Worth, Fl.: Palm Beach Community College. 4 videocassettes (170 min.); sd., col.; ¾ in

Pinnel-Stephens, June and Barbara Jones (June/July, 1999). 'Libraries a Misunderstood American Value, *American Libraries*, 30(6): pp. 76–79.

Schechter, Stephen (Spring 1990). "The Library as a Source of Civic Literacy," *The Bookmark*, pp. 176–182.

Siegle, Joseph, Michael M. Weinstein, and Morton H. Halperin (Sept.–Oct. 1994). "Why Democracies Excel," *Foreign Affairs,* 83(2): 57–85.

Torrey, Jesse. *The Intellectual Torch* (1815); reprinted Woodstock VT, Elmtree Press, 1912), as quoted in Ditzion, Sidney H., *Arsenals of a Democratic Culture*. Chicago: ALA, 1947. p. 58.

Turfan, Barbara, et al. (1995). Emerging Democracies and Freedom of Information; proceedings of a Conference of the International Group of the Library Association (IGLA), Oxford, September 1994. London: library Association. 174p.

Tyckoson, David A. (2000). "Of the People for the People: Public Libraries Serve Democracy," *American Libraries*, vol. 31, no. 4, pp. 40–42.

UNESCO Public Library Manifesto (1994). International Federation of Library Associations and Institutions (IFLA) http://www.ifla.org/VII/s8/unesco/eng.htm. [viewed March 4, 2006]

MANAGEMENT OF AGRICULTURAL RESEARCH INFORMATION AND KNOWLEDGE: A CASE FOR THE SCECSAL REGION

Justin Chisenga

ABSTRACT

The major by-products of agriculture research are information and knowledge, which in the case of most African countries are codified and made available in the form of grey literature. However, the grey literature is not easily accessible both from within and outside the agricultural research organisations. This is due to a number of factors, among them the weak mechanisms for the documentation and dissemination of the outputs of agricultural science, and the general lack of capacity among agricultural information specialists and institutional capacity for agricultural content management. In addition, in most cases not that many documents are produced and a large number of them are locked up in drawers and cabinets, thus making their distribution and accessibility very limited. Agricultural research organisations in the SCECSAL region can benefit significantly from participating in the activities being conducted under the new AGRIS strategy. The strategy provides a framework for documenting, disseminating and sharing agricultural research information and knowledge using ICT-based tools and methodologies, and information management standards. In addition, AGRIS also emphasises capacity building in agricultural information management and is supported by a series of online training modules produced under the Information Management Resource Kit (IMARK) initiative, and complimented by face-to-face training workshops held in collaboration with national and regional partners.

1 INTRODUCTION

Agriculture forms the mainstay of the economy in most developing countries (Beye, 2002, p. 1). In 1997 it contributed on average 40% of the Gross Domestic Product (GDP) and more than 60% to foreign exchange earnings in 1977. In spite of this being the case, Africa and other continents have not been experiencing growth in agricultural yields. This is due to a number of factors, among them the decline in external agricultural assistance from multilateral organisations. Further, there has also been a reduction in funding for agricultural research. Yet, agricultural research holds the vital key to improving food security, reducing poverty and sustaining broad-based economic development (Beye, 2002, p. 2).

Agricultural research includes also research on fish, trees, as well as crops and livestock and natural resources (ISNAR, 2002), and the primary benefit from agricultural research is improved production (Johnson, 2001). However, the major by-products of agriculture research are information and knowledge. Agricultural research and the information generated from such research are important stimulants for accelerating agricultural production development in a country (Kaniki, 1992, p. 83). To carry out their work, agricultural research organisations also require various resources, among them information and knowledge. Therefore, efficient provision of access to relevant information and knowledge to agricultural research scientists could contribute to quality research, through which "a country is able to select appropriate technology and information, which if applied can help productivity" (Kaniki, 1992, p. 83), and thus contribute to the overall growth of the country's economy.

2 A CHALLENGE FOR AFRICAN AGRICULTURAL RESEARCH INSTITUTIONS

2.1 Visibility of Outputs of Agricultural Research

Agricultural research information and knowledge has traditionally been codified and made available mainly through scientific articles in learned journals, originally in printed and increasingly in electronic form. Other outputs of research have been the "grey" or fugitive literature in printed or electronic format (e.g. institution reports, technical documents, conference proceedings, seminar papers, theses and dissertations), which have often not been captured in easily accessible forms by the institutions that produce them. However, institutions are increasingly realizing the importance of these archival collections of documents, which are being digitized, stored, and made accessible from e-repositories, in the form of full-text documents as well as associated metadata.

In spite of the availability of various mechanisms for the dissemination of agricultural research information, the research generated in developing and emerging countries is "missing" from the international knowledge bases because of financial restrictions affecting its publication and distribution (Gibbs, 1995; Arunachalam, 1994), and Africa is the most affected continent. Most agricultural research information from Africa is largely available as grey literature, mainly in the form of research/technical reports and papers presented at conferences and seminars. Very little research output finds it way into the world's well-established international scientific journals. The mechanisms for the documentation and dissemination of the outputs of agricultural science in Africa are in general weak and as a result the outputs of research are *often inadequately* recorded, and are not communicated to the farmers, policy makers and others who need to adapt and apply them (FAO, 2004, p.1). One contributing factor to this state of affairs is the absence of capacity, both human and institutional, for managing grey literature, which increasingly is being generated in digital format. Agricultural research organisations need to adopt a suitable strategy for capturing and managing grey literature (both in print and digital formats) and for making this literature visible to all potential "consumers".

While it is easy to find research outputs (scientific articles) in journals by scientists from developed countries, it is not the same for research outputs from Africa. Articles in well-established scholarly journals are indexed in various international databases such as Science Citation Index, CAB Abstracts and AGRICOLA, which increases the "visibility" of their contents. Overall, it is very difficulty to increase the visibility of research from the less advanced countries due to many factors, among them the following identified by Cetto (2002):

- Publication in mainstream journals faces the problems of over-subscription and recorded prejudice against submissions from developing country scientists.
- Few local journals are published and these journals have in general poor distribution and visibility, and are normally underrepresented in the international databases and indexing services.

In addition, most agricultural research libraries and documentation centres only include published materials, such as books, in their catalogues and do not carry out abstracting and indexing activities for grey literature. Further, most library catalogues, especially in the public agricultural research institutions, are not computerised and therefore cannot be accessed via electronic networks such as local intranets, extranets and the Internet. The result is that there is limited visibility and access to agricultural information resources being generated in Africa.

So, a principal challenge facing agricultural organizations involved in science and technology is that although their core competencies are in research and development, there is an *imperative* to be effective in accessing information and disseminating their outputs. Many opportunities are provided by the new information technologies, but many agricultural organizations are not rising to the challenge adequately. Key constraints are firstly institutional capacities (lack of resources and appropriate organizational structures), secondly human capacities (lack of awareness and skills), and lastly the networks that offer poor outreach to key audiences. Enhancing institutional capacities will require new organizational structures, new skills and/or new staff, new information content in digital format, and the acquisition of new technologies. Minimising the impact of this change would require that stakeholders learn lessons from others and as far as possible use existing technologies.

Taking the above situation into account, a suitable solution for agricultural research organisations in Africa is one that addresses the problem of lack of capacity in agricultural information management while at the same time ensuring visibility of the outputs of agricultural research. This paper makes the case that the International Information System on Agricultural Sciences and Technology (AGRIS) and its associated network of participating institutions is well placed to do this.

3 INTERNATIONAL NETWORKS FOR MOBILIZING AGRICULTURAL SCIENCE AND TECHNOLOGY INFORMATION

3.1 AGRIS – the new strategy

FAO has been committed to effective documentation and communication of agricultural science and technology for developing countries for over 30 years under the AGRIS network. AGRIS was established in 1974 by FAO in response to demand from member states to facilitate information exchange and to bring together world literature dealing with all aspects of agriculture. The system became operational in 1975 as an international initiative aiming to build a common information system for science and technology in agriculture and related subjects, based on a collaborative network of institutions (FAO, 2002). One of the founding principles of AGRIS was that it was to provide a centralised collection of bibliographic details of outputs and activities of national agricultural research programmes, especially non – conventional (grey) literature. Although AGRIS has been partially successful in achieving its goals, a stocktaking exercise undertaken in 2002 led to some major observations about the status of the network. In particular, it concluded that it was difficult to access the original documents from AGRIS references, there was extremely incomplete global coverage of agricultural grey literature in the central database, many existing AGRIS centres did not link in any significant way to the wider scientific community in agriculture, and lastly many independent national bibliographic databases and information systems had arisen outside the scope of AGRIS, often with no involvement of FAO.

Following this review and taking into account developments in information and communication technologies, FAO in collaboration with the Member Countries developed the following new principles for the AGRIS network in 2002:

- a ***decentralised*** approach with greater emphasis on national partnerships with greater autonomy but with improved links;
- a greater ***diversity*** of research-oriented organisations participating in a strengthened global AGRIS network;
- a strengthened role in ***capacity building***, including improved linkages between the AGRIS network and other FAO initiatives in Member Countries;
- a focus on management of ***full text*** of documents in agricultural science and technology information resources;
- a greater availability of ***associated information*** about activities, organisations, and people in agricultural science and technology;
- a continually improving set of ***web-enabled*** AGRIS methodologies and tools (with a focus on the establishment of standards), aimed at effective exchange and retrieval of science and technology information in a multilingual environment, developed and disseminated by FAO in consultation with Member Countries and AGRIS partners.

The above principles placed emphasis on improving electronic publishing of documentation (full-text documents) in agricultural science and technology, linking information about institutions, scientists and researchers, and activities, and using Web-enabled AGRIS methodology and tools to manage and disseminate digital documents. As apposed to the old arrangements whereby one organization (national AGRIS input centre) in a country coordinated inputs into AGRIS, the new strategy allowed for individual research organisations to directly contribute and share their information/knowledge resources with the international AGRIS community. This arrangement also made it possible for institutions to collaborate, share their information resources and work towards a distributed national and regional AGRIS network. Further, the new AGRIS strategy supported and promoted the concept of establishing open access repositories (open archives).

The new vision was intended to lead to the creation of a collaborative network of collections of resources and publications, working with web-enabled technologies for the Internet and CD-ROM. Participation in this network was to be open to any organization able and interested to participate in AGRIS, and these organizations were then renamed "Resource Centres", leaving behind the notion of centralized national hubs.

An electronic conference across the AGRIS network moderated by FAO in 2003 led to a set of fifteen recommendations related to capacity building and the processing and presentation of information content, all which were implemented during 2004/05.

3.2 Resource materials for capacity building

There is a widely recognized need for high quality resource materials to support capacity building in agricultural information management. A wide range of organizations including FAO are collaborating on developing such materials for trainers and for learners in support of capacity building programmes/activities related to participating in and accessing scientific and technical information through initiatives and networks such as AGRIS.

A group of seven organizations have formed a Steering Group that supports and guides a partnership-based e-learning initiative known as the Information Management Resource Kit (IMARK), which is training individuals in effective management of agricultural information (http://www.imarkgroup.org). The goal of the IMARK initiative is to mobilize and build upon existing resources to create a comprehensive suite of distance learning resources for information management and exchange, which will support agencies, institutions and networks world-wide, and to allow them to work together and share information more effectively within a virtual community of practice. IMARK covers several major subject areas in information management and each module treats one of the major subject areas. The modules introduce the latest concepts, approaches and tools for information management, using interactive tutorials specifically designed for individual self-paced learning. The learning materials are being developed as a series of modules on CD-ROM, supplemented by an Internet-based online community, providing a virtual discussion forum for contributors and learners to exchange views, share information and request help from each other.

IMARK modules are being developed using the latest methods in e-learning, providing an interactive environment for self-paced learning.[14] The modules that have been developed so far all have direct applications in developing human and institutional capacities in digital information management, and these are:

- Management of Electronic Documents
- Digitization and Digital Libraries documents.
- Investing in Information for Development
- Building Electronic Communities and Networks

3.3 AGRIS – new strategy into action in African countries

In Africa, FAO and partner organizations focused on developing the capacity building element of the new AGRIS strategy, while also addressing the need for advocacy for adoption of the new approach. IMARK modules are being used to support the roll-out of the new AGRIS strategy in the context of a blended learning approach which uses the IMARK curriculum and materials to support face-to-face workshops with self-paced distance learning. Given that IMARK modules were initially produced in English only, capacity building activities were concentrated in Anglophone Africa. Since May 2004, several face-to-face training workshops have been held in the SCECSAL region.

Activity in Eastern/Central Africa was led by the Association for Strengthening Agricultural Research in Eastern and Central Africa (ASARECA), through its Regional Agricultural Information Network (RAIN). A regional training-of-trainers workshop on *Electronic Production of Agricultural Documents and Bibliographic Database/Management* held in Kenya in 2004 for 22 participants from nine countries (Burundi, Democratic Republic of Congo (DRC), Ethiopia, Kenya, Madagascar, Rwanda, Tanzania, Uganda and Sudan). Since that time, national AGRIS training workshops have been held in Kenya (in collaboration with the Kenya Agricultural Research Institute – KARI), Tanzania (in collaboration with the Department of Research and Training of the Ministry of Agriculture and Food Security) and in Sudan, in collaboration with the Agricultural Research Corporation.

Activity in West Africa was led by the Ghana Agricultural Information Networks Systems (GAINS) based at Institute for Scientific and Technical Informa-

[14] http://www.imarkgroup.org/

tion (INSTI) of Ghana. In March 2004, GAINS hosted a regional training-of-trainers workshop on *Electronic Production of Agricultural Documents and Bibliographic Database/Management* for 20 participants from the Gambia, Ghana and Nigeria, in May 2004.

The objectives of the training workshops were to introduce participants to modern trends and initiatives in agricultural information management, to introduce participants to the new AGRIS vision, and to equip participants with skills to enable them to manage outputs of agricultural research (electronic documents) using WebAGRIS tools and methodologies. Leading on from these training initiatives, pilot national AGRIS networks in the new vision are now being established in Ghana and Kenya, with participation of multiple resource centres and wider uptake and use of methodologies and tools.

Now that IMARK materials are available in French, capacity building activities are being strengthened, and plans are being developed for the development of pilot national networks.

3.4 Regional and international institutions and networks

A group of organizations at the regional and sub-regional level has provided leadership and support for the development of capacities in the area of agricultural information management. The Forum for African Agricultural Research (FARA) has held a series of meetings in 2004–05 around the topic of building a regional agricultural information system (RAIS) in the FARA region". The meetings have been aimed at examining the potential role of the RAIS in the context of activities by international organizations and the emerging information/communication strategies of the three sub-regional organizations ASARECA, CORAF (West and Central African Council for Agricultural Research and Development), and SADC (Southern African Development Community). The parties all recognized that their collective goal was to add value to and enhance national systems (NAIS), because such systems are generally weak in Africa, often operating in unfavourable policy environments, with poor and high cost of connectivity, and limited capacity and infrastructure. Bearing that in mind, it was decided to establish a RAIS for Africa, centered on common sets of information, training and infrastructure support.

These activities in Africa have been part of a broader picture at global level, whereby the Global Forum on Agricultural Research (GFAR) has been orchestrating a series of activities and meetings in 2003–5 focused on information and communication management for agricultural research and development (ICM4ARD). Separate regional consultations, including one in Africa, culminated in the 1st Inter-Regional Consultation held in June 2004, out of which arose a ICM4ARD Global Partnership Programme (GPP) to support regional and national ARD organizations. The outputs of the GPP were to be (i) strengthening of the advocacy role of the National Agricultural Research System (NARS) leaders, (ii) capacity development of regional and national ICM specialists, and (iii) greater integration of ARD information systems, and (iv) development of appropriate governance structures for global and regional information Systems.

These four themes were further examined and refined at an international consultation in Rome in October 2005 in terms of achieving maximum synergies between the existing national, regional and global initiatives and capacities. Out of this consultation has emerged the decision to re-launch AGRIS under co-ownership, with the primary objective still on strengthening national networks but using the sub-regional and regional organizations to provide support and leverage lesson learning opportunities between countries.

4 COHERENCE IN CONTENT MANAGEMENT

4.1 Agricultural Information Management Standards

Sharing information and knowledge in an electronic environment requires the use of common exchange standards. FAO has played a key role in the creation and provision of common agricultural information management and exchange standards, and has undertaken a number of initiatives under the WAICENT Framework to facilitate setting of standard and promote the concept of "coherence" in agricultural information including the following three major initiatives (FAO, 2006, p.3).

Under the new AGRIS strategy, FAO is committed to facilitating the development and support of free tools and standards to provide AGRIS network members with a complete set of applications for distributed data input, management, and dissemination of metadata on information objects (FAO, 2002b). The new AGRIS strategy can easily facilitate management, sharing and integration of the outputs of agricultural research from the SCECSAL region into international networks while at the same time providing access to information and knowledge resources on the local intranet.

- The **Agricultural Metadata Standards Initiative** (AgMES), launched in November 2000, facilitates the development and use of standardized agricultural metadata terms for enhancing location and exchange of agricultural information on the Web. Several systems and applications within and outside FAO have operational metadata schemas using AgMES elements.
- The **AGRIS Application Profile** is a format that allows sharing of information across dispersed bibliographic systems derived from the AGMES standard for the AGRIS international information system for the agricultural sciences and technology.
- **Terminologies and thesauri:** The multilingual AGROVOC thesaurus standardizes the indexing process in order to make searching simpler and more efficient, and so allows the user to locate the most relevant resources.
- The **WebAGRIS** toolset manages metadata, and allows links to full-text documents available in electronic format. It uses WWW-ISIS software, developed by the Institute for Computer and Information Engineering in Poland, in close cooperation with FAO-WAICENT, with an Interface based on HTML forms. WebAGRIS uses common standards of data input (metadata standard data structure), and dissemination formats (export formats – XML, HTML, ISO2709), as well as subject categorization schema and thesauri, i.e. AGROVOC.

The above standards are being used to facilitate the common exchange and description of agricultural information documents and resources within the current AGRIS network. To facilitate collaboration and sharing of information on the standards and related initiatives, FAO created the Agricultural Information Management Standards (AIMS) portal, which was launched in 2005 (http://www.fao.org/aims).

Fig. 1: AIMS Portal

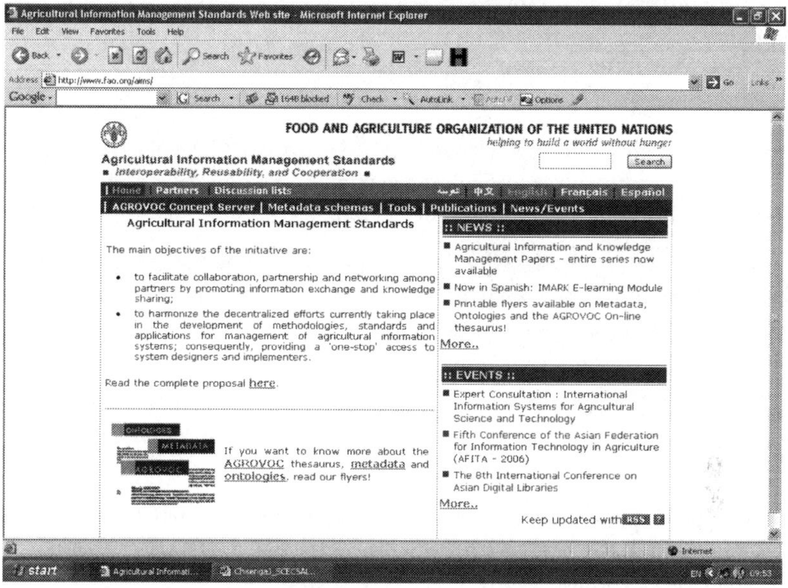

5 CONCLUSION

Organizations in the SCECSAL region with a stake in agricultural information management need to adopt and use mechanisms supported by international standards in the management and exchange of agricultural information and knowledge resources. They also need to participate in collaborative international networks such as AGRIS to enhance the visibility of their research outputs. Active participation in AGRIS activities and the adoption and use of AGRIS-supported tools and methodologies, and associated information management and exchange standards, will facilitate the exchange and access to agricultural information and knowledge resources among agricultural research organisations in the sub-region, via local intranets and the Internet. This approach will also make the outputs of agricultural research in the sub-region more visible to the global community, and thus raise the profile of agricultural research organisations in the sub-region. Providing access to full-text information resources in digital format will also contribute to the bridging of the content divide that exists between the developed countries and the developing countries.

REFERENCES

Arunachalam, S. (1994). Accessing information published in the third world – should spreading the word from the third world always be like swimming against the current? *Journal of Scientific & Industrial Research*, vol. *53*, pp. 408–417.

Beye, G. (2002). *Impact of foreign assistance on institutional development of national agricultural research systems in sub-Saharan Africa*. Rome: FAO. (FAO Research and Technology Paper 10).

Cetto, A. M. (2000). *Sharing scientific knowledge through publications: what do developing countries have to offer? World Conference on Science: Science for the Twenty-first Century, a New Commitment.* Paris: UNESCO: pp. 148–150.

Chisenga, J. (2004). *Application possibilities of agricultural information portals. Johannesburg*. Rand Afrikaans University, Johannesburg, South Africa. [D. Litt. et Phil. (Information Science) thesis].

FAO. (2006). New approaches to information access under WAICENT [Paper presented at the 24th FAO Africa Region Conference, Bamako, Mali, 30 January–3 February 2006]. Retrieved February 4, 2005, from ftp://ftp.fao.org/unfao/bodies/arc/24arc/J6885E.pdf

FAO. (2005). The AGRIS Application Profile for the International Information System on Agricultural Sciences and Technology: Guidelines on best practices for information object description. Retrieved November 28, 2005, from ftp://ftp.fao.org/docrep/fao/008/ae909e/ae909e00.pdf

FAO. (2002a). *Directory of Agricultural Research Institutions in Africa 2002.* Rome: FAO.

FAO. (2002b). AGRIS – A strategy for an international network for information in agricultural sciences and technology within the WAICENT framework. Retrieved November 29, 2005, from http://www.fao.org/docrep/MEETING/005/AC502e.htm

FAO (n.d.). AGRIS/CARIS information centre homepage. Retrieved November 30, 2005 from http://www.fao.org/agris/

FAO. (2004). Report of the FAO Expert Consultation on Mechanisms for Documenting and Disseminating Outputs of Agricultural Research in Sub-Saharan Africa, 12–14 May 2004, CAB International Africa Regional Centre, Nairobi, Kenya. [Unpublished report].

Gibbs, W.W. (1995). Lost Science in the Third World. *Scientific American*, vol. 273, pp. 76–83.

ISNAR. (2002). Agricultural research organisations on the Web (AROW). Retrieved November 29, 2005, from http://www.isnar.cgiar.org/arow/

Johnson, R. C. (2001). Word to Web publishing for agricultural research. Retrieved November 29, 2005, from http://www.regional.org.au/au/asa/2001/5/a/johnson.htm

Kaniki, A. (1992). Meeting the needs of agricultural researchers in Africa: The role of unpublished reports. *Information for Development*, vol. 8, no. 2, pp. 83–89.

Katz, S. (2005). *Coherence in Agricultural Information Systems* by Stephen Katz made at the Expert Consultation: International Information Systems for Agricultural Science and Technology – Review of Progress and Prospects, 19–21 October 2006, Rome, Italy. [PowerPoint presentation]

Rudgard, S. (2004). FAO's approach to scientific and technical information in agriculture. (PowerPoint presentation). Retrieved November 29, 2005, from http://sist.cirad.fr/fichiers/200403_Mpl/FAO.ppt

A DIGITAL LIBRARY IN A RURAL MALARIA RESEARCH CENTRE IN AFRICA: THE KENYAN EXPERIENCE

J. Kaduda, C. H. O. Olola, T.O. Oluoch, and D.M. Mwazi

ABSTRACT

Medical libraries play a key role in data and information management in medical research and healthcare. The rapidly changing information technology has enhanced the management process, enabling availability of a plethora of publications online globally. However, the widespread use of information technology is seldom realized in developing countries. The overall aim of this study was to evaluate and discuss lessons learnt in setting up a hybrid library in a medical research institution. This was a retrospective study in a busy medical research hospital in Kilifi, Kenya. Two library information management (manual and digital) models were evaluated. The evaluation of information management tools involved medical records, virtual libraries, registers, communication, network and online search systems. User sensitization in change management was not a trivial event. The pace of digitalization of medical libraries in developing countries is slow due to lack of appropriate staff skills, unaffordable cost of information technology and communication (ICT) facilities. However, collaborations with medical research agencies abroad have enabled the transfer of tremendously improved ICT at medical libraries and research institutions as a whole. The available library request and pediatric admissions data demonstrate the existence of correlation between the monthly requests and admissions. More requests are observed during the high admission periods across the year.

1 INTRODUCTION

Digital Libraries play a very crucial role in any research or higher learning institution. A lot of publications are now available online and can be delivered to the end user fast and conveniently over the Internet. The Internet revolution has made it possible for a number of African based scientists to access the most current publications just like any other research institution in the world. The history of libraries in Africa dates back to the colonial days when the three East African countries formed a regional reference resource known as the East African Literature Service in order to save costs. Its first centres were at Makerere University's Mulago Medical School and Muguga in Central Kenya. (Kiathe, 1988)

With the expansion of library service, the quality of service delivered has been compromised over time. A few biomedical libraries are still run by government supported institutions such as the Kenya Medical Research Institute (KEMRI) and the University of Nairobi's College of Health Sciences.

This paper discusses how a hybrid library (digital and manual) has been set up at the KEMRI/Wellcome Trust Research Laboratory (KEMRI/WTRL) Unit based in a rural district along the Kenyan coast. The research activity at the Unit has focused on Malaria and a number of clinical, laboratory and community based research are currently undertaken. The need for up to date publications has increased over the years forcing the Unit to invent a system that would evolve with time to embrace the changing technology. The paper briefly describes the earlier paper based library which has now been integrated with an online electronic system. It has evolved to consolidate various biomedical information resources to provide a rich database, which is very up to date and readily available primarily to the Malaria Research Scientist.

The advent of the local area network and eventually the satellite equipment installation has enabled a rapid growth of a digital integrated database, which is rich in document resources and innovation of tools which have enabled access locally and worldwide of the same resources. Unique in a way, because the system has been customized such that the repository is rich in, but not limited to, the primary area of focus of the Unit – Malaria.

In broad terms the system makes use of e-mail, a web interface, an integrated database system, and a manual paper system which originally existed before the spread of the intranet and internet on the researcher's desk, which still draws onto other, still existent manual system to make the document database very rich.

The Unit is located at the Kilifi District Hospital. Kilifi is one of the poorest districts in Kenya with a high infant mortality rate. Eleven percent (11%) of children in Kilifi district die before the age of 5 [Snow et al, 1994]. The mortality rate for all children under 5 admitted at the Kilifi District Hospital stands at 6.5% [unpublished hospital surveillance data, 2002]. Malaria is the most prevalent disease, only rivaled by HIV Aids. The district suffers from poor road network as well as an under-developed telecommunications infrastructure among other things. There is no established public library within the district, from which scientific information can be obtained to support research. Internet services are hampered by the unreliable and costly telephone link between Kilifi and Mombasa.

The Unit has been in existence since 1989 and currently hosts a number of top Kenyan scientists and those from collaborating institutions, mainly from the United Kingdom. The local community benefits from the existence of a pediatric research ward as well as an intensive care ward run by KEMRI.

2 BRIEF DESCRIPTION OF THE KILIFI LIBRARY PAPER BASED SYSTEM

Before the Virtual library came up, the library users used to get their articles mainly from paper journals in the library, they would get the available journal and search for articles they needed and photocopy.

The users also made their own requests for articles from Oxford University through the librarian in charge. After the request was serviced, the librarian sent them directly to the owners. The requests were not centralized then. The process in a nutshell entailed

- Sending request to librarian using a format printed on the card.
- Librarian processing the request before dispatching them to the University of Oxford Librarian.
- University of Oxford locating the article, scanning it in and returning to the user as an attached file in PDF format.

Personal paper holdings of the organizations members listed in Endnote (a reference management tool) were merged and the only person who had access to it was the librarian because there was no network then. So when the user made a request the librarian could check in the database and if it was available she would open the reference and check in the label field for the name of the scientist who owns the paper, then the librarian would borrow the article from the owner and photocopy then she informs the user who had made the request to collect it from the library.

3 THE INTEGRATED SYSTEM

The hybrid Data Flow Diagram (DFD) below illustrates how medical/healthcare articles and/or books requests are processed at KEMRI/WTRL unit in Kilifi, Kenya. Requests are handled through two distinct channels. Books are requested via a librarian and/or a designated researcher, who then regularly submits batches to the Oxford University through a designated librarian. Journal articles (or any others) requests are done through a librarian, who also first utilizes access subscription rights to search for the articles or polls other departments in e.g. KEMRI headquarters library, before resorting to placing the request(s) to the Oxford University's librarian.

Before a system user (requester) initiates a request, a thorough check on the availability of the needed article/book via resources (internet, library, personal holdings etc) is done. After a request has been completed and serviced, the librarian, in most cases, makes PDF copies and places the same in a folder (on the Unit's server) called "personal holdings" for ease of access by future requesters.

4 INFORMATION MANAGEMENT AND DISSEMINATION

Information management is conducted through a number of techniques in the Unit and some of the major tools used are:

Medical records registries

In clinical practice, healthcare and medical research, informatics is most useful in the fields of electronic medical records (EMR), telemedicine, clinical decision systems, and improving access to information [Arunachalam 1999; Shortliffe, 1999; Benson 2002]. Records management procedures vary from one healthcare and research institution to another. Apart from medical records being used primarily to document care given to patients, they are also used, in many healthcare settings, as source documents for other purposes such as billing patients, conducting epidemiological studies, quality control, decision support and legal claims (van der Lei 2002).

Apart from the Kilifi medical library being the main information resource centre, a great deal of research information is maintained and obtainable from the medical records registries. The Kilifi unit runs two medical records registries, namely the pediatric research and hospital based medical registries. In addition, both registries are custodians of hard copies of patient's medical notes. Both EMR and non-EMR notes are requested through designated medical records staff in the Unit.

Registers

A register is maintained in the library to handle and record various requests attributes. The attributes are collected when lending out books and contains the following columns, name of borrower, title of the book, catalogue number, date borrowed and date returned, signature.

Accession Register

This is a Register for recording the library collection. It contains date, accession number, author, title, class number, catalogue number, publisher, price, source, remarks, and location.

Electronic and non-electronic articles: Hybrid of DFD and Flow-chart

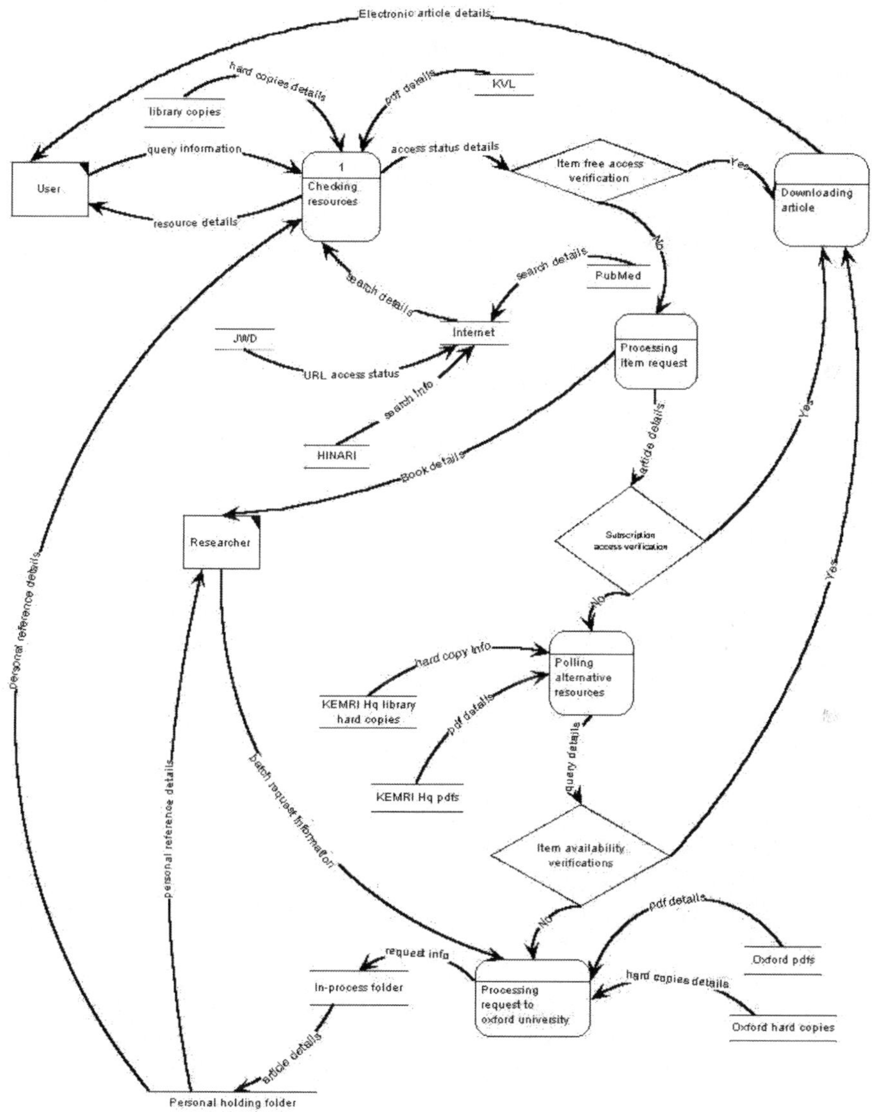

The Kilifi virtual library (KVL)

KVL is a system built using FileMaker Pro database management software. It offers scientists an interface for searching and downloading the unit's publications, the latest articles from journals to which the unit subscribes, in addition to other vital facilities.

When the librarian requests for an article from a journal to which the unit has online access, the librarian downloads it and places it in Kilifi Virtual Library and informs the user to download it from there.

When the librarian requests for articles from Oxford University, and incase they are sent as electronic copies, the librarian stores them in the KVL and informs the user to retrieve the same from there.

5 INFORMATION RETRIEVAL TOOLS

There are various search and query tools used in the digital library in Kilifi. A good number of these tools have been used due to user familiarity with them and also because of the readily available local information on basic support, having been built over time. A few others have been designed to assist the users in making good use of the locally customized system, allowing them to draw information and avoid duplication of searches, efforts and therefore use of unnecessary bandwidth beyond the local area network (LAN). Apart from the electronic searching tools, there is an existing manual library system for borrowing, which controls and monitors the retrieval of documents to and from the users.

6 SEARCH AND QUERY ENGINES

PubMed has been one of the principle tools with a web interface to connect users to the indexed *Medline* database. The search allows a user to access an extensive range of abstracts on bio-medical information. They can then seek full documents, usually in PDF format through the institutional subscription or requisition through the manual document retrieval system.

Endnote is also popular amongst scientists in Kilifi. It facilitates searches on many other indexed databases apart from the *Medline*. Endnote allows users to organize downloaded citations and abstracts in an order, which classifies the information for easy retrieval. Other tools such as *reference manager* also offers similar features but is not widely used within the Centre.

Hinari came about with a goal of bridging the divide on information acquisition by researchers in developed and developing countries. This was done by allowing access to over 2000 publications of biomedical literature at a very low cost. The Kilifi Digital Library has managed to gain great advantage by accessing this very rich resource through the Multilateral Initiative Malaria Communication (MIMCom) Network at no cost at all, adding thousands of papers to its already existing biomedical literature database.

Journal Web Database (JWD) is one tool, which needs mentioning. This is a local catalogue of papers, which allows the digital library users to know what papers are available within the existing collected document literature, and if not available where they can be searched for. JWD compliments the whole system as it provides simplified steps in decision making when trying to search for a topic of interest. It also indicates whether a journal is only available to subscribed members or can be accessed for free.

7 THE COMPUTING NETWORK INFRASTRUCTURE

The Unit has a Local Area Network (LAN) consisting of 3 servers and 105 workstations. The network spreads over the area through Ethernet cabling. Currently hubs which run at speeds of 10MBps distribute points to the networked workstations. These are slowly being replaced by switches which can negotiate speeds of 10/100MBps. There are fiber optic cables interconnecting far flung buildings. The operating system on the two main servers is Novell NetWare and the Mail system is run off GroupWise 5.5 server software. This system document management feature allows users to share documents through shared folders. It also has the capacity to publish these same documents over the internet, and can be accessed by logging in into its Web interface through an individual's account. A dedicated database server running FileMaker 5 server software hosts all the online systems, including the Kilifi Virtual Library which is part of the larger Kilifi Integrated Data Management System (KIDMS). This server runs on a Windows 2000 advanced server Network Operating System.

The LAN Infrastructure

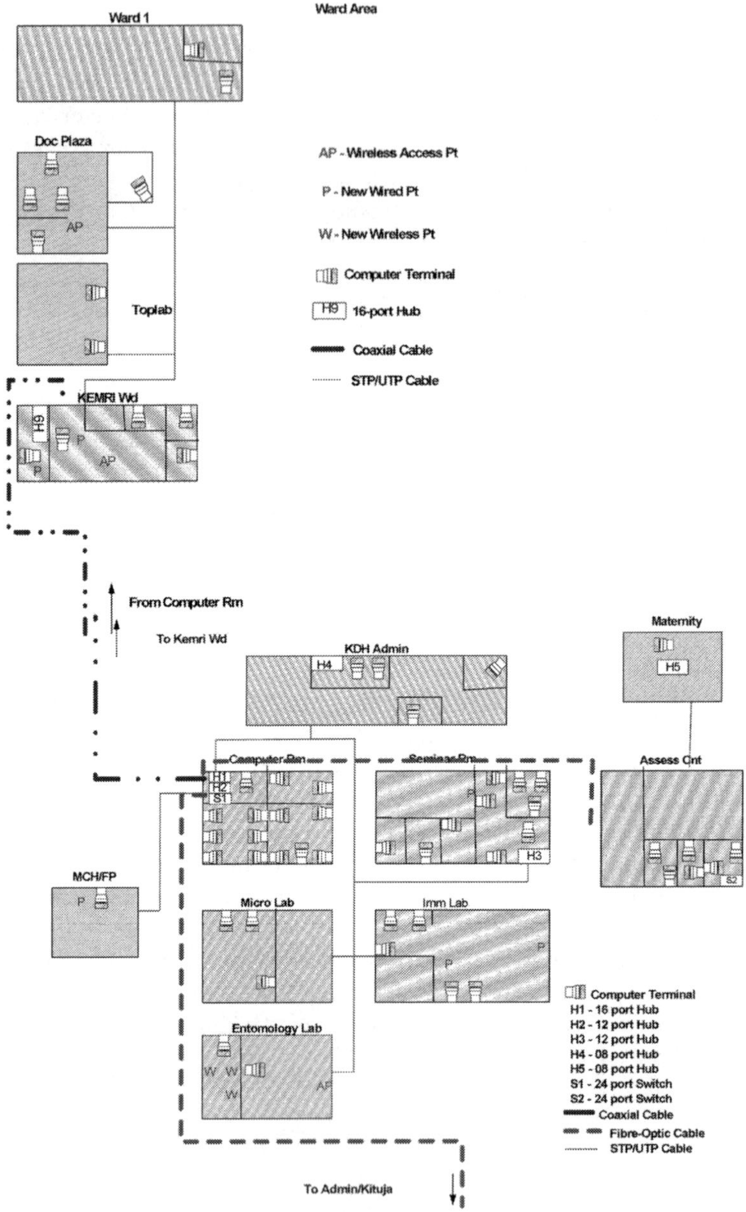

Figure 1

8 THE EXTRANET

The Kilifi Unit is one of the MIMCom network sites in Africa. This network provides Internet connectivity to a number of Malaria research institutions across Africa and has been operational since July 1999. Each site has a 2.4 m satellite dish which enables communication with the hub station in London for onward connectivity to the Internet backbone (see Schema – figure 2).

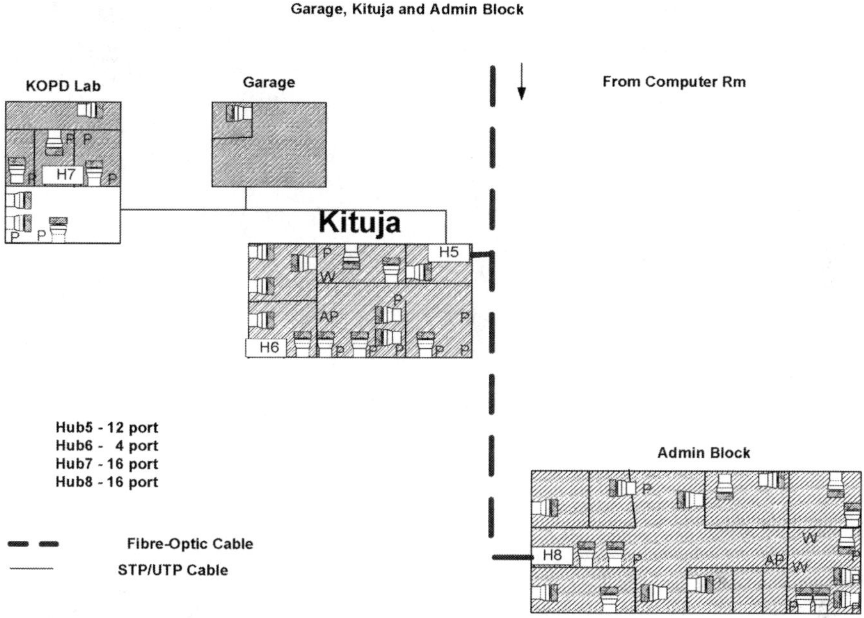

The network design is such that the various sites can share extra bandwidth that is not in use by other sites at any one time thereby ensuring efficient utilization of bandwidth. This has proved to be vital for communications from rural and remote research sites where Internet connectivity had been very difficult or non-existent in the past. Kilifi currently enjoys an uplink bandwidth of 64Kbps and downlink bandwidth of 128kbps (with a burst excess of 320 Kbps).

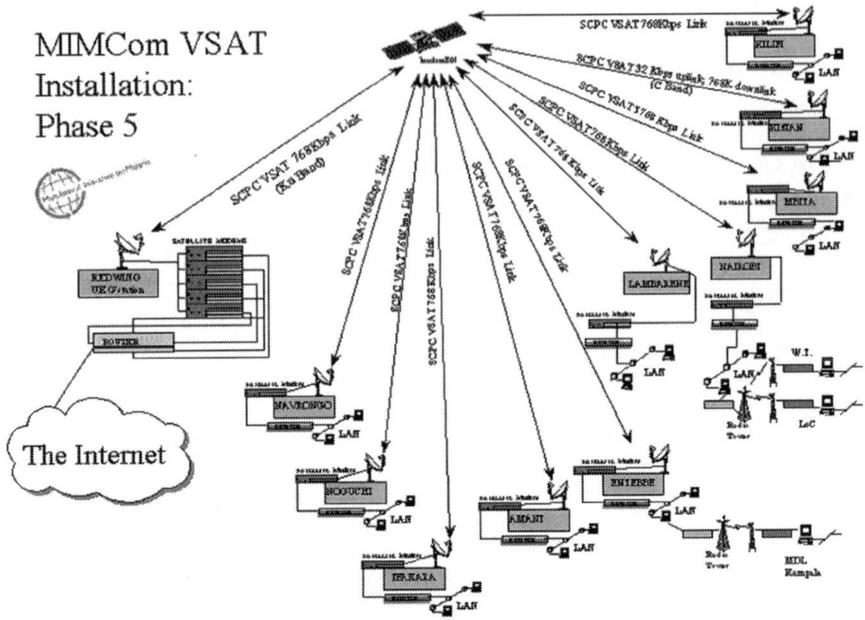

Figure 2

9 SCALABILITY

The system has had an equal share of its triumphs and disappointments. In the initial stages there was a steep learning curve to provide the necessary input towards constructing and innovating for the Digital library. There was initially very little information to go by on consolidating the web interface towards building an intranet to leverage existing resources i.e. draw interfaces and publish papers which have been subscribed for the unit. However informal training did the trick and this work was embarked on. However this did not take place in earnest until the Kilifi Integrated Database Management System was born. The KIDMS gave birth to the KVL. Although an evaluation of the system to assess the impact of the digital library on the quality of research done has not been conducted, improved access to current publications has significantly contributed to the production and publication of high quality papers.

The scaling of the system is underway. Plans of making an intranet which will be shared between the two offices (500KM apart) are being developed, whose main aims are:

1. provide documents for discussion amongst the scientists;
2. provide a documented forum of discussion; and
3. provide a portal of exchange of documents between the centers.

Most of these services will however depend on bandwidth control, management and availability. Of late, there has been a great challenge in bandwidth control and management. Bandwidth is increasingly becoming expensive and its control to enable research have its day has become a priority to Data Managers. However, proper tools will go a long way in achieving these objectives.

10 THE LIBRARY VS. HOSPITAL ADMISSIONS PATTERNS

One observation which can also be made and further investigated, concerns the requests patterns for documents against the seasonality of malaria within the centre

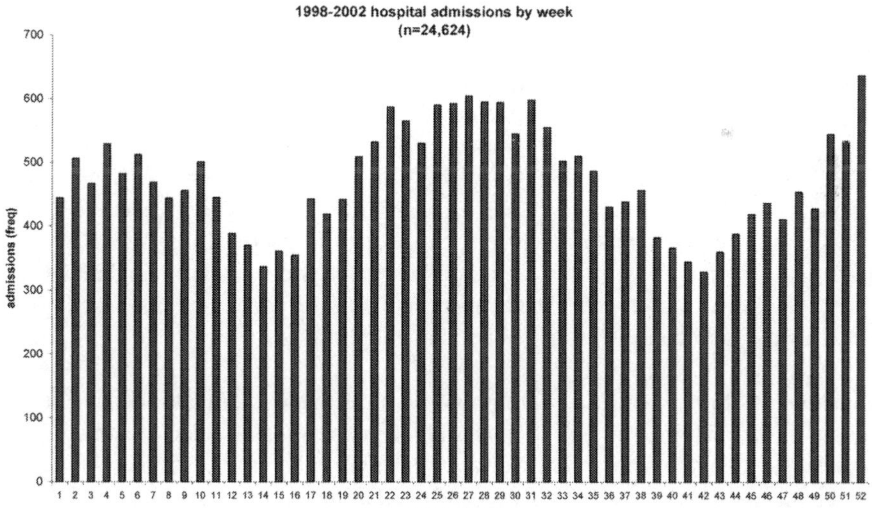

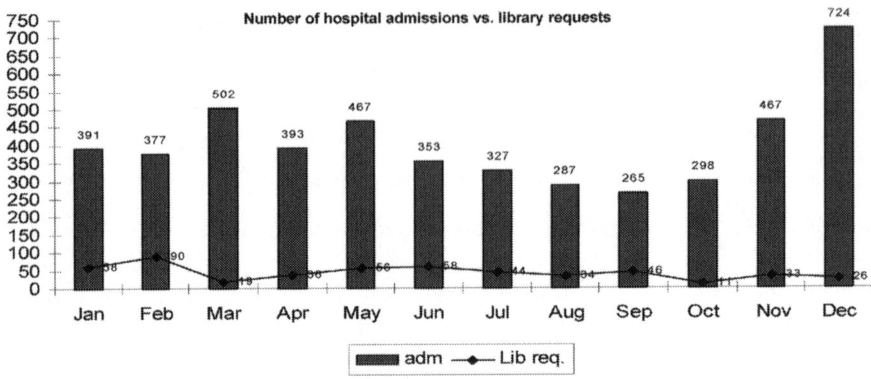

Figure 3

In general, there is some correlation with the pattern of monthly library requests and the pediatric admission. More requests seem to be serviced during the high admission periods across the year.

11 CONCLUSION

Some of the major challenges include getting users sensitized to use the system as intended. There was a lot of apathy from the bulk of users who were comfortable with the traditional systems but this is changing as user education continues. Lack of user support also undermines streaming in of feedback to enable improvement of the system from the developers.

Developing web-based systems is still a new concept within the Kilifi Unit. There has been little input in skills, which would have otherwise made a big contribution towards having a better interface, and innovations, which would have gone a long way in the design of a digital web database in line of E-Projects, which exist in developed countries. Facilities too constrain these objectives further, and there is an urgent need to address this.

The advent of the Internet connectivity via satellite communications has gone a long way in bridging the gap of disparities of institutions in Kenya and equivalent research institutions within developed countries. However, there is a lot which needs to be done to ensure the availability and maintenance of these facilities. A lot of the issues like training are being addressed through workshops of system Operators and database engineers, through arrangements coordinated by MIMCom.

The MIMCom communication project has beaten the hurdle of poor telecommunication infrastructure, and enabled research to acquire a facility which would have otherwise been a dream within most African research institutions.

However there is also a need to leverage the communication facilities and consolidate these biomedical information documents, index them for the use of these common sites, in the region and the world, with special emphasis on work done with the African Bio-Medical research chapter. This will go a long way in addressing duplication of resources and redundancy. Multicentre studies will bear fruits into developing unified policies on health targeting Africa. All this can be made possible by "humanizing", keeping in reach this communication facility to the African scientist and enabling a level playing field with his counterpart in the developed nations.

REFERENCES

Kiathe, R. (1988). "Association for health information and libraries in Africa and African Index Medicus: their contribution to medical education", *East African Medical Journal*, vol. 75, no. 6.

Arunachalam S. (1999). "Informatics in clinical practice in developing countries: still early days", *British Medical Journal*, vol. 319

Shortliffe, E. H. (1999). "The evolution of electronic medical records", *Academic Medicine*. 1999; vol. 74, no. 4, pp. 414–419.

Benson, T, (2002). "Information in practice", *British Medical Journal*, vol. 325, pp. 1086–1089

Van Der Lei, J, (2002). "Closing the loop between clinical practice, research and education: the potential of electronic patient records." *Methods of Information in Medicine*, vol. 41, no.1, pp. 51–54

Snow, R.W. and Mung'ala V.O., (1994). Forster, D., Marsh, K. "The role of the district hospital in child survival at the Kenyan coast", *African Journal of Health Sciences*, vol. 1, pp. 11–15.

THE MANAGEMENT AND ADMINISTRATION OF MANUSCRIPT COLLECTIONS WITHIN LIBRARY ENVIRONMENTS IN EASTERN AND SOUTHERN AFRICAN REGION

Nathan Mnjama

ABSTRACT

The management and administration of manuscript collections in many African libraries poses considerable challenges. The root cause of the problem stems from failure on the part of librarians to distinguish the peculiar features of archives and manuscripts from the ordinary library materials. Librarians have very often failed to realize that the management and administration of manuscript collections requires different types of skills and treatment. For instance, it is common practice to find manuscript collections placed in the same category with special collections or rare collections. It is also common practice to find manuscript collections being managed by librarians as opposed to trained professional archivists and records managers. While there are areas of convergence in the management and administration of library and manuscript collections, there are certainly major differences in way manuscripts are acquired, processed, stored and accessed. Moreover many libraries lack clear manuscript acquisition policies and as a result have ended up acquiring unsolicited manuscripts which re now underutilized or are irrelevant to their immediate clientele. This paper further argues that time has come for libraries to re-examine their manuscript collection policies, staffing requirements for manuscript collections, access conditions and disposal practices. The paper argues that out although many libraries acquire archives and manuscripts; they are very often ill-pared to face the challenges that go along with managing archives and manuscripts. The paper provides some practical guidelines for managing archives and manuscripts within a library setting where resources and facilities may not be ideal for the management, storage and use of archival materials.

1 INTRODUCTION

The management and administration of manuscript collections in many African libraries poses considerable challenges. The root cause of the problem stems from failure on the part of librarians to distinguish the peculiar features of archives and manuscripts from ordinary library materials. Librarians have very often failed to realize that the management and administration of manuscript collections requires different types of skills and treatment. For instance, it is common practice to find manuscript collections placed in the same category with special collections or rare collections. It is also common practice to find manuscript collections being managed by librarians as opposed to trained professional archivists or records managers. While there are areas of convergence in the management and administration of library and manuscript collections, there are certainly major differences in the way manuscripts are acquired, processed, stored and accessed. Moreover many libraries lack clear manuscript acquisition policies and as a result have ended up acquiring unsolicited manuscripts which re now underutilized or are irrelevant to their immediate clientele.

This paper argues that time has come for libraries to re-examine their manuscript collection policies, staffing requirements, access conditions and disposal practices. The paper argues that out although many libraries acquire archives and manuscripts, they are very often ill-prepared to face the challenges that go along with managing archives and manuscripts. The paper provides some practical guidelines for managing archives and manuscripts within a library setting.

2 KNOWLEDGE MANAGEMENT AND RECORDS MANAGERS/ARCHIVISTS

The focus of this conference is on knowledge management and some of you would wonder if archives and records management has anything to do with knowledge management. Indeed there is a link between archives, records management and knowledge management. Archives Management is concerned with the management of non current records while records management is the application of scientific and managerial principles to the management of records from the time of creation to up to the time of their final disposition. If we agree that knowledge management is the utilization of information and other organizational resources for the benefit of the organization , then archives and records management constitutes part of that wider domain of knowledge management. William Saffady one of the greatest authors of archival science suggests knowledge management is concerned with the systematic, effective management and utilization of an organization's resources. Well, more than twenty years ago, Frank B Evans one of the prominent American Archivists also observed that "archivist must master by study of the holdings themselves most of the administrative history and the subject content of the local archival holdings which are, by definition, unique. All archivists also need an understanding of how institutions and organization, both public and private, originate and develop, of types and patters of internal organization and functions, of recordkeeping and record systems past and present, and of the relationship of documentation in all of its forms to organizations and functions." It can therefore be concluded that knowledge management and records management are different yet complementary activities. In seeking to establish a link between knowledge management and records management, the Government of New South Wales (2003) observed that "Knowledge management focuses more on people, while records management focuses on records and evidence. However, while knowledge cannot exist without people, people gain knowledge from many different sources of information, including records. Records are an important source of knowledge because they are unique to an organisation: they relate directly to the business context." New knowledge cannot be created without extensive reference to archival materials. Nor can the accumulated collective knowledge of a society be transmitted intact to succeeding generations without its preservation and organization. These are indeed the core functions of archival work.

3 THE DIFFERENCES AND SIMILARITIES BETWEEN LIBRARIES AND ARCHIVES

Archives centres and libraries have several similarities as well as differences. While libraries receive or collect single items such as books or periodicals, archival centres often receive large or small consignments of non-current records which are very often the product of an activity or records that that have been brought together by a scholar or other citizens in the course of activities. For this reason, archival collections tend to be organic in nature and each item is closely associated with other items within the collection.

Secondly, while librarians organize their collections under some form of predetermined classification system such as Dewey Decimal, Library of Congress or any other, archival materials can only be organized under the principle of provenance which simply states that records of one organization should not be intermingled with those of another, even if the records are related or cover the same subject area. Moreover, archival materials must further be organized and maintained in the order in which they were created- the principle of original order. These two principles must always be obeyed even if they do not make much meaning to the archivist or librarian. It is only in rare cases when the archivist or librarian may consider other forms of arrangement.

The other major difference with library is collections is the very fact that while a library may acquire more than one copy of an item, archival materials are rarely duplicated elsewhere and as such each archival item is rare and irreplaceable

The major similarity between archives and libraries is the fact that both libraries and archives are memory institutions. They are both engaged in identification of information resources, they collect and provide access to information, libraries to published information and archives to records. They are thus knowledge based institutions. The discussion that follows examines specific areas which study observed.

4 SURVEY RESULTS

A simple questionnaire was mailed electronically to all university Libraries whose e-mail addresses were obtained from The Directory of University Libraries in Africa. Many of the questionnaires were returned undelivered. Only five libraries completed the questionnaire. The results of the survey revealed that:

a) Most libraries in the region stored their collections in strong rooms which were not air-conditioned or which depended on centralized air conditioning.

b) Most libraries collected manuscripts, maps, plans photographs, phonographic records, videos, audiotapes, microforms, DVD's.

c) the problems encountered by libraries in the management of manuscript collections include: lack of proper storage equipment, shortage of storage space, unacceptable user behavior or carelessness when handling manuscripts, use of ink pens, interfiling of documents by users, issues of users who want to use their own digital cameras, users requesting for large volumes of materials to be photocopied, inadequate supervision by library staff and theft or loss of manuscripts.

d) The major source of manuscript collections were from parent organizations, donations from private individuals and organizations, and in a few cases direct purchase from auctions.

e) Most libraries had no clear policies for acquisition, appraising or selecting manuscripts prior to acquisitions.

f) All the libraries surveyed lacked well defined preservation and conservation policies.

g) Most libraries have an interest in digitizing their collections, but lacked the equipment or other resources.

h) Some of the manuscript collections were managed by non-archivists,

i) There was no clear distinction between manuscript collections and general Africana collections.

j) Some basic retrieval tools such as general guides, catalogues and in one instance a searchable database had been developed.

k) No specific disaster and preparedness plans were in place for manuscript collections held in libraries.

The discussion that follows looks at ideal environments for managing manuscript collections in libraries.

5 ARCHIVES AND RECORDS MANAGEMENT COLLECTION POLICY

William Saffady (1974:204) argues the effective and efficient management of records must be supported by an infrastructure of policies, structures, procedures, tools, training and resources. It is for this reason that the Archives/Manuscript Unit of a library must derive its authority from a policy statement or charter issued by the library management setting out the objectives and mapping out the plan for the programme. Ideally, this policy statement should be approved by the library management and issued in the form of a directive. It should specify the need for the programme, the objectives, the proposed structure of the programme and the level of administrative and technical support required.

In addition the library management should clearly define the boundaries of its archives programme. Traditionally, archives programmes were limited to collecting historical or simply non-current records of their parent organizations and accepting donations here and there. With the proliferation of paper, and an increase in human activities, it is of vital importance that the library declares its stance on which formats of records are to be collected, the broad subject areas to be covered and the likely costs to be incurred in the acquisition of each collection. Failure to do so will impact on the archivist's ability to provide an efficient service.

There are reasons why libraries should formulate such a policy. In the first instance, resources must be allocated for running the archives programme. Secondly, the establishment of the post of an Archivist within the library set up and other support staff must be approved by the library management and an administrative framework established. Thirdly, a well defined career path for the archivist and other support staff need to be developed if these professionals have to be retained within a library establishment

6 ACCESS TO ARCHIVAL COLLECTIONS

The findings of this study indicate that there are variations in the provision of access to manuscripts in the region. While some libraries have developed access policies, others have not. Without an access policy, it will be extremely difficult to determine which records should be made available and those that should be restricted. It is common practice in many countries to follow the same restrictions for public as private manuscripts deposited by individuals. It was also observed that some of the manuscript collections originate from private organizations. As many of the manuscripts deposited in libraries are from private organizations and individuals, national archival legislations would not normally govern access to such collections and in the absence of written donor agreements administering access to such collections becomes extremely difficult or left to the discretion of the librarians who are unaware of the intricate requirements of the rights of citizens of access to information and the rights of individuals to enjoy certain private rights. In order to formulate access policies, there is need to re-examine acquisition policies and donor agreements and ensure that a clear understanding on which types of records can be opened at the expiry of agreed retention periods, while other records many be subjected to extended closure.

Supervision of users was also noted to be of major concern to manuscript curators. The need for effective supervision of users can not be overstated. Archival materials are rare, unique and irreplaceable. This calls for close monitoring of users at all times.

Records and Manuscript Disposal

The disposal of manuscript collections was another aspect this study sought to determine. While it is common practice to weed out out-dated books, manuscript collections were rarely weeded out among the libraries surveyed. Once an institution has acquired archival materials, this becomes its baby for the rest of that institutions life. Perhaps the question that we should ask ourselves is: What should libraries do with manuscript collections which have not been accessed for several decades? What criteria should librarians/archivists use in weeding out manuscript collections? Do they have a right to dispose of collections which they did not create in the first instance?

7 PLACEMENT OF THE ARCHIVES FUNCTION WITHIN THE LIBRARY ADMINISTRATIVE HIERARCHY

Perhaps one of the thorniest issues that need to be addressed is the question of the placement of the Archives Unit within the administrative structure of the Library. Nicholas Burckel (1975:385) opines that "the staffing of the archives and its place in the organization of the college are perhaps the most important determinant of how successful it will be." Where should the archives service be placed? To whom should the unit be answerable? Should it be answerable to the Technical services or Reader services? Although any of these arrangements is possible, each has its own limitations. Any of the following options may be considered.

An Archives Service under the direction of the Librarian. In some universities, it is common practice to find Library archives placed under the Library Librarian. This was the observation made by the late Kufa (1994:78) when he wrote saying "at some universities archives do not have a status and an identity different from that of the special materials sections in libraries". Placing the Library Archives Service under the Library Librarian might lead to the service being neglected as the Librarian may be pre-occupied with the administration of library materials as opposed to records management. On the other hand, the archives service might never grow as it will be seen as an offshoot of another section, rather than a major library activity. Experience gained elsewhere indicates that where Library archives services have been wrongly placed, they have ended up inadequately funded or allowed to die a natural death.

8 APPOINTMENT OF A LIBRARY ARCHIVIST/RECORDS MANAGER

In order to ensure that recorded information is accessible and can be managed professionally, it is essential that an Archivist be appointed to take direct responsibility for the unit. The responses obtained from the survey indicate that some libraries have appointed professional records managers and archivist to oversee their archives collection while in others the management and care of the archives collections is still under the responsibility of librarians. It cannot be overstated that it would be futile for the Library to embark on an n archives programme without a trained archivist. No wonder Donald Simpson (1975:22) advises "do not embark on a sea of records management with an inexperienced navigator" Ideally, the archivist or any other person responsible for the collections should be a person educated to Diploma/Masters Level in Archives and

Records Management and should have the ability to work methodically and reliably. His or her main duties should be:

- To direct, plan and administer the Archives activities
- To preserve, repair and provide access to the archives,
- To compile, publish guides and other retrieval tools to Library archives,
- To acquire through purchase, donation, bequests etc. on behalf of the Library any records, book or other materials which in the archivist's opinion has enduring or historical value.
- To devise procedures for the listing, scheduling and destruction of records no longer needed by the institution.
- To regulate the conditions under which researchers may use the archives
- To provide authority and equipment for making and authentication of copies of documents and extracts from the archives for the purpose of research or as evidence in court of law.
- To perform such other functions as are necessary for purposes of directing, managing and controlling the archives.
- To advocate and promote the use archives to the Library community.

Depending on the size of the archives held, the Archivist will need to be supported by a team of well trained officers at appropriate levels.

9 APPOINTMENT OF AN ARCHIVES AND RECORDS MANAGEMENT COMMITTEE

While the appointment of the professional archivist constitutes the first step in the effective management of manuscript collections in libraries, the need to appoint an archives advisory committee can not be overstated. The creation of an Archives and Records Management Advisory Committee of the Library should be constituted as soon as possible. The committee should ensure that the Library Archives pursues the objectives and policies set in the policy statement and that it has the resources to do so. Initially, the main function of the committee should be to approve measures designed to set up the Archives Programme. Once the programme has been launched, the specific functions of the Committee should include:

- Approving manuals and other publications prepared by the archivist.

- Approving retention/disposition schedules
- Compiling and revising reading room rules and regulations
- Hearing appeals from the researchers as far as access to records is concerned
- Assisting and communicating key problems or issues to the Library Administration.

10 THE BUDGET

Many archives programme fail due to inadequate funding. Any Library contemplating establishing an archives service must be prepared to provide the necessary funding to support the programme. No wonder Mc McCarthy (1975:7) argues that" poorly or inadequate supported programmes have debilitating effect on staff morale, on the institutions image and most important on the use of historical materials." Funds will be needed for purchase of specialized storage equipment, payment of staff salaries, restoration facilities, maintenance costs, archival boxes, insurance, acid free papers etc.

11 CONCLUSION

This article has highlighted some of the major elements that are needed to operate an effective archives programme within a library environment. It has indicated that the major elements include policies, procedures and programmes. To be successful, there must be goodwill among the Library staff in order to ensure that the programme remains vibrant once initiated. Without the support of all the users of the centre, the programme is bound to fail.

REFERENCES

Burckel N. C. (1975). "Establishing a college archives", *College and Research Libraries*, vol. 36, no.5, pp. 384–392

Choongo M W (1998). "Justification for setting up an archives at the library of Zambia: problems and prospects, *African Journal of Library, Archives and Information Science*, vol. 8, no. 2, pp. 77–88

Evans F.B. (1967). "Archivists and records managers: variations on a theme", *American Archivist*, vol. 30, pp. 45–58

Kemoni H. and Wamukoya J. (2000). "Preparing for the management of electronic Records at Moi Library, Kenya: A Case Study", *African Journal of Library, Archives and Information Science*, vol.10, no. 2, pp. 125–138

Kufa J. (1994) "Wither library archives", *South Africa Archives Journal*, vol. 36, pp. 78–81

McCarthy P.H. (19975). "Overview; essentials of archives or manuscript program", In: Lytle, R. *Management of archives and manuscript collections for librarians*, Chicago: The Society of American Archivists, pp. 5–20

New South Wales (July 2003). Knowledge management and records management, record keeping in brief No. 26 Available at: http://www.records. nsw.gov.au/publicsector/rk/rib/rib26.htm (Accessed on 14th January 2006)

Oyiti M. (1998). Records and archives management in academic institutions: A case study of the Library of Botswana. Master's in Library and Information Studies Thesis. Library of Botswana.

Saffady W. (19974). "A library archives and records management programme: some operational guidelines." *College and research Libraries*, vol. 35, no. 3, pp. 204–210

Simpson D. (1975) "The don'ts of good records management programme", *Records Management Quarterly*, vol. 9, no. 1, pp. 20–21

Ugwunze V. I. (1992). "An examination of records management in the library of Lagos registry", *African Journal of Library, Archives and Information Science*, vol. 2, no. 1, pp. 39–48

MAKING A CONTRIBUTION TO THE CIVIL SOCIETY: KNOWLEDGE MANAGEMENT AND THE INFORMATION PROFESSIONAL

Stephen A. Roberts

ABSTRACT

This paper looks at the rise of knowledge management (KM) as a theme for the information professional noting briefly the theoretical and intellectual context. The discussion proceeds by developing and offering some structures for analysis and action in terms of developing the KM paradigm in different sectors of application in an African and developing world setting. The paper reflects on some of the currently debated themes at the global and regional level and will explore how information professionals can both profit by and contribute to a wide range of professional, social, cultural and economic debates which characterize the modern society at large (embodied in the state and the market) and its more specific foci the emergent Civil Society (in NGOs and community organizations all set within in a matrix of family, social and citizen relationships).

1 INTRODUCTION

The term 'information professional' has a pretty good ring about it. It is an umbrella term which has gathered together a number of well founded occupations. The majority will have come from library services and will have joined together with special librarians and information service providers. It will include a number of archivists and records managers. It will also include documentalists and those who call themselves information scientists. On these terms many information professionals will be employed in the public sector; some will work in the private and commercial sector, and an increasing number will work in the voluntary sector including NGOs. The greater majority of African countries now have some means of sustaining this identity. The participants of XVII Standing Conference of Eastern, Central and Southern African Library and Information Associations (SCECSAL XVII) showed the personal strength behind this, although the agendas discussed showed an awareness of current weaknesses and gaps, they as well as indicated opportunities for development. However, the use of the term is still self-referential. It has to be said that it is not well understood or appreciated by those at large in the wider information society and in the growing information economy. Those working in computing and information communication technology (ICT) largely focus on the hardware and software platforms and carry out their work through the prism of information systems at both the generic and specific levels.

Those working with and actively using information in the business world respond to the concerns of those previously mentioned as well as having a strong organization and business process focus. These business practitioners tend to focus on very specific kinds of content. However, within the business world there is clearly scope for using and actively having to deal with much more complex information. It is in this context that the business world at large has welcomed and seized the ideas of knowledge management which have formed part of the information world's discourse in the last decade. Beyond these two areas where information is as essential feature of their context, there are many other areas and sectors where information handling activities form essential parts of the landscape. Nonetheless, those practitioners and specialists who do work extensively with information (the wider membership of the information society) are not prone to reference themselves as 'information professionals'. This does not mean that this term could not be suitable, but in reality they rarely call themselves as such. They are more likely to name themselves in accordance with other professional or occupational labels (in Africa they could be for example: teachers, community workers, advisors, administrators, aid workers, media personnel and journalists. This situation is not likely to change! Whether this leaves the so called information professional suffering from isolation is a moot point.

Beyond these groups (largely representing the better educated and more economically active populations) lies the greater citizen public at large. It is perhaps towards this majority group that the self-referential information professional must align, as they it may represent the group with the strongest cause to espouse. This idea has not been lost on those we will now define as the 'information professionals'. A librarian or a public information provider has always been conscious of the wider and more citizen friendly aspect of their profession. And in reality the group has consistently looked outwards to the wider world, even though their message has not always been heard or received. It is around this point of professional equilibrium that we can plan out an argument for discussion. Given the African perspective that concerns the conference we need to bear in mind not only the wider global and professional environment, but also how its influence will be received ' on the ground' in the African context. So, we really ask not only about the nature and scope of the broader trends towards knowledge management (to be clarified and discussed), but how can they be interpreted and acted upon in the continental context and in the setting of Civil Society.

2 DEVELOPMENT AND CHANGE: STATUS, STRUCTURES AND LEARNING IN INFORMATION PROFESSIONALISM

Information professional education has developed for well over one hundred years. In the library setting it has moved from and through phases of dissemination of technique, consolidation of craft practices, specific professional education and professional education within a wider academic setting. It is in this fourth phase that it now finds itself and it is perhaps moving towards a new fifth phase where its wider cultural (indeed global) significance is recognized. It would be comforting to think that this fifth stage may have a lot to do with the emergence of the knowledge idea in its various guises.

The claim to the term 'information professional' is only valid if it is founded on a well developed basis of professional recognition, structures and education.

Professional recognition has been achieved: the public recognises the role most notably through the library as an institution (even if they neglect it). National governments and international bodies (notably IFLA and regional bodies like SCECSAL) give recognition through legislation, policy statements, provision of resources (always too little) and through voices of representation. The links to publishing, the book trade, education, research and culture are well established. In Africa the structures have yet to fully emerge in many states, although in some areas they are moving ahead in multiple form (Nigeria, and RSA) and in most a basic outline is nascent (Tanzania, Uganda, Namibia, Botswana) or emergent (Kenya).

Libraries (the majority for public use) provide the structure both in terms of physical presence, organizational form, sectoral identity and mission, goals and objectives. These organizational resources form a structural capital upon which the profession has built its identity and which provides an engine for change. This provides us with a metaphor of an ever growing and rich knowledge capital, which we in turn wish to apply to the growth of social, cultural and human capital. This theme is enlarged later in this paper.

It is recognised that education plays a potent role in validating the profession and professional ethos. Profession is part vocation (a calling to serve), familiarity with a body of rigorous knowledge, and the guardianship of knowledge and practice for public and individual purpose. This latter aspect is very important as it sends out signals of reputation, trust, confidence and ethical solidity. It thus effects how information professionals behave and even more importantly how they are perceived by others (the public, the users, the clients). The point to make here is that the growing identity and role of the information professional has gone hand in hand with changes and developments in self-knowledge, exclusive knowledge, and the dissemination of knowledge. We could say that the more the group has evolved the stronger its professional identity has become: knowledge strengthens and generates expansion. Menou (1997) has addressed this issue specifically in the African context suggesting the need for a universalism of outlook combined with a deep understanding and sensitivity or local and regional needs.

The knowledge relationships within the field and the professional role have been strengthening: there has been progressive internal growth and differentiation. We have experienced over one hundred years of professional knowledge growth. This growth has reflected the changing information professional role we have considered at the start. Whilst knowledge and its growth has a certain fluidity and flexibility, when we move from the realm of ideas to the arena of people in practice certain rigidities are present and even inherent. A person with an idea can be either resistant or flexible: in other words they can exercise free will and choice if they so desire. It is the contrast between imagining and doing. Information professionals can imagine doing any number of things. But in practice and reality their scope to act is usually much less.

It is this contrast that poses a challenge for the information professional on the threshold of the knowledge era. We will be able to show they have the ideas, the potential and the ability to act, but their scope is limited in practice and by circumstances. There is a chance now to address this in regional (African)terms and in the frame of the developing world, by posing the question of how we can respond to the question embodied in the title: Making A Contribution To The Civil Society: Knowledge Management and the Information Professional: This theme was a part of the SCECSAL XVII agenda. The many individual reactions to it contributed to the summary resolutions of the event. These will be the measures for information professional progress in this region of Africa.

It is now the moment to introduce a view of knowledge and knowledge management to the discussion. We need to see how this idea can be owned by the information professional and to what extent they can extend their role to become either knowledge management professionals or (more realistically) information and knowledge professionals. The exploration can begin through the natural relation between information and knowledge.

3 EVOLUTION OF THE KNOWLEDGE CONCEPT

As the role and scope of the information professional has changed so has the body of professional knowledge itself. To draw a rough parallel with the profession. The first phase focused on techniques (the development of library classification (Dewey post-1876; UDC post-1900); the development of administrative processes for the emerging public libraries in the UK and the Dominions, in a number of continental European countries and in the USA, and progress in bibliography. The second phase of consolidation of craft practices occupied the first three decades of the twentieth century: sectoral diversification and increased specialization was taking place. The third phase was evolving naturally from the second. The development of professionally based education and other forms of professional organization both strengthened the craft and deepened its application and knowledge base. In some ways the USA was a leading focus of innovation: professional education and organization was already robust by the early 1940s. The UK was slower to respond but the post-war reconstruction gave a strong impetus. These developments were to lead on to a fourth phase in which a consolidation was achieved by the shift of professional education to the higher education / academic sector. This phase can be marked out by a real growth in professional knowledge derived from active practice and the gradual growth of inquiry, investigation and research following the scientific and social scientific model and / or rigorous inquiry in the arts and humanities.

By 1980 the fourth phase had consolidated and become the recognised paradigm for professional practice, education and knowledge creation. All these currents were strengthened by the recognition that craft practice needed to be reinforced by a more rigorous approach to management of people, organization and resources. The need to gain recognition and to propagate the values of the field lead to a surge in the policy development model for the field. Focus on policy and strategy could bring about wider application of techniques of library and information management in an increasing range of organizations and settings. Indeed the information management paradigm was slowly challenging and even replacing the historic one of library management and services. The professional field was turning to look outwards with greater vigour and even confidence.

By the 1980s the ICTs were having much wider impact in both business, organizations and society at large. Although yet not quite all-pervasive in the developing world the 1990s, this was to become the crucial decade of innovation and change. At the start of the new millennium the trends were clear to see and new directions and challenges were opening up. By 2000 a fifth phase was becoming evident with a convergence and fusion of trends that had been building since mid-century. We are now getting to grips with this fifth phase of the professional environment. We live now in this period of professional adjustment and it defines the agendas which the conference has gathered to address. In summary the following trends can be observed and noted. The profession as hitherto defined by institutional form and the husbandry of published information content is metamorphosing towards a profession which can deal directly with many and diverse organizations, with a progressively varied range and form of information content.

The management of information in any form is becoming the central focus, irrespective of content, delivery, and context. This leads to an inevitable reduction in and redundancy of boundaries between places and people. It suggests new possibilities of communication, information transfer and the growth of networks of activity. The impact of computing, digital technologies and telecommunications is becoming profound and widespread offering radically new models of communication and information, which are nevertheless able to adapt to the strengths of the existing models.

There is a progressive and outward shift of focus from the reader of the document to the user of information. This is coupled with a richer model of the user from a transient and localized demand to a deeper and more consistent individual world of information which can be managed by way of collaboration and support. We are moving from the discrete user to the holistic model of the knowledgeable person with richer identities of the empowered citizen of multiple needs and responsibilities. Steps along this way may take us to the model of the user life cycle or the whole information life of the user. This will lead towards the need and indeed the right of all citizens to have access to a relevant knowledge base required for living. In the African professional experience at large much of this is still unarticulated and aspirational. The book and the document still remain a key priority for education, for information inputs to wealth creation, for the spread of literacy and for cultural enrichment (reading, writing and for mass literary communication). Nevertheless, the region can witness a small yet growing body of information professionals who do and will have the capacity to innovate a knowledge management process.

In this section we set out to define the context of knowledge management by stating that professional knowledge has evolved steadily through a number of distinct yet related phases. Our own professional discovery is itself a model for tracing the wider aspects of knowledge management, which will be dealt with in the next section. What needs to be done now is to take this internal knowledge and confidence built up over a prolonged period and see how it can be applied collaterally to the wider world for the solution of universal problems. What the information professional has learned has to be shared and applied with confidence and vigour on the world stage.

4 KNOWLEDGE AND ITS MANAGEMENT: STRUCTURES AND CONCEPTS

There are a growing numbers of writers and commentators on knowledge management: more in the field of business and management generally, as well as some significant information professional commentators, some of whom are educators (like the author) and others who are reflective practitioners. Well for my purposes are Nonaka, Stewart, Boisot, Sveiby, Prusak and Leonard Barton, in addition to such business strategic theorists as Porter and Earl. For the present purpose a reduced and simplified view of structures and concepts will prove adequate, since our main goal is to prescribe some areas of practical application in the contexts of African development and the Civil Society.

The capacity to know and to realize what is known for constructive purposes lies in the development of the species (homo sapiens) through the physical, biological, chemical and mental properties of the human brain itself and its relation to the body and its functions. The higher functions of speech, language, senses and mental process allow learning, processing of external information and stimuli as well as reflection and powers of choice and decision. Growing self awareness and realization has increased and shaped human capacity as well as provided opportunities for mental growth and intellectual development, to enable both primary processing for action (the purposive use of information resources) and cognitive processing to assist the making sense of events (manifest in spiritual and cultural development and to a capacity for formal considerations such as found in philosophy and other forms of intellectual and scientific activity).

It is this range and reality that provides the backdrop for what might be called various kinds of professional skill, technique and application. Within this frame one can be whatever is desired or can be achieved. In the current case it has allowed the distinct development of the information professional in one form or another. Let us assume that this line of discussion is a legitimate basis for what follows: essentially a pragmatic means of constructing an argument and a consensus for information professional activity in a social and collective setting (a civilized society in which Civil Society can be fulfilled).

A pragmatic definition (or starter definition) for the information professional's knowledge management can focus first on content and material. This is both familiar and appropriate for professional information handlers. We can construct a map of content from the simple to the general and more complex on a vertical axis. To this can be added a range of horizontal axes at each point on the linear / vertical axis (the knowledge focus is most relevant here).

The elements of the vertical axis are in ascending order:

DATA

Units of information in their simplest forms such as single observations, measurements, numerical identities, symbols, records of events etc.

INFORMATION

Aggregations of data in numerical, linguistic or symbolic form which have a meaningful capacity and which inform the receiver or user in a substantial way about things and matters in a specific way.

INTELLIGENCE

Data, information and sometimes knowledge which may be actually or potentially useful, but often requiring supplementation, confirmation and inference before its meaning can be fully ascertained or assured.

KNOWLEDGE

Things which are known as a result of experience and action and which are normally derived form sensory and intellectual input, which may be revealed through evidence in the form of data, information and intelligence.

Knowledge often requires a temporal period for its construction, confirmation and affirmation. Knowledge can be enhanced through reflection, review and critical analysis as well as though exchange, sharing and collaboration. In the longer term knowledge is formed by constructive social engagement and socially constructed engagement.

WISDOM

A form of well considered and proven knowledge which is valuable to conserve and apply particularly to make effective decisions in uncertain circumstances.

ACTION
Things which are done and carried out and which serve as a source of experience.

Information professionals (our definition) have been involved in these constructs to differing degrees. As librarians they have had little engagement with data; this field is the primary domain of the business information and business IT specialist, database constructor, the administrator, the functional specialist (e.g. accountant, marketeer, logistics manager etc.) and operations specialists.

The librarian and the library and information services specialist is the historical core group of information professional. Taking the theme that much information production, handling and transfer is through the medium of documents (published or internal, ephemeral or more permanent) it has fallen to book people and librarians to undertake activity in this area ... By ranging over documentary sources and extracting content (document and information retrieval) librarians have extended their range to information service and provision by analysis, aggregation and dissemination. This extended activity can or has earned them or has lead them to acquire the accolade of information manager. It has also provided a basis to make some claim to the area of knowledge manager: a claim which some might regard as premature! I have yet to attempt a confirmation or a denial! In the African context it is vital that this capacity is built. Technology is a vital aid but a poor substitute for the mental and cultural preparation that this information and library experience bestows. In Tanzania at first hand it can be experienced through the efforts of the TLS, at the Bagamoyo training school, and in the information services developing within both government and Tanzanian civil society. So too can it be seen in Uganda and Kenya, Malawi and Namibia to name but a few.

In so much as work with intelligence can and should involve work with documentary sources the library and information professional can make some claim to be a more extended form of knowledge worker. Intelligence work brings to the picture new dimensions of working with tacit, hidden and obscure sources. It also requires sifting, appraisal, projection, judgment and work with uncertainties and probabilities. Whereas the traditional library and information professional works with explicit, published and public information taking the nature of the content as given, the intelligence worker has to use inference, make links over gaps by assumption and corroboration and often deal with a less than voluminous or perfect evidence base. We might ask if this transition leads us towards danger and crosses some ethical and professional frontiers and limits.

Nevertheless, enough has been said now to plant the definition of information management into the picture.

INFORMATION MANAGEMENT

This term has come to mean the systematic approach to the identification, acquisition, processing, storage, analysis, retrieval, distribution and dissemination of data, information and intelligence (and to some extent knowledge) in order to exploit information as a resource making it resourceful for strategic purposes, extracting value and attaining impact.

The management of information implies a necessary engagement with and management of the media in which the information is contained. This provides a basis for incorporating librarianship and documentation within the sphere of information management. In order to obtain the maximum benefits information management tasks have become professionalized to make the best use of technologies, systems, methods and techniques.

Amongst the critics of knowledge management we can note Tom Wilson from the UK who has stirred a note of controversy. It is certainly true that once we information professionals move beyond the realm of the recorded, published, tangible, explicit and empirical view of information we raise the nature of our game and expose ourselves to risk, uncertainty, turbulence and change. Wilson tends to confine a realistic view of 'knowledge management' to the confines of information management, thus implying management of risk and the possibility of clear answers to questions. His arguments are powerful and attractive. But, they do tend to put an end to the development of information professional activity by posing a limitation.

My understanding and feeling is that we still need to change (along with the world and society itself) and allow ourselves a response to challenges. In a way we have allowed ourselves to get quite deeply into what I loosely call the fifth phase of information professionalism. To make sense of any idea of knowledge management it is absolutely clear that information management does and has to form the basis, but Wilson's skepticism (even opposition) has to be challenged and taken forward. Certainly a crystalline view of what constitutes knowledge management is going to help.

KNOWLEDGE MANAGEMENT

This represents a progressively more coherent, strategic and purposive effort to extend the base of information management (and its business equivalent in Information Resource Management (IRM) to encompass knowledge in all its forms, aspects and varieties.

The totality of knowledge resources may be referred to as intellectual capital and are combined with human, structural and customer capital resources to obtain the maximum benefits from all human knowledge.

Its foci include the management of existing knowledge resources through sharing, leveraging, collaborating and learning in order to create new knowledge to provide a basis for innovation and progress and increases in economic, social and cultural welfare.

5 CAPITAL: KNOWLEDGE AS VALUE AND POTENTIAL

Information professionals must develop their field and make their contribution to society. So far they have risen to the challenges of managing information, a foundation for the growing possibilities of exploiting knowledge. It seems a natural proposition to envisage their ability to work within the development of knowledge. The claim is strengthened by the nature of knowledge as content and through the ways in which communication processes enable the development of knowledge. If information is a resource which can be managed, then through the necessities of content and process, knowledge is a resource that can also be managed from the same professional perspective. As we will see below, when financial resource constitutes the primary form of capital it is accountants who play the key role in its management. When the dominant form of capital is knowledge those who have a foundation in managing information content and process also have the potential to manage knowledge. Therefore, by analogy, they may also establish a key role where knowledge is a primary form of capital. Any critique of knowledge management should not fail to recognize this.

The analysis for the transition from a dominant financial capital to a dominant knowledge capital has developed from a study of economic history and economics as much as anything else. From the Mercantilists of the 16th Century to the Industrial Revolution and Adam Smith and then beyond to a line of thought through J.S. Mill, Fredrick Engels, Karl Marx to J.M. Keynes the relationship between financial capital, primary resources, people as labour, and wealth creation has been the orthodoxy for both economics and cultural and political interpretation. The microeconomics of the market and the theory of the firm and classical demand and supply analysis reigned supreme. In the wake of the First and Second World wars and the sequences of depression and reconstruction, the economic debate was also reconstructed. Keynes' contribution from the 1920s onwards was critical to the development of a new macroeconomic theory which linked money supply, rates of interest and levels of employment and taxation to wealth creation and economic management. He propounded a new political economy based on the idea that if the state could set the right conditions at the macro level the markets and enterprise could do what they do best motivated by demand, potential for profit and satisfying the requirements of investors for a return. And, hopefully meeting the needs of customers.

After 1945 Keynesian economics was given its head and in many ways delivered more and better than the older systems had done against a background of global and social change. This naturally formed the backdrop to de-colonization and a post-imperial world. It formed the modern history of Africa and has gone on to work its effects when and where given a chance. Notwithstanding the Cold War after 1945, the perceived hegemony of new US Imperialism coupled with the powerful economic strength of that country, the emerging global world is perhaps owing more to Keynes than to the earlier classical theorists and more recently, the Monetarists of the neo-conservatism and the New Right of the 1970s.

To this emergent setting we can add over the recent half decade (on the negative balance) a rising demographic curve, persistent pockets of global poverty, continued local and regional conflict, a harshening environment, global warming and climate change, depletion of energy resources, acute civil, social and health crises. One can go on with this listing, but it is enough to make the point … and worse still, that the African continent bears the brunt of witness.

However, there is also a positive balance. The development movement has made progress over the last 50 years at least in methods and methodology if not always in execution and results (yet). Scientific, medical and technological progress too has brought many benefits to Africa (although not yet widely enough disseminated). The greatest successes have been evident in computing and telecommunications, not least through the Internet and the WWW. In economic growth there have been stories of economic success: initially the 'tiger economies' of South and East Asia, and more recently the great advances made by China, with India in fast pursuit. In Latin America the possibility of moving to global intermediate status is evidenced by Brazil and Mexico. The North-South axis has become a highly visible theme of political and economic discussion.

Political and educational reform is uneven and often very slow. There are also large areas where plans are laid down but progress is lacking: world trade negotiation is one of these and with the idea of globalization now unstoppable (largely) must come reciprocality and fairness, as in reality markets may be the only practical mechanism for mobilizing and regulating such vast projects. This may not amount to a fairer version or vision of capitalism, but where there is some dynamism there is always potential for improvement.

This world of a continuance of Keynesian economics (of central influence and a responsible role for the public sector) coupled with the new liberal market ideas (capitalism in its new evolution with its backdrop of regulation and better governance) and a backdrop of globalization made reality through the exploitation of the ICTs is the stage for the next decades (as far as we can predict and barring an unforeseen catastrophe). It is also the backdrop for the need for managing knowledge and the possible rising of "information professionals of the fifth phase" to assert their claim to contribute to the generation and management of knowledge.

6 KNOWLEDGE: AN ANALYTICAL FRAMEWORK

With a stated view of knowledge capital we can return to analyse the horizontal axis. Human capital_provides the foundation. This is the source of intellect and intelligent behaviour. Social capital represents a form of human capital as a resultant of concerted social and organizational engagement. Human capital and social capital are powerful sources of knowledge capital. The aggregate knowledge embodied in human capital can be called knowledge capital. The term intellectual capital can be used for the products of the use of knowledge capital, which represent the results of concerted and purposive intellectual effort which can be embodied in specific and often explicit forms. Explicit forms can be regarded as intellectual property which can be protected through legal copyright. The 'capital' characteristic implies a store of value which can be exploited for a longer or even continuous period, even without significant deterioration. Structural capital can be considered as the organizational dimension of intellectual capital or intellectual property. Customer capital embodies the idea that social relationships with partners can be considered as a resource which can provide more enduring value to those who create, use and exploit it. Customer capital is a sub-case or relation of social capital.

HUMAN CAPITAL

People (Labour, Human Resources, Organizational Staff) continue to be the fundamental asset for social and economic development and for the creation of present wealth and future potential investment. It is the source of intellect and intelligent behaviour.

Human capital firstly refers to the primary (demographic) resource and the way it is nurtured and developed (through upbringing, experience and education) to become a realizable asset in its contemporary setting. Secondly it refers to the potential contained in the current actual resource and implies the ways in which it can be used (exploited, leveraged etc) in the future.

KNOWLEDGE CAPITAL

This is a generic term for the aggregate of knowledge possessed by the resource of human capital. It is a product of inheritance, experience, learning, innate human intelligence and its application. Its application is a source of wise action (wisdom) and informed action in general.

It is derived from a multitude of sources. The information professional is especially interested in that knowledge which is derived from information and knowledge sources and resources which can be or have potential for accumulation and transfer. Its antecedents are to be found in data, information, intelligence and varieties and states of knowledge.

The way in which knowledge capital is made resourceful through the structures of the information and communication cycle so that it can be identified, stored, accessed and leveraged for practical and beneficial purposes is a key focus.

INTELLECTUAL CAPITAL / INTELLECTUAL PROPERTY

This is to be considered as the product of human minds and action related to needs and the fulfillment of goals. Intellectual property is the result of intellectual achievement. It can be represented as products of knowledge which have the properties of goods: it can contribute to activities and amongst other things to the creation of wealth and beneficialities.

Intellectual property is considered in many cases to be capable of ownership and of relatively exclusive possession, but it may also be represented more commonly by what can be held to be universal intellectual property (in the sense of human heritage or cultural capital and more recently the human genome)

Intellectual property as an artifact of knowledge can take many forms:

Published works
Unpublished writings and works
Copyrights to published and unpublished works
Artistic production
Cultural performance
Scientific knowledge at various stages of its production and transmission
Brands of goods
Trademarks and logos
Patentable inventions
Technologies
Techniques (with a proprietary origin)

Intellectual property is clearly related to creativity and its creative origins derived from human capacities working with knowledge and experience.

Intellectual property clearly has potential for commercialization and therefore will have considerable economic significance in many cases

STRUCTURAL CAPITAL

Structural capital can be considered as a property of the organization and its environment: the organization could be a business, a public body or a voluntary organization, amongst very many different types.

The structural capital can be considered as those aspects and elements of organizations which are a combination of the significant, the individual particularities, and the adaptations and developments of common properties which can in theory be applied to all or many organizations.

Structural capital can be exemplified *inter alia* by the following:

Organizational structures which have adapted well to the organizations needs and upon which other functions depend;

Common technologies which have been introduced, implemented and enhanced to meet the functioning and purpose of the organization and its clients and stakeholders;

Procedures and processes which have been developed and applied within the organization, so that they are highly fit for purpose, critical and well adapted;

Aspects of the organization and its behaviour which have been developed and enhanced through learning and experience so that they have special value and functionality in their context;

Unique assets possibly blending together technologies, procedures, and a varied mix of resources to meet particular needs and purposes.

Structural capital can embody intellectual property but in such a way that knowledge is used through process and action

CUSTOMER CAPITAL

Customer capital is represented by and embodied in the clients and stakeholders of the organization.

It represents a form of external human capital (clearly) but more precisely represents the actual and potential relationships which can exist and be developed from business, trading, contractual and organization to client relationships.

Historically, customer capital has been known as 'goodwill' : the propensity of clients to repeat, strengthen and sustain relationships with an organization.

Goodwill and its contemporary embodiment as customer capital recognized the actual and potential mutuality that can arise from relationships.

The realization of its existence and beneficiality associated with it has lead to the idea that it can be improved and enhanced and increasingly thereby take on valuable characteristics as a resource.

In estimating the value of a business for sale it has been customary for accountants to make a financial estimation of goodwill.

In the contemporary environment customer capital is seen as more active and extensive and has become as much process-related as an asset.

The realization of customer capital has been extensively accelerated by the deployment of new information and communication technologies to support the business process especially in the areas of selling, marketing and distribution.

The use of organizational and business information systems internally and now externally in web and telecommunications-supported environments is the focus for customer capital management. Knowledge about the client and the customer can be leveraged and deployed: it manifests data, information and knowledge as a resource.

It is possible to define internal customer capital where organizations are large or complex enough to permit its growth by allowing internal reciprocal relations to take place (e.g. business units, internal markets)

So much for basic concepts and definitions. Now, we must address the resultant professional activities at a similar level of detail and scale.

7 APPROPRIATE KNOWLEDGE MANAGEMENT: A TASK FOR INFORMATION PROFESSIONALS

Hitherto, we have set out the scope for information professional work and presented the scope for knowledge as content and substance. There is a credible case for suggesting that information professional work can and is evolving towards the more complex and wide ranging area of knowledge work.

The information professional task in knowledge management is to ensure that the third element of the definition we have used is delivered:

"Its foci include the management of existing knowledge resources through sharing, leveraging, collaborating and learning in order to create new knowledge to provide a basis for innovation and progress and increases in economic, social and cultural welfare".

What is the management agenda associated with this trend of professional activity? This might take the form of considering actions of the following kind: And more specifically, what and how might this be experienced in African conditions? Mchombu (1997) has contextualized the role under the broad aspiration for democracy and democratic change. Some illustrations how this might be relevant are given for each heading in the box below.

Carrying out audits of information, knowledge and communication activity
Participating fully in developing internal and external structures and infrastructures for information and communication management and supporting knowledge development
Environmental scanning and knowledge gathering from external sources
Using information and communication management to elicit, record, store and disseminate knowledge within a setting

Targeting knowledge to where it is needed internally and externally
Undertaking leading and supporting actions to develop, conserve and enrich knowledge capital in its main dimensions within an established framework
Working in an information professional capacity with all other parties and stakeholders internally and increasingly externally
Developing knowledge activities at the strategic level in the setting by ensuring involvement at the strategic level
Contributing to actions and activities which will lead to the creation and development of new knowledge resources
Supporting the realization, dissemination and export of knowledge based innovations, products and roles
Ensuring that an all pervasive knowledge culture is engendered and supported in the setting
Develop and maintain methods and techniques to support the knowledge culture using all levels of material and technology as appropriate
Assist in the development, training and education of members and stakeholders to support a knowledge culture
Actively support the culture of learning organization, knowledge based activity and the community of practice

In order to accomplish this agenda of knowledge management, significant activity in three areas is essential. These are:

- The development of the learning organization
- The structuring of processes within organizations to permit learning in the broadest sense and the development of knowledge resources
- Ensuring that competences are embodied in the settings to enable and maintain the existence of communities of practice

The learning organization can be characterized as follows:

A DEVELOPMENTAL GOAL

The term 'Learning organization 'is often applied to formal organizations which are going through a state of development and transformation.

'Learning organization' and 'Knowledge organization' are sometimes used synonymously. The more an organization adopts and adapts to new circumstances and new goals the more likely it is to perfect certain processes which will sustain its emergent state.

The educational metaphor is appropriate because in order to learn it is necessary to communicate well and this involves processes of discovery and imparting what is known through sharing and exchange.

It is already established that these processes are significant in the knowledge management environment since they can be shown to lead to the discovery, leveraging, mobilization and generation of new knowledge.

Explicit knowledge can be utilized relatively easily especially if it is subject to adequate levels of information management.

However, tacit knowledge often requires discovery and elicitation before it can be leveraged, exploited and utilized.

Establishing conditions in which a variety of learning experiences can take place is significant in knowledge management.

An organization which prioritizes its own learning and enables learning offers the best conditions for knowledge management in the widest sense.

The structuring of processes takes typical forms:

TOP DOMAINS OF LEVERAGING
(Source : Barth in Turban et al. (2002))

Sharing knowledge and best practices
Instilling responsibility for sharing knowledge
Capturing and re-using best practices
Embedding knowledge in products, services and processes
Producing knowledge as a product
Driving knowledge generation for innovation
Mapping networks of experts
Building and mining customer and knowledge bases
Understanding and measuring the value of knowledge
Leveraging intellectual assets

KEY ASSETS IN KNOWLEDGE DEVELOPMENT

INNOVATION

Knowledge and innovation are inseparable
Developing an environment for innovation
Supporting innovation processes

EXPERIENCE

Realizing human potential through experience
Open for learning

SHARING

Maximizing possibilities for communication
Active sharing as a productive experience
Breaking down barriers and liberation
Pushing limits

COLLABORATION

Discovering possibilities for collaboration
Maximizes interfaces and potentials
Encourages respect and trust

LEARNING

Holistic experience
Varieties of forms of learning favoured
Favours communication, collaboration and sharing

Ensuring competencies by building capacities within organizations and knowledge management settings helps create and strengthen learning organizations. This domain is crucial to the development of Civil Society but is fortunately one that is achievable. It could even thrive in the intermediate and appropriate environments of the developing world.

COMPETENCIES

If knowledge development is a desired requirement there is a strong indication that competences in knowledge management have a very prominent place in the setting.

These competencies can be both individual and collective constituents: the more they are identified, enhanced and developed the greater the possibilities for learning and leveraging.

The development of knowledge competences should be reflected in the values, mission, goals, aims and objectives of the setting (whether it is an informal social group, formal group or organizational structure).

Individual competencies are necessary but these need to be established in a wider context of structures, processes and behaviours. Individual competencies are strengthened through collective engagement (sharing, co-operating, mentoring etc.).

Knowledge development and communication go hand in hand. The individual normally acquires skills and knowledge through experience and exchange with others. Of course, a certain amount of individual, even solitary activity may be necessary to acquire preliminary levels of information and knowledge but interaction is vital after an initial phase. From this proposition growth and communication are significantly related: this is apparent biologically and socially.

Practically the information professional as a knowledge manager (worker) has to match the identities of information with appropriate skills and competences. There are thus appropriate applications for data management, library skills, information service delivery, archiving and records, documentation, ICT skills and competences, analysis and intelligence skills, investigation and research and more generally for information management.

The knowledge managers make their contribution to knowledge development through the deployment of these specific competences and actions.

COMMUNITIES OF PRACTICE

The community of practice is a convenient way to describe both a goal and a structure for knowledge development.

Communities of practice provide reinforcement and stimulus for the acquisition and deployment of competences as well as favouring the leveraging of knowledge.

A community of practice can be both an intermediate or final structure in a knowledge/learning organization environment.

Certain features include:

Common values, purposes and goals
A strong social identity
Evidence of learning organization competences
Structure and structural capital which reinforce learning and knowledge development
Substantial tangible information assets
Substantial evidence of interface activities and techniques / technologies which leverage deeper knowledge in more visible, tangible and accessible forms
Rich in communication structures and open environments
Visible indicators/indications of information and knowledge processing and management
Evidence of use of knowledge capital
Members with explicit information / knowledge roles

This view of knowledge management in practice provides a model for using existing information professional expertize, methods and experience and positioning them towards an enlarged field of engagement. In this way the information professional may truly aspire towards the title of knowledge professional. Clearly, there is a sense of colonization at work or of overcoming resistance to a greater formality and organization of information and knowledge work in different settings. But, this is what information professionals have always aspired to and have sensed the frustration of exclusion.

The information professional as knowledge worker will become less a separate species and more a member of the common tribes of occupations. The knowledge model with its emphasis on sharing, collaboration and mutual interest should underpin this convergence. It is natural enough to think it might be so. And, if it is not happening it will remain a potent indicator of a barrier to rationality and sense, which will make overcoming it all the more important and challenging.

8 INFORMATION PROFESSIONALS AS RESOURCES: A ROLE TO PLAY IN CIVIL SOCIETY

If the knowledge professional agenda (discussed above) can be addressed it suggests a very firm and secure future information professionals, who if they can realize this agenda, deserve to be called knowledge professionals. The opportunity awaits them. It will have taken them a long way form their original roots in librarianship and documentation, but in a fashion which is completely consistent within a framework of progressively greater orientation to and engagement with users.

Knowledge management provides the opportunity to move out of the shadows into the business world, the public sector and the Civil Society. In the UK the London School of Economics has established the Centre for Civil Society: I have this organization as my basis for definition. Let me quote their key definition:

> Civil society refers to the arena of uncoerced collective action around shared interests, purposes and values. In theory, its institutional forms are distinct form those of the state, family and market, though in practice the boundaries between state, civil society, family and market are often complex, blurred and negotiated. Civil society commonly embraces a diversity of spaces, actors and institutional forms, varying in their degree of formality, autonomy and power. Civil societies are often populated by organisations such as registered charities, development no-governmental organisations, community groups, women's organisations, faith-based organisations, professional associations, trade unions, self-help groups, social movements, business associations, coalitions and advocacy groups.
>
> Source: http://www.lse.ac.uk/collections/CCS/what_is_civil_society.htm

The Civil society is distinctly different from the two polar forms of private and commercial market society on the one hand and government and the public sector on the other. The family and the individual are distinct complexes but clearly are more closely related to the civil society of the definition since its work is likely to increase their engagement and empowerment. Through this social participation and greater social cohesion will be gained.

9 TARGET THEMES: AFRICA AND THE DEVELOPING WORLD

This paper has been prepared specifically to set the scene for the cluster of conference sessions discussing knowledge management and the Civil Society. The development of the Civil Society implies the construction of an Open Society, with a participative, democratic and representative framework. It implies a motivated, capable and competent social body which upholds certain basic civil and human rights. It requires the building up of people through education and frameworks of opportunity so that they can play a responsible part in the development of society, through all institutions, but especially those that thrive on voluntary and social commitment where ownership of issues and values goes hand in hand with effort and responsibility. In African society there is an emergent base to build the civil society in the form of church and religious organization (nurturing voluntary and charitable activity, and through the network of organization created by NGOs and development agencies. This milieu can be regarded as a learning environment in which knowledge management can be enhanced and expedited.

To meet the needs of society and the institutions of Civil Society there must be and needs to be the means to fully exploit information and knowledge and to communicate between those who have it, need it and can exploit it by adding value. Information and knowledge professionals have a clear role to play in this. To give focus to this I want to lay out an information agenda. It has two dimensions which mutually interact. On the one hand it prescribes areas of information attention which citizens need: on the other hand it provides a series of goals towards which information professional work has to aspire. If both these requirements can be met the tasks of managing knowledge which have been outlined earlier are more likely to be met. Furthermore, a benchmark statement is offered for present African conditions.

Information empowerment
Citizens need to have rights to information with appropriate guarantees. Access to education ensures basic and increased levels of literacy of all kinds. There needs to be a sufficient and growing stock of information resources and means of availability and communication. Social and economic progress necessitates information empowerment as a primary means. (Literacy is widely understood to be fundamental: literacy rates are improving, but need to be matched by documentary supply as well as general media growth)

User needs and requirements
The citizen and the individual need to be aware of their needs and requirements for information and knowledge in both a potential and actual sense. (Urban areas have some advantages over rural areas. Increased literacy may help to develop demand and enable needs and requirements to be stated)

Citizen and community information
Information and knowledge are coterminous with the idea of active citizenship and with a progressive and changing society. Information is a social good and as such should be a community resource. The individual citizen and the community can best interact and support each other in an enriching information environment. (Civil society institutions have a great role to play as catalyst for needs and activities and as providers. Libraries need to work with and within their communities to develop and sustain activities)

Information rights and the need to know
These conditions are fundamental to empowerment and need to be enshrined constitutionally and to be deliverable in practice. Information professionalism has to take up the task of supporting these in an ethical and responsible manner. (The assurance of constitutional rights, civil right and information rights is the basis. In most African states there is considerable work to be done. If the structures exist then they need to be activated and exploited.)

Freedom of Information (FOI)
Good governance is essential to and protective of development. FOI ensures that governance is transparent and therefore democratic in outlook as well as in practice. This will help to promote cohesion and confidence. (The development of good governance has been emphasized at the highest level. It is a challenge to achieve and sustain it in any country anywhere. If it can be achieved its effects will be beneficial)

Information access and privacy
Whilst information rights, empowerment and FOI will encourage access to public and social information, it will be necessary to ensure privacy, confidentiality and security of information where it is appropriate. For example, in relations between private individuals, between the individual and the state and where communication is lawful and there is no likely endangerment to public good or national security. (These are conditions which emerge from achievement of the pre-conditions reviewed already. If sustained they provide indicators of a viable civil society and an open society in general)

Data and information protection
The application of computers to information processing has been the catalyst for data and information protection. The ease of manipulation and transmission of data and information over networks has made such protection essential. (As the ICTs are developed in Africa the highest standards of operation need to be in-built from the outset)

Legal frameworks for information
These have become ever more important as the information society and the knowledge society becomes a reality. The more important and resourceful information becomes the greater the need for legal frameworks. What is important if the legitimacy and justification for such framework. Intellectual property, information goods and structural capital all necessitate legal frameworks, which may be additional to the established traditions for copyrights, literary and cultural censorship and slander or blasphemy. (Good governance and an emergent civil society will encourage suitable legal frameworks and engender respect for their operation and implementation.)

Role for public information provision
A knowledge society (and a Civil Society) is an increasingly public society. The responsibility for public information provision is thus a consequence and clearly a potential source of benefit and capital (Libraries and educational institutions are essential and need to be visible. But public information concepts need to be rooted in all institutional and organizational structures)

Provision of access to the ICTs
The information society and the knowledge society are increasingly technology based and technology dependent. The provision of ICT access is an economic as much as a technical challenge. It is such a significant resource that it carries a significant public dimension. However, it is likely that significant provision of technology and access is a task which will fall more and more to the commercial and market sector. This raises governance and public policy issues which are at the heart of the Open Society as much as the Civil Society. (As general economic development is raised the technology base will follow. Mobile telecommunications and mass media will be potent forms of innovation and information distribution)

Levels of information and computer literacy
With the rise of the ICTs will come a demand for access and use. This will require acquisition of skills on a wide scale and competences to fully exploit them. (Basic education is the key to this type of literacy. It is capital intensive. Reductions in some technology costs will be beneficial to African societies)

Tackling social exclusion (including the consequences of underdevelopment)
Citizens who do not have a place in this information agenda will find themselves significantly excluded from society in many of its aspects. The assurance of rights can be seen as an essential step in preventing exclusion. Exclusion is clearly a waste of human and social capital. The information professional's role must address all aspects of social exclusion. (Reducing exclusion is a long term goal although a short and medium term need. Acceleration in the development of civil society institutions is possibly the only realistic model for progress)

Resourcing: management and the responsibilities of providers
Information professionals have always claimed that their activities are under-resourced and many of them may have been under-managed. There may be little room for optimism and improvement here. But, the increasing pervasiveness of information and knowledge resources and activities will lead to some increase and a greater sharing of basic resources. (Where resources can be found they need to be made effective. Institutional corruption is believed by many to hold back and to undermine efforts: it needs to be tackled at all levels. Realistically, progress will remain slow but maintain momentum).

If information professionals as knowledge managers can successfully promote this agenda they will help lead in the creation, development and maintenance of Civil Society. They will create the environment in which the institutions of Civil Society will effectively contribute to the development of learning organizations and to a knowledge base learning society. This offers significant benefits for the quality of the general development process.

It is essential to note that there is little novel in these issues, which has not been well covered and discussed in professional arenas since the 1960s. Rightly, they form the basis and substance for information professional education. Many of these issues were raised from the 1960s onwards as the idea of national information policy was advanced as an input to development planning. The work of the UN and UNESCO has been significant (UNISIST and the General Information Programme) in the 1970s. IFLA and FID promoted the idea actively in the 1980s. National information planning enjoyed some successes but tended to falter for various reasons or simply the effort became dispersed as more agencies necessarily had to be involved. National libraries in African countries have found the model useful and have achieved in practice where conditions were favourable.

At best the issues emerged at the third or fourth tier of the process: after general economic development strategy and planning, which was followed by strategic sectoral planning (in health, education, energy, physical infrastructure etc.). Education plans certainly provide opportunities for publishing (I can cite the experience of Kenya and Tanzania) and libraries have realized opportunities (Tanzania provides an excellent model). Contributors to SCECSAL XVII provide a rich fund of examples. From this point on regional and local plans and development assume importance. Where organizations and communities can become involved there have been good instances of 'take-off' to use the classic development term favoured by Rostow and Myrdal.

However, this retrospect does uncover a significant finding. Initial perception might imply that the further down the development chain is your project, the less likely it is to survive and succeed (I am sure there are many who can cite the contrary but there is an intuitive truth in the assertion). But, the Civil Society idea is some forty years or two generations down the line as a conceptual focus from the development chain model (mainly to do with visibility and labeling : it was always out there!). What Civil Society does as a model is to suggest the orthodox hierarchy can be inverted and therefore given new visibility and priority.

With the new energy available to the information professional and the opportunities provided by the dynamics of societies and the new information and communication technologies, the time is ripe for a fusion of knowledge management and the activities of Civil Society. We look forward to hearing about this from our session contributors who can provide practical evidence.

10 AN AFRICAN REFLECTION: AN EXTERNAL VIEW

No one knows better than SCECSAL delegates about the African reality. There can be no substitute for their on the ground and front line knowledge. But, those who look-on and who support and contribute in some way from outside Africa have a part to play.

Images of famine and terror have been a trigger for support from other nations and people collectively and individually. The mass media enable the diffusion of images and information across the whole scale. The bad news often forms the basis of awareness, an interest, a contribution or a campaign. But, good news also gets through and this informs and encourages. As a consumer and observer of the UK media we get in general a wider view both historical and geographical, social, economic and political, as well as artistic, cultural and human interest. We have (in the UK and Europe) the resources of information and media and good access to them to at least make us informed and even knowledgeable.

Whilst individuals can play a role, we outside Africa also expect organizations from the public sector, the private sector and our civil society to play their role on our behalf in the substantive development of African societies.

For the UK the chairmanship of G8 and the EU in 2005 was seized on as an opportunity for exposure and action, not least in the areas of debt relief, world trade negotiations and the global market, migration, health provision, famine relief, social development and aid through bodies like DfID, as well as a greater exposure to environmental issues of drought, climate change and global warming and the dire consequences which follow inaction. Drought effected regions of Africa (e.g. Sudan, Somalia, Chad, Kenya) suffer both political or military conflict or both. Indeed climate change is set to become a major attention focus in 2007 following a number of influential reports and commentaries made in 2006, such as the Stern Report in the UK (HM Treasury and Cabinet Office, 2006).

The private sector (as the generator of wealth and provider of goods and services) has a role to play too. Setting aside the darker side of its past record we can see new awareness in terms of corporate responsibility, reforms of markets, investment policies, trade agreements and promotion and in some areas a willingness to work more closely with relevant organizations and governments.

In the wider sphere bodies such as Oxfam, Danida, MSF and many other civil and religious trusts and charities can play a significant role. In addition they provide the means and the model for adaptation to local African conditions and be effected themselves by autochthonous and indigenous models. These exogenous organs of Civil Society have to be the catalyst for necessary endogenous development. As information professionals you have to take these ideas forward from the SCECSAL conference and ensure that information resource and knowledge capital play their part in development.

It is to the Civil Society that we need to focus attention on achievements so far and in potential for the future. There is no doubt in my mind that the institutions of the Civil Society provide a viable and hopeful model for African development and society. We have mapped out how the information professionals can play an established part and how in the area of knowledge management they can be the most significant collaborators.

So now, enough has been said by way of discussion to conclude this keynote paper by highlighting some actions which can be developed to help bring about a vigorous Civil Society in each African country.

11 ACTIONS: SOCIETY

Community development has to be prioritised through effective leadership and by leaders in the community. Public education is the main resource to support this. Human capital will be developed. The contexts for developing indigenous knowledge will be created.

The focus on the community will create conditions to mobilize social energy and engender a climate for taking initiative in many of the key fields. The institutions of Civil Society are the primary vehicles for these actions. The creation and success of some will become the model for many.

Minimum thresholds of public society are required, humans rights and freedoms must be assured, respected and protected. If these are absent or failing the effectiveness of Civil Society will be reduced. Information rights, public access to information and personal information empowerment have to be assured.

Information literacy and empowerment can consciously be developed through the educational systems. The information professional has clear responsibilities here already, but has then to be prepared to reach out and support the growing institutions: meeting their needs for information and assisting them in the development of knowledge management. These institutions have to discover their power to develop through knowledge activity.

12 ACTIONS: ECONOMY AND TECHNOLOGY

The general economic good health of countries and their constituent societies has been the motive of development policy since the colonial era. What has been done by way of achievement needs to be maintained and developed. The economic future is substantially about increasing the volume of activity and ensuring equitable distribution of gains.

The leading developed economies and a number of the emergent ones (where they can) carry a responsibility to provide aid and assistance as well as to ensure that the global economic structures (investment, debt relief, trade law and agreements and technology standards) are there to assist rather than thwart general economic development.

There is no shortage of theory and policy development, but still many difficulties in economic management and development on the ground. We cannot review all the key aspects here but we are all aware of them.

The process of overcoming difficulties and development aid in general has been achieved through civil societies which can provide models for the future. But what has to come is the indigenous development of civil societies and institutions. The better the economic outlook the easier and more encouraging it will be for civil societies in practice.

In the interim, the model of knowledge development includes the proposition that "we do not know what we know" and a belief that there are actions which many can take and which are simple to implement, which can increase the stock of knowledge. This is a resource that can be tapped even if the level of economic development is lower. The institutions of Civil Society are ideal nurseries for this intermediate activity.

In both the globalized and the localized worlds the potency of the information and communication technologies has been realized at the levels of both policy and practice. In African society there is still a very long way to go, but the environment and possibilities are changing. It was not such a long time ago that a British school considered it an achievement to have one or at best a few computers. Nowadays the computer is nothing if it does not have that broadband Internet connection. The next decade will see changes in Africa although they will not arrive evenly. But the measure of computers and computer access is a corroborative measure of progress towards the knowledge society.

13 ACTIONS: CULTURE AND COMMUNICATION

The ICTs are bringing the newest means of communication to progressively more and more people. Their application to the institutions of the civil society will be highly beneficial and provide a wider range of tools to access, generate and disseminate knowledge. Of course, the overall communication environment embodies the mass media (printed and broadcast) and the creative and cultural industries as well as the regulatory framework and the impact the media have on the public at large. In this area many African countries have a way to go.

Communication media are potent causes and effects in culture in all its forms. To be effective all work with information and knowledge resources is integrated with the wider cycle of information and communication. Any role that the information professional can play in this effort is worthwhile, either as a knowledge worker in an organization, as a contributor the infrastructure and as an advocate and communicator for the organization.

14 ACTIONS: THE PROFESSIONS

This paper began with a look back to the evolution of the information professional. This is now the moment to pause and reflect on what has been achieved and what there is still to do. The participants at the conference can engage with this task. A little SWOT analysis would prove useful. There is a strengthening although not a full infrastructure in Africa; professional self-knowledge can help to address the weaknesses; the field of knowledge management can find application everywhere, because it is literally at the heart of everything; and we have ourselves to blame if we cannot recognize and act on the threats which undoubtedly exist.

15 PRACTICAL STEPS FORWARD

This overview of the background to a range of actions is part of the agenda which clearly faces the information professional and directs them directly to the task of building knowledge activities and placing them at the disposal of the Civil Society.

It is the task of the conference and the participants to take the steps necessary to measure out progress in the coming years, and at least to realize that by the date of the next SCECSAL meeting there are clear achievements to record.

REFERENCES

Barth, S. (2002). Knowledge as a function of X. *Knowledge Management*, February 2000. Cited by: Turban, E., McClean, E., and Wetherbe, J., *Information technology for management: transforming business in the digital economy*. New York: John Wiley.

Boisot, M.H. (1998). *Knowledge assets: securing competitive advantage in the information economy*. Oxford: Oxford University Press.

Earl, M.J. ed. (1996). *Information management: the organisational dimension*. Oxford: Oxford University Press.

HM Treasury and Cabinet Office. *Stern review on the economics of climate change*. London: HM Treasury and Cabinet Office, 2006. (Prepared by group under the chairmanship of Sir Nicholas Stern). Available under : http://www.sternreview.org.uk/

Leonard-Barton, D. (1995). *Wellsprings of knowledge: building and sustaining the sources of innovation*. Boston: Harvard Business School Press.

Mchombu, K.J. (1997). Information support for democratisation in Africa. In: John Feather ed. *Transforming libraries and educating librarians: essays in memory of Peter Havard-Williams*. London: Taylor Graham, pp. 41–56.

Menou, M.J. (1997). Culture, information and the education of information professionals in Africa. In: John Feather ed. *Transforming libraries and educating librarians: essays in memory of Peter Havard-Williams*. London: Taylor Graham, pp. 25–40.

Nonaka, I. and Takeuchi, H. (1995). *The knowledge-creating company*. Oxford: OUP.

Porter, M.E. (1985). *Competitive advantage: creating and sustaining superior performance*. Free Press/Collier Macmillan: New York/London.

Prusak, L. (1997). *Knowledge in organisations*. Boston: Butterworth-Heinemann.

Stewart, T.A. (1997). *Intellectual capital: the new wealth of organisations*. London: Nicholas Brealey Publishing.

Sveiby, K.E. (1997). *The new organisational wealth: managing and measuring knowledge-based assets*. San Francisco: Berrett-Koehler.

Wilson, T.D. (2002). The nonsense of "knowledge management". *Information Research*, vol. 8, no. 1.

INFORMATION VACCINE: INFORMATION AND UGANDA'S REDUCTION OF HIV/AIDS

Kendra S. Albright, Dick Kawooya and Judy Hoff

ABSTRACT

The spread of HIV/AIDS in Africa over the last two decades has seriously impaired the continent's health care services and overall welfare. Unlike many other African nations, however, Uganda has developed and implemented a unique approach to combating this problem. Part of Uganda's success has been attributed to a formalized Information, Education, and Communication (IEC) strategy, lowering estimated HIV/AIDS infection rates from 18.5% in 1995 to 4.1% in 2003. The purpose of this study is to understand how access to health care information contributed to Uganda's success. The types of information and dissemination methods offer an understanding of what information contributes to behavioral change and prevention of HIV/AIDS transmission. Interviews were conducted with over 300 organizations involved in the dissemination of HIV/AIDS information to examine the types and methods of dissemination. The results of this study are presented and discussed in light of their role in the overall IEC strategy.

1 INTRODUCTION

The number of people living with HIV/AIDS has become a global pandemic. Currently, there is no cure for the disease, which kills millions each year. Sub-Saharan Africa is the hardest hit region of the world in terms of HIV/AIDS. With over 10% of the world's population, Sub-Saharan Africa accounts for 64% of the people living with HIV/AIDS and 77% of the deaths from AIDS in 2005 (UNAIDS, 2005). In response to the AIDS pandemic, policies are being developed in many African countries focusing on information, education, and communication (IEC) strategies as a means of prevention. With no vaccine or cure in sight, information is a key weapon in the battle against HIV/AIDS. Through the widespread dissemination of HIV/AIDS information, the people of Sub-Saharan Africa can gain the knowledge needed to change their behavioral response to the AIDS epidemic.

Uganda is one of only a few countries in the world that has successfully reduced its rates of HIV/AIDS at the national level. Part of Uganda's success has been attributed to a formalized Information, Education, and Communication (IEC) strategy, lowering estimated HIV/AIDS infection rates from as high as 18.5% in 1995 to as low as 4.1% in 2003. This study is part of an ongoing study to understand how and why this strategy of access to health care information has contributed to Uganda's success. By examining the types of information and methods for dissemination offers we can better understand how information contributes to behavioral change.

The Uganda AIDS Commission (UAC) has estimated that there are approximately 1,500 organizations involved in the dissemination of HIV/AIDS information in Uganda. These include governmental (Government.), non-governmental (NGOs), faith-based organizations (FBOs), community-based organizations (CBOs) private companies, multi- or bi-lateral organizations, and other international organizations. Information that is disseminated focuses on a variety of topics including Abstinence, Faithfulness, and Condoms (the ABCs), among other topics. Albright and Kawooya (2004, 2005) identified problems in the flow of information within and between these organizations (Albright and Kawooya, 2004, 2005). The type of information and how it is being disseminated by these organizations has not been examined and the organizations themselves are not aware of what is shared between the organizations and the general public. The purpose of this study was to find out the answers to these questions. Specifically, there were three main purposes:

1) To identify the types of organizations involved in the dissemination of HIV/ AIDS
2) To catalog the types and formats of information that is being disseminated by these organizations;
3) And to examine what information is shared between them.

This study examines the types of organizations involved in HIV/AIDS information dissemination, the types of information they disseminate, and how it is disseminated, both to other organizations and to the general public. By classifying the types and methods of information that these organizations disseminate, the contribution of information to the decline of HIV/AIDS can be better understood.

2 LITERATURE REVIEW

Uganda is one of only a few countries in the world that has successfully reduced its rates of HIV/AIDS at the national level. There appear to be several factors that have allowed Ugandans to integrate their understanding of HIV/AIDS into an appropriate and specific cultural context resulting in a dramatic reduction in the prevalence of HIV/AIDS. Through a combined approach of national policy and community response, the Uganda people have changed their behavioral response to AIDS.

Uganda differs from other countries:

- Dramatic decrease in prevalence rates of HIV/AIDS and in the number of new cases reported
- Specifically: behavioral changes resulting in a dramatic decrease in the number of non-regular partners (Low-Beer and Stoneburner, 2003) and reduction in sexual networks

This finding is supported by other research. The number of non-regular sexual partners was 60% lower in Uganda 1995 than in Kenya in 1998 and Zambia and Malawi in 1996 (Stoneburner and Carballo, 1997; Stoneburner & Low-Beer, 2000).

Green et al. (2002) found that adults in various African countries considered reductions in casual sex and abstinence to be the greatest response to AIDS. Condom use, although reported, was not considered to be as important. Furthermore, condom use in Uganda has not been reported to be higher than in other countries (Low-Beer & Stoneburner, 2003).

Personal channels are the main source for communicating information about HIV/AIDS in both the urban and rural areas of Uganda (Low-Beer & Stoneburner, 2003). Between 1989 and 1995 there was a shift from mass and institutional communication to personal communication channels in Uganda for communicating information about HIV/AIDS (Low-Beer & Stoneburner, 2003). Mass and institutional communication channels account for the majority of HIV/AIDS communication in all other countries reported by Low-Beer & Stoneburner (2003).

3 METHODOLOGY

Contact information for organizations involved in HIV/AIDS information was obtained from the Uganda AIDS Commission. Semi-structured, face-to-face interviews were conducted with over 300 selected organizations. Types of HIV/AIDS information that were disseminated by these organizations (e.g., information about the disease, ABC, caring for someone with AIDS, etc.) and their methods used to distribute that information (e.g., media, print, drama, etc.) were identified and cataloged. Funding and source of materials disseminated by these organizations, as well as the primary recipients were also examined.

Types of HIV/AIDS information that were disseminated by these organizations (e.g., information about the disease, ABC, caring for someone with AIDS, etc.) and their methods used to distribute that information (e.g., media, print, drama, etc.) were identified and cataloged. Funding and source of materials disseminated by these organizations, as well as the primary recipients were also examined.

The study was conducted in the summer of 2004. Data were collected from over 310 organizations across 22 districts. The sample was drawn from the inventory of HIV/AIDS agencies from a 2001 study released by Uganda AIDS Commission (UAC) titled *Inventory of Agencies with HIV/AIDS Activities and HIV/AIDS Interventions in Uganda.* Seven hundred and sixteen (716) organizations were listed in the inventory. Organizations encountered in the course of the field activities but were not in the inventory were surveyed and entered in the study inventory. Some 62 new organizations were added bring the total number of the study inventory to 778. Initially, data collection was to be done through electronic mail (e-mail), telephone, or physical visits to organizations. Telephone surveys are a recent phenomenon in Uganda, however, especially for business transactions like research. The method was abandoned early once its utility was tested and doubted by the research team, although future studies may have more success with telephone research as more Ugandans become familiar with the telephone as a medium for conducting business. However, our experience suggests that telephone rates in Uganda and for Africa generally, are prohibitive for a large study. We also found problems with e-mail in that addresses were far out of date from the 2001 list from which we had to work. Therefore, most of the organizations in the study were interviewed face to face.

A total of 310 organizations were included in the study, or 40% of the total 778 organizations identified. Based on the sampling framework, Kampala, Mbale and Tororo were automatically enrolled given the presence of a large number of organizations with HIV/AIDS interventions. This study included two researchers and 7 research assistants. The Principal Investigator managed the administrative aspects of the project from Tennessee and the Co-PI, originally from Masaka, headed up the research in the field in Uganda. Six research assistants were hired to work in the field, while one worked in Tennessee, coordinating the data transferred from Uganda into the database at the University there. The Research Assistants in Uganda were given one week of training before beginning the data collection. Training focused on the background of the study including objectives, instrument and methods, ethical obligations, procedures and careful review of the consent form and questionnaire. At the end of the training, Research Assistants were informally evaluated to establish their clear understanding of the study, processes, and ultimate goal. The survey instrument was tested and slight errors were identified and corrected.

Data collection started in Kampala soon after the training and lasted slightly more than three weeks before moving to upcountry districts. For nearby districts, Research Assistants would leave Kampala in the morning, visit organizations, and return in the evenings. Because of road conditions, travel to and from target districts Kampala is difficult. As a result, for districts more than 100 miles from Kampala, two teams of three Research Assistants were established and each team visited different parts of the country so that when one team was in the Western part of the country, the other team was in the Eastern.

Teams met every week except for a few weeks when teams were far removed from Kampala. For most organizations, appointments were set up by telephone or other means. Upon securing appointments, organizations were visited and the survey administered. Some organizations preferred to just complete the survey instrument rather than participate in an interview. Here, the survey was dropped off for later pick up. For a few organizations, particularly those with national operations and, therefore, branch networks, the standard procedure involved seeking clearance from national headquarters in Kampala before proceeding to branches or affiliates. Most of these organizations have developed elaborate and, at times, more stringent application procedures than those instituted by Ugandan Government. Such organizations mostly required providing an application package complete with a study protocol, ethical statement(s), study tools, application letter, Government and parent institution's clearances and, for some, payment to offset staff time for participating in the study. These bureaucratic procedures sometimes rendered organizations inaccessible until later in the study period. Consequently priority was given to organizations with little or no bureaucratic procedures. Understandably most HIV-AIDS organizations are overwhelmed with "clients" who must be served as a matter of priority before attending to researchers. Uganda's successful campaign means that organizations also have to deal with large numbers of researchers/ investigators majority of whom are trying to establishing what contributed to Uganda's success. The establishment of organizational research policies is a good remedy to those challenges.

Once data were collected they were checked for accuracy and entered into an SPSS spreadsheet. Of 48 total surveys e-mailed, only one was completed and returned. All other surveys were conducted by face-to-face interviews or contacts. Preliminary data analysis has been conducted using descriptive frequencies, cross-tabs, chi-square, and ANOVA and MANOVA. What follows in the findings is a report of those results that stood out in the study as statistically significant.

4 RESULTS AND DISCUSSION

There were eight different categories of organization types that were collapsed into four major categories including:

- NGOs (including national, international, and local) (44%);
- Government (including Central and Local government) (20%);
- FBOs (16%);
- CBOs (16%); and
- Other (4%).

The breakdown of these four groups is presented in Figure 1. NGOs accounted for the largest type of organization with nearly 44% of the representative organizations. This was followed by Government organizations with slightly over 17%. FBOs and CBOs each accounted for approximately 16% of the representative organizations. All other organizational types were grouped together and accounted for only 4% of the remaining organizations.

There was one private company that reported but was eliminated from the study because the category was so small. Although there is some overlap between these categories, the organizations were asked to select the one category they believed best represented their organization.

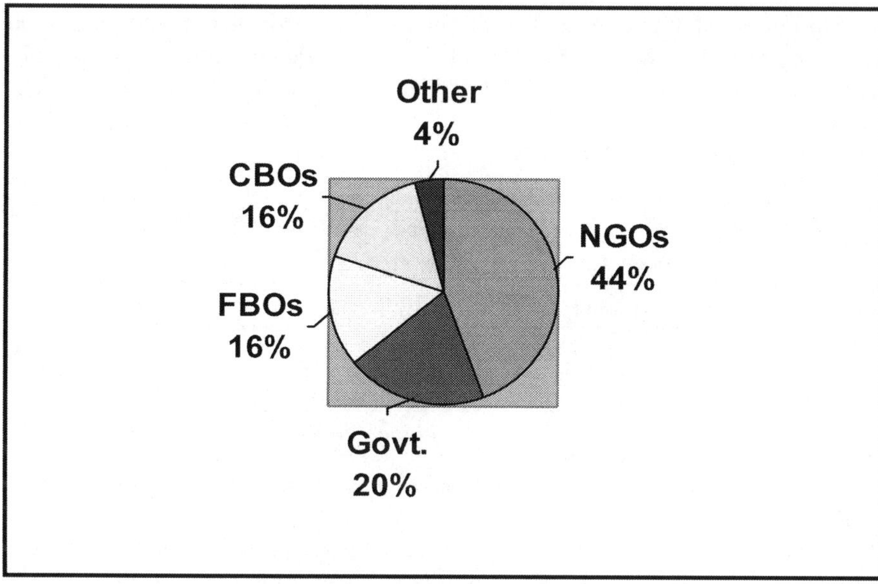

Figure 1. Study Participants by Organization Type

The types of information disseminated by organizations included:

- General information about HIV/AIDS;
- HIV;
- AIDS;
- Transmission of HIV/AIDS;
- Symptoms of AIDS;
- Abstinence;
- Age of Sexual Debut;
- Faithfulness;
- Condoms;
- Circumcision;
- Orphans;
- Contraceptives;
- Treatment of AIDS;
- Management of Symptoms;
- Caring for Someone with AIDS; and
- Sexually Transmitted Diseases (STDs).

When crossed with organization type, the results were very interesting. Two categories of organizations were significantly more likely to disseminate certain kinds of information more than any other organizations (Figure 2). These included FBOs, which disseminated information on Abstinence, Faithfulness, and Orphans and were significantly less likely to disseminate information on condoms and contraceptives, and Government organizations, which were statistically more likely to disseminate information on Condoms and Contraceptives than any other organization type.

Organization Type	Type of Information Disseminated
Faith-Based Organization	Abstinence
Faith-Based Organization	Faithfulness
Faith-Based Organization	Orphans
Government	Condoms
Government	Contraceptives

Figure 2. Type of Information Disseminated by Organization ($p \leq .05$).

There were other significant findings about faith-based organizations. FBOs are significantly more likely to serve and disseminate information to other FBOs than to any other organization type. They are also significantly more likely to disseminate information on abstinence, faithfulness, and orphans than any other type of organization. They are very significantly less likely to disseminate information on condoms and contraceptives (at the $p=.000$ level) and they consider information on condoms to be significantly less important than do all other types of organizations. FBOs are significantly less likely to disseminate information to CBOs and they believe that the general public is significantly more likely to get HIV/AIDS information from Local Government than from any other organizational source.

A very important finding of our research focused on the format by which information was disseminated. Interview participants were asked to select the formats for dissemination of HIV/AIDS information. Choices included:

- Radio
- Television
- Newspaper
- Recorded music
- Drama (plays, etc.)
- Movies
- Books
- Comic books
- Brochures, pamphlets

- Reports
- Magazines (popular, general information)
- Journals (scholarly)
- Other

Although participants were asked to select all formats that apply, the top two reported formats for information dissemination included radio and drama. This is not surprising given the oral tradition of Ugandan society and the high rates of print illiteracy. It suggests, however, that given the drop in prevalence rates of HIV/AIDS in Uganda, information is effectively transmitted through oral tradition.

The origination of information for dissemination also produced some interesting results. Although funding, source of materials, and primary recipients were examined, the results were inconclusive. Many of the organizations either did not know where their materials came from or they concluded that they came from the headquarters office of their organization. Therefore, organizations whose materials may have been produced outside of Uganda were not aware of their origin.

From our previous research, we knew that the Uganda AIDS Commission was interested in whether organizations involved in HIV/AIDS activities were familiar with the UAC, so we asked this question. We found that in general, the answer was yes: 76% of the organizations included in our survey knew about the UAC and 24% did not. Of those that were familiar with the UAC, organizations were significantly more likely to disseminate information on condoms and treatment of AIDS than organizations that were not familiar with the UAC. Further, organizations that were familiar with the UAC were significantly more likely to disseminate information via:

- Radio
- Television
- Newspapers
- Reports
- Films
- Brochures, pamphlets

Interestingly, those that were NOT familiar with the UAC were significantly more likely to disseminate HIV/AIDS information through drama. Organizations that were familiar with the UAC were also significantly more likely to be aware of and to participate in the AIDS Partnership. When we look at the breakdown of organizations that are familiar with the UAC we find that the Faith-Based Organizations again stand out. Only about two thirds (67%) of FBOs were aware of the UAC and the partnership compared to the other types of organizations. More Government organizations (80%) and NGOs (78%) were aware of the UAC.

There were several other key findings to report. The first finding is the perception of where organizations think the public gets its HIV/AIDS information. Government organizations are significantly more likely to perceive that the public gets its HIV/AIDS information from Central and Local Government. Faith-Based Organizations are also more likely to perceive that the public gets information from Local Government than other sources. Community-Based Organizations, however, are significantly more likely to believe that the public gets its information directly from them.

The second key finding here has to do with the information sharing between organizations. Government organizations are significantly more likely to share information with central government than any other organization and NGOS are significantly more likely to share information with Local Government and Community-Based Organizations than with any other organization. Faith-Based Organizations were less likely to disseminate to CBOs than any other type of organization.

5 CONCLUSION

There were several important findings of this study. First, the type of information that is disseminated differed significantly depending on the type of organization disseminating the material. In particular, Faith-Based Organizations were significantly more likely to disseminate information on abstinence and faithfulness than any other type of organization. Government organizations were more likely to disseminate information on condoms and contraceptives. Although these results are not surprising, it raises questions regarding the varied effectiveness of the different dissemination approaches; does the rate of HIV transmission vary by the recipients of different information types?

A second important finding of this study is the format of information dissemination; radio and drama are most widely used to disseminate HIV/AIDS information in Uganda. This is not surprising in light of the oral tradition of Ugandan society. It is interesting, however, within the context of the reduced rates of HIV/AIDS prevalence in Uganda. It raises questions regarding the effective use of culturally appropriate dissemination methods; does the use of oral transmission methods lead to better dissemination of information that contributes to the reduction of HIV/AIDS?

Third, the results support the reported success of the IEC strategy. The shared dissemination of information between Government, CBOs, and NGOs suggests that information is widely shared across levels of government and other sectors of society, offering evidence of the multi-sectoral, IEC policy of the Ugandan approach. The perception of most organizations is that the Government is the greatest disseminator of HIV/AIDS information, from Central Government through to the lowest levels of Local Government. The vertical structures offered by Governmental dissemination of HIV/AIDS is supplemented and enhanced by the horizontal dissemination throughout society through NGOs, CBOs, and FBOs.

6 FUTURE RESEARCH

Based on the findings of this study, new questions can be raised regarding the effectiveness of HIV/AIDS information and formats for dissemination. In order to better answer the questions identified in the Conclusion, it would be useful to investigate the rates of HIV/AIDS prevalence among recipients of information from various groups. Faith-Based Organizations are of particular interest, since it is possible that their users may receive more limited information coming primarily, if not solely, from FBOs. It would also be interesting to examine the use of drama by FBOs in the dissemination of HIV/AIDS information to see what effect that has on the individual recipients. FBOs emerged in this study as having several unique characteristics that upon further investigation could yield important evidence in the battle against HIV/AIDS.

7 ACKNOWLEDGEMENTS

The authors wish to thank the University of Tennessee for supporting this work through the award of a Scholarly and Research Incentive Fund (SARIF) grant and the College of Communication and Information for providing additional grant support.

REFERENCES

Albright, K. S. and Kawooya, D. (2005). "The Role of information in Uganda's reduction of HIV/AIDS prevalence: individual perceptions of HIV/AIDS information". *Information Development*, vol. 21, no. 2.

Albright, K. S. and Kawooya, D. (2004). The Role of information in Uganda's reduction of HIV/AIDS prevalence: the Rakai Project and World Vision cases. *Proceedings of the 67th Annual Meeting of the American Society for Information Science & Technology, November 12–17, 2004, Providence, Rhode Island*, Silver Spring, MD: ASIS&T.

Green, E., Nantulya, V., Stoneburner, R. and Stover, J. (2002). *What happened in Uganda?* USAID Case Study Paper. Washington, D.C.

Low-Beer, D. and Stoneburner, R.L. (2003). "Behaviour and communication change in reducing HIV: is Uganda unique?", *African Journal of AIDS Research*, 2, 1, 9–21.

Stoneburner, R. and M. Carballo. (1997). *An Assessment of emerging patterns of HIV incidence in Uganda and other East African countries*. Arlington, Virginia: Family Health International AIDS Control and Prevention Project.

Stoneburner, R.L. and Low-Beer, D. (2000). Elements of sexual behaviour change associated with HIV prevalence declines in Uganda: comparative analyses of HIV and behavioral data in Uganda, Kenya, Malawi and Zambia. *XIII International Conference on AIDS, Durban, South Africa, 9–14th July 2000*, Abstract No. ThOrC721.

Uganda Aids Commission. (1997). *Inventory of agencies with HIV/AIDS activities and HIV/AIDS interventions in Uganda*. Kampala, Uganda.

UNAIDS/WHO. (2005). *AIDS epidemic update*. New York: Joint United Nations Programme on HIV/AIDS.

SOCIO-CULTURAL DETERMINANTS OF HIV/AIDS INFORMATION IMPACT: EXPERIENCES FROM BABATI DISTRICT IN TANZANIA

Paul Akonaay Manda

ABSTRACT

This paper examines the socio-cultural contexts that influence the impact of HIV/AIDS information on changes in sexual behaviors and attitudes in Babati district, Tanzania. The study integrated both qualitative and quantitative research designs. The sample of 131 respondents comprising of 50 male and 81 female was purposively selected from three villages in Dareda ward. Primary data was collected using face to face interviews, focus group discussion, dissemination workshop and in depth interviews with key informants. Data analysis involved the use of cross tabulation and qualitative descriptions. Results revealed that HIV/AIDS information provision though inadequate is flowing into the communities. The providers of HIV/AIDS information include the district council, village government, private and religious health institutions, civil society organizations, schools, faith based organizations and other community groups. The identified major sources of HIV/AIDS information are mass media such as radio, television and newspapers. Major factors that limit the positive impact of HIV/AIDS information include the weaknesses in the information infrastructure, information provision not structured to enhance local ownership of the process and service provision. Others are cultural norms on multiple sex partners, gender inequality and high rates of poverty made HIV/AIDS information less effective and led to individual decisions that tend to increase HIV/AIDS transmission rather than its reduction. The study recommends HIV/AIDS Information and Knowledge Management Strategy (IKM) for Babati district, in Tanzania.

1 INTRODUCTION

1.1 Background to the problem

"With the critical mass of infected persons already present in Tanzania and little discernible change in sexual behavior, the HIV/AIDS epidemic is probably the single greatest threat to Tanzania's future" (UNDP, 2000). The first three cases of AIDS were reported in Tanzania in 1983. By December 1994 a cumulative total of 53,247 cases had been reported. In the 1980s the AIDS epidemic was mainly an urban phenomenon and associated with activities of truck drivers and prostitutes. In the 1990s the disease spread to rural areas. On the 31st December 1999 the former President of Tanzania William Benjamin Mkapa declared HIV/AIDS a national disaster and asked the government, political, religious, civic leaders and non-governmental organizations to institute measures that will put the nation on a war footing against HIV/AIDS pandemic. The main mode of transmission of HIV in Tanzania over the years has been through heterosexual sex. The NACP 2001 surveillance report revealed heterosexual sex accounts for 78% of all HIV/AIDS cases and that five districts showed unusually high prevalence among blood donors. These districts were Kilombero (34.6%), Babati (33.9%), Muleba (33.7%), Kinondoni (33.3%) and Singida rural (27.5%).

1.2 Problem statement

What is the impact of information on individual decisions on risky behaviors and attitudes relating to HIV/AIDS? Data collected from the study on the flow of HIV/AIDS information in Babati District, Manyara region, Tanzania revealed that HIV/AIDS information though inadequate is flowing to the communities. However empirical findings from this same research showed no relationship between HIV/AIDS information flow and changes in risky sexual behaviors and attitudes. The sexual behavior changes targeted include the use of condoms, single partners and abstinence. This paper critically examines the socio-cultural contexts that enhances or inhibits the positive impact of HIV/AIDS information on changes in sexual behaviors and attitudes among communities in Babati district, Tanzania.

1.3 Literature review

Wougnet (2003) and Kickbusch (undated) observed that although it is believed that sufficient HIV/AIDS information is available the increased social economic stratification in the communities creates differential access patterns and rates. For example, because of women's low social economic status in most rural African societies women have insufficient access to accurate information on HIV/AIDS transmission, prevention, diagnosis and treatment services.

Kichbusch concludes: "While access to information and preventive health services were necessary and important, they have not been sufficient to reverse the epidemic"

Literature review (Sohail, 2002; Shaheed, 2001; Lugalla, 1999; Kaijage, 1992, Kickbusch, et al. undated) has indicated a need for interventions for sexual behavior changes to be based on the socio-cultural contexts of a given locality or community. It is observed that sexual behavior and attitudes are shaped by a variety of social and cultural factors in specific localities. Consequently the success of HIV interventions may depend on the understanding of the socio-cultural contexts among other factors. For example, Wougnet (2003) argues that national response design strategies in Africa do not address the underlying cultural and social practices that make women vulnerable to HIV infection:

> "The influence of Africa's cultural environment and the patriarchal nature of our social interaction and norms as well as the physiological make up of women has created adequate room for women's vulnerability and the manifestation of HIV/AIDS in Africa ... the pattern of and nature of the infection among women and girls is largely fuelled by the factors of gender inequality and poverty"

However studies in Zimbabwe and South Africa (Kickbusch, et al) have shown that HIV/AIDS infections were highest among people with highest literacy rates:

> "... the risk of becoming infected rises with the level of education, perhaps associated with greater income and mobility and hence increased probability of having multiple sex partners ... while education is important simply attending school, being able to read, and having access to information are not sufficient to prevent the spread of HIV/AIDS"

1.4 Research Question

This paper discusses why HIV/AIDS information provision is not positively related to changes in sexual behavior and attitude patterns within the social-cultural milieu of Babati district?

2 RESEARCH METHODOLOGY

2.1 Research context

This research was conducted in Babati district, one of the five districts in the recently (2003) established Manyara region. Field work was conducted in Bermi, Loto and Seleto villages in Dareda ward.

2.2 Sample

Sample study was drawn from a population of villagers, students, employees of hospitals, schools, and other training institutions. Convenient and purposive non-probability sampling techniques were employed. Purposive sampling enabled researchers to obtain a sample that is fairly representative of the major socio-economic characteristics found in the communities and assumed to influence access and use of HIV/AIDS information. A sample of 131 respondents consisting of 50 (39%) males and 81 (61%) females was selected. The age of respondents ranged from 15 to 66 years. 34% of respondents were between 20–29 years, 24% between 30 and 39 and 22% between 40–49 years. Fifty four percent of the sample had attained form four and 15% form six levels of education. The dominant occupation was home making and this was reported by 31% of all respondents. Twenty eight percent of respondents indicated farming as their main occupation. Other social groups were students (15%), petty traders (11%), teachers (6%), nurses (8), and carpenters (9%).

2.3 Methods of data collection

Data for the study was collected through face to face interviews, Focus Group Discussions (FGDs), in depth interviews, key informant interviews, participant observation and dissemination workshop. Face to face interviews was conducted with Local Government Authority officials at district, village levels, CSOs officials, religious and local leaders.

2.4 Data analysis

Data analysis employed quantitative and qualitative techniques. Quantitative data was analyzed using bivariate techniques mainly cross-tabulation. Data obtained from focus group discussions, observations and key informant interviews were analyzed using qualitative techniques.

3 FINDINGS

3.1 HIV/AIDS status, information programmes, activities and providers

HIV/AIDS Status in the district

The overall prevalence of HIV infections among blood donors in the district was 20.3% in 2003.

Table 3: Prevalence of HIV infections among blood donors in Babati district 1997–2003

Year	# of blood donors	% HIV positive
1997	1,137	9.5
1998	3,182	20
1999	4,007	20
2000	2,800	10
2001	4,544	29
2002	2,770	29
2003	1,865	20.8

Source: DMO Office, Babati District Council

The high transmission areas included most of the emerging trading centres such as Babati town, Bashanet, Gallapo, Magugu, Bonga, Dareda, Mamire and Mwada. Factors that contributed to the transmission of the disease in the district included: unprotected sex, multiple sex partners, sexually transmitted diseases, alcohol and drug abuse, cultural practices such as widow inheritance.

3.2 HIV/AIDS Information Providers

Major HIV/AIDS activities in the district are undertaken by the District Council and a number of NGOs such as LAMP and Farm Africa (which externally funded). In the study area HIV/AIDS activities are undertaken by village governments, civil society organizations such Local Initiative Support Organization (LISO) (local NGO), Dareda School of Nursing and Midwifery, Dareda Secondary School, St. Joseph Dareda Vocational Training Centre, the Diocese of Mbulu-Roman Catholic Church and primary schools.

3.3 Access to HIV/AIDS information

The major sources of HIV/AIDS information reported by respondents include radio, health personnel, television, local leaders, peer, family members, NGOs, CBOs and schools. Results support previous research findings (Sudha, 2005, Muswasi, 2000; Ndeki and Ulepp, 1994). The dominance of radio as a major source of HIV/AIDS information on the various aspects of the disease was partly explained by increasing access and affordability of radio in the rural areas. Television though mentioned as the second most important source of HIV/AIDS information is however an anomaly because the study area had less than 10 television sets. Respondents could have seen information on TV somewhere else other than in the study area. Health personnel was the third most important source of HIV/AIDS information and this was understandable because health personnel were required to provide such information especially to pregnant women. Leaders, peers, family members, NGOs, CBOs and schools were insignificant sources of HIV/AIDS information although logically one expected that since these were institutions that were close to people they could have played a more prominent role in the provision of HIV/AIDS information. However, it was also possible that these institutions were themselves not informed and knowledgeable about HIV/AIDS. The study also indicated that although respondents generally receive information on various aspects (i.e. Prevention, treatment, care and support for PLWHA) respondents seem to be more informed on some aspects than others. For example respondents seemed to be more informed on HIV/AIDS prevention than on care and support of PLWHA. The major explanation being that HIV/AIDS prevention has been the focus of organizations and institutions fighting the disease for years now. However as more people are now living with the diseases in the communities the focus is also turning to issues of care and support for PLWHA and information on this component will be critical.

Table 4: Sources of HIV/AIDS information by % distribution of respondents

	Type of HIV/AIDS information			
Source of HIV/AIDS Information	**Prevention**	**Treatment**	**Care of PLWHA**	**Support for PLWHA**
Radio	81%	70%	65%	44%
TV	41%	34%	34%	28%
Health personnel	35%	32%	35%	34%
Leaders	29%	21%	24%	27%
Peer	28%	20%	13%	15%
Family members	22%	14%	12%	15%
NGOs	18%	13%	12%	12%
CBOs	5%	2%	4%	2%
Schools	2%	1%	1%	2%
No access to information	3%	13%	21%	34%

With the current flow of HIV/AIDS information in the study area and the fact that a large proportion of the sample (38%) have been touched by the disease (either have lost some one close to them or are HIV-positive) were people knowledgeable or at least better informed about HIV/AIDS? Results indicated that respondents were informed and were knowledgeable about the general issues around HIV/AIDS. For example, on how the disease was transmitted 97% reported sexual intercourse which was followed by blood transfusion (51%), 49% use of non-sterilized needles and syringes. However only 15% reported that the diseases could be transmitted through mother-child and only 5% reported sharing of needles and razor blades as possible ways of transmitting the disease. Respondents were also found to be less informed about HIV/AIDS prevalence rates in the district and neighboring villages. Only 18% of respondents knew that in 2001 Babati District was ranked number three with 33% of HIV/AIDS positive blood donors. Twenty one percent of respondents knew that Dareda Centre less than five kilometers from the study area was among the high transmission areas in the district. On condom use only 28% reported to know how to use condoms.

4 DISCUSSION

The critical issues addressed is whether HIV/AIDS information provided was enabling people to make informed decisions on issues relating to HIV/AIDS. Findings indicate that in spite of most people having access to some HIV/AIDS information on the transmission and prevention behavior and attitude patterns indicated limited positive influence of information on these patterns. Why was information less effective in influencing individuals' decisions on issues relating to HIV/AIDS? Several contributory factors are discussed.

4.1 Information infrastructure

A well structured information system is an important component in the generation, processing, packaging and dissemination of information in any social system. In the study area HIV/AIDS information infrastructure was found to be inadequate. Public library has not been established in the district. The only functional library was the one with the Dareda Nursing School (access is only for the school) and the small information centre at LISO. The district council's HIV/AIDS activities and programmes have not clearly entrenched the provision of information as an important component. The entire programme has a centralized form of governance with the district directing the villages and all others with limited feedback mechanism. The district itself was getting its model of operation from above (TACIDS). Therefore the district model lacked the participatory framework and the end-users who were the target group did not own the program. The district plan took a top-down approach without any needs assessment done prior to its implementation. For example, the HIV/AIDS programmes in the district and villages did not established key repositories of information and knowledge from local communities to identify key individuals and culturally appropriate delivery techniques.

The organizational structure of the district program had no inbuilt structure that allowed efficient coordination and sharing of knowledge between and across different communities of interests. It had no strategy for managing HIV/AIDS information and knowledge at village and district levels. Consequently most of the key stakeholders in the civil society organizations were of the opinion that village and district committees were ineffective and they argued that it was better to go directly to the people.

Current and accurate HIV/AIDS information avoids misinformation about the disease while sharing of strategies and networking are critical aspects of information provision but all these were lacking. Developing collaboration and coordination strategies to improve HIV/AIDS information creation, collection and dissemination need to be addressed if information is going to have the desired impact. Within a collaborative and sharing framework best strategies for the generation and dissemination of HIV/AIDS information will be developed within the local culture. Research results showed that institutions and organizations in the district (government and civil society organizations) were undertaking activities without a forum for the exchange of ideas and sharing of experiences. Furthermore the organizational structure of the district HIV/AIDS information system requires leadership which is visionary. Currently the district HIV/AIDS coordinator is the District Community Development Officer and in the villages the Village Executive Officer is the secretary of the village HIV/AIDS committee. Experiences else where have shown that some local leadership may not provide the vision and strategic thinking required to enable communities better informed on HIV/AIDS issues. Therefore leadership is an important element in the strategy to manage HIV/AIDS information but unfortunately that type of leadership with the required expertise and commitment to deal with issues of HIV/AIDS in general and specifically with information management was found to be a rare phenomenon at village, district and institutional levels.

4.2 Cultural patterns

Findings of the research showed that certain dominant cultural norms (whether traditional or modern) embedded in the social systems of the local communities made HIV/AIDS information less effective in influencing individual decisions on issues relating to HIV/AIDS. Thus unless consistent efforts are made to address these cultural and normative values HIV/AIDS information might not influence decision making process. Major cultural issues analyzed include those relating to sexual and gender relationships. Data from this research showed that when it came to sexual relationships the men decided. Sexual relationship was the second most important cultural dimension which appeared to make HIV/AIDS information fail to influence individual decisions on HIV/AIDS. Traditionally in the study area the social construction of sexual relationships were slightly different from what was prevailing. Respondents observed the decline of morality on sexual relationships now than it was in the past. While there was some truth in this assertion the past could neither claim a very high moral ground on the issue of sexual morality. During the study it was observed that instead of the traditional night dances disco dancing, video shows, increased use of alcohol and drugs by young people were the norm. Others are choir groups and official celebrations (e.g. uhuru torch functions). There certainly is nothing wrong with such functions whether traditional or modern but these provide an environment that often leads to increased sexual activities. Data also indicated that currently men-women love and sex relationships were financially motivated. Examples were given of well to do men (in terms of income and position) with multiple sex partners taking advantage of poor women. Some respondents observed that it was socially acceptable for men to have several women partners while women with more than one partner were regarded as "prostitutes". Findings also revealed that most of the respondents believed that adults were generally not good role models on sexual behavior patterns. The traditional perception of sex in the study area would not have been a major stumbling block to the use of condom because there are no any cultural inhibitions to the use of condoms. However key informants revealed that although generally condom use was on the increase as shown by the number of condoms used during night ceremonies unfortunately condom are usually used during the first sex encounters but not the following encounters where preference was sex without condoms.

4.3 Social economic situations

Social factors such as low education, poverty, unemployment, family breakdowns need also to be addressed simultaneously with the provision of HIV/AIDS information for it to have the intended impact. For example the increased flow of HIV/AIDS information will not in itself address the issues of poverty, decay in morality which could be among root causes of why some segments of the society are getting engaged in prostitution or have multiple sex partners. Why do some individuals with high socio-economic status (SES) have multiple sex partners as already observed? Data showed that because of poverty young women were forced to exchange sex with money! But in contrast those taking advantage of the poor young women were often well to do men! Additionally respondents were of the opinion that the modernizing agencies such as the VETA (formerly AMREF with its social club), the process of urbanization taking place in the trading centers and the influence of Babati being a regional headquarters, the rural electrification project which was completed in 2004 and the improvement of the district and rural roads had both positive and negative impacts. First these modern institutions and services increased the flow of HIV/AIDS information. However these modern institutions unwittingly increased HIV/AIDS transmission in the area. The increased physical mobility and migration tended to increase interaction. For example, a group of workers on the road and electrification projects without their spouses or partners was a very risky group especially when they had the financial power to influence love or sex relationships. Ideally local communities and the new comers should have been the target of sustained HIV/AIDS information campaigns and education. Additionally because of rapid and unplanned urbanization in the form of rapidly expanding trading centres people (mainly young people) moved to these urbanizing centres in search for employment and when employment was not available they became involved in socially unacceptable behavior such as drug abuse and prostitution.

5 CONCLUSIONS AND RECOMMENDATION

5.1 Conclusions

This examination of why HIV/AIDS information is not making a positive impact on sexual behavior and attitude changes has raised a number of important issues from which conclusions can be drawn. First, though inadequate HIV/AIDS information is flowing to communities in the study area. Basically there were few success stories in the study area. Second, major explanations for the limited positive impact of HIV/AIDS information on sexual behavior and attitude change include: inadequate, inappropriate information resources and infrastructure and cultural patterns on gender and sexual relationships and social-economic conditions. Third, based on the above unless the weaknesses of information infrastructure, social-economic and cultural dimensions are simultaneously addressed, information may continue to play a marginal role in the process of influencing individual decisions relating to sexual behaviors and attitudes. For example HIV/AIDS information provision in the study area is not structured to enhance local ownership of the process and activities. Furthermore, the cultural norms on multiple sex partners and gender inequality made HIV/AIDS information less effective. Sexual actions might differ along the trajectories of age, culture and gender. Culture is evolving and dynamic but whatever its form it has a relatively strong bearing on the potential impact that HIV/AIDS information can have in changing peoples attitudes and behavior. Therefore the strategic provision of HIV/AIDS information has to simultaneously address these other cultural norms and behavior patterns whether traditional or modern which inhibit the effectiveness of HIV/AIDS information. If these are not addressed as is the case in this study area information will have limited positive impact. Finally, high levels of poverty influenced individual to make decisions that tended to increase HIV/AIDS transmission rather than decrease.

5.2 Recommendation

Based on the research findings it was evident that HIV/AIDS information was not efficiently managed (creation, collection, dissemination and use) in Babati district. The study therefore proposes an **HIV/AIDS information and knowledge management strategy (IKM) for Babati District.** This is based on research findings and on the emerging consensus among practitioners and researchers that information and knowledge (including access and sharing) are the key to controlling the spread of HIV/AIDS. The study area as observed was a rural and relatively poor setting with no functioning information infrastructure and a social-cultural environment that made the flow of HIV/AIDS information inefficient and ineffective. The challenge therefore is to design HIV/AIDS information and knowledge strategy for Babati district so that its communities become HIV/AIDS informed and knowledgeable. In this context although libraries and information centers are an integral part of the information system they are by no means the only key players. The following HIV/AIDS information and knowledge management (IKM) strategy for Babati district is therefore being proposed to address some of the gaps identified to increase the efficiency and effectiveness of HIV/AIDS information flow. The HIV/AIDS IKM strategy for Babati district has three main components: IKM vision; framework and strategy. In designing the HIV/AIDS IKM Strategy for Babati District ideas and insights were borrowed from presentations by McDowall and Fourie (2005) on information and knowledge management.

HIV/AIDS information and knowledge management strategy (IKM) for Babati District

A: **IKM VISION STATEMENT:** To have HIV/AIDS informed and knowledgeable communities in Babati District

B: **IKM FRAMEWORK**

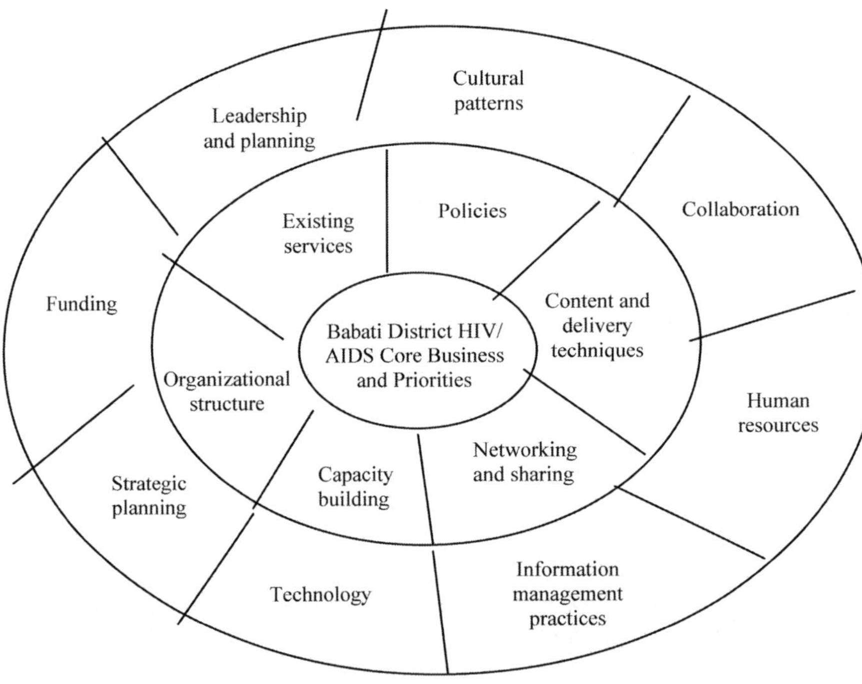

1. **Inner ring: Babati District HIV/AIDS information and knowledge priorities and Core Business:** Generation, collection and dissemination of HIV/AIDS information and knowledge at local levels on prevention, transmission, counseling, treatment and care.

2. **Middle ring: Critical HIV/AIDS information and knowledge areas for Babati District:** Content, format of resources and methods/techniques of HIV/AIDS information and knowledge delivery; Networking and sharing HIV/AIDS information and knowledge (key stakeholders: government and non-governmental organizations); Competencies and skills in HIV/AIDS information and knowledge; Organization, planning and leadership on HIV/AIDS activities; Existing services and Policies.

3. **Outer ring: Information and Knowledge Management Enablers:** Technology: use of multi-media, storytelling, communities of practice, oral traditions; Information and knowledge management practices: content and process management: access to HIV/AIDS information and tools (including ICT) for management: establishment of repositories and information centers; Human resources: capacity and competency building, training at district and village levels; Collaboration and communication: governmental, civil societies, experts, key people in the communities etc; Culture, behavior and local communication systems; Leaderships and planning: Engaging and committed; Funding: mobilization and management of finances (internal and external)and HIV/AIDS Policies and organizational structures at district and village levels.

C: IKM STRATEGY

Needs assessment: Identify needs in terms of generation, collection, processing, packaging, repackaging and dissemination of HIV/AIDS information and knowledge at local levels (use surveys, interviews, workshops etc). Identify key issues and priority areas. The process has to be participatory and locally owned. Clear objectives, plans and indicators have to be set for evaluation.

Approaches: Inclusive and participatory for all stakeholders

Governance (structure): Establish permanent and full-time HIV/AIDS Secretariat at District Council (with 3 permanent members). Establish a full-time position of HIV/AIDS coordinator in each village. The governance structure has to be flexible and participatory. Establish a HIV/AIDS committee for each village which is representative and formed of committed members.

Measurement: The use of surveys, meetings, reviews and evaluation against set objectives (return on investment) and measurable indicators.

Cultural normative patterns and social-economic dimensions: Identification of cultural normative patterns and values (both organizational and community) and social-economic factors that could facilitate or inhibit the free flow of HIV/AIDS information and knowledge

Standards and existing policies: HIV/AIDS policies, health policies and organization structures at local levels.

REFERENCES

Babati District Council. (2005). Comprehensive plan for reducing HIV/AIDS spread in Babati district 2004/2005.

Carael, M., J. Cleland and L. Adeokun (1991). "Overview and selected findings of sexual behavior surveys." *AIDS*, vol. 5 (Suppl.): pp. 65–75.

Gould, Bill and Huber Ulli (2002). HIV/AIDS, poverty and schooling in Tanzania and Uganda. Liverpool. Workshop Paper. January 2002.

Health Scope Tanzania (2002). *District capacity assessment: detailed analysis report*. Dar es Salaam, TACAIDS, January 2002.

Kaijage, F.J. (1992) "The AIDS crisis in Kagera Region, Tanzania, in a historical perspective", In: *Behavioral and Epidemiological Aspects of AIDS Research in Tanzania*, edited by Japhet Killewo, George Lwihula, Anita Sandstrom and Lars Dahlgren, Workshop proceedings, Dar-es-Salaam, Swedish Agency for Research Cooperation with Developing Countries (SAREC) Documentation Conference Report, Stockholm, Sweden.

Kickbusch, J. et al. "Health, literacy, empowerment and HIV/AIDS: striking a balance on an uneven playing field" UNESCO. (Undated). http://www.ncls.gov/libinter/infolitcon and meet/papers/kickbusch-fullpaper.pdf.

Lugalla, J.L.P. et al. (2004). "The availability and acceptability of intervention strategies against HIV/AIDS infection in the Kagera Region of Tanzania." *Internationales Afrika Forum,* vol. 4, no. 33.

Mbananga Nolwazi (2004). "Cultural clashes in reproductive health information in schools", *Health Education*, vol. 104, no. 3, pp. 152–162.

McDowall, P and Fourie, L (2005). Regional information and knowledge management workshop, 28th November–2nd December 2005, Arusha, Tanzania.

Muswazi Paiki (2000). “HIV/AIDS information resources and services: a Swaziland case study”. *Library Review* 49, vol. 10, pp. 34–39.

Mwakalobo, Adam. Implications of HIV/AIDS on rural livelihoods in Tanzania: the case of Rungwe district. University of Massachusetts, (Workshop Paper) May 2003.

National AIDS Control Programme (2002). HIV/AIDS/STI surveillance report January–December 2001. Ministry of Health (Paper # 16), Dar es Salaam.

National AIDS Control Program (2003). Surveillance of HIV and syphilis among the antenatal clinic enrollers 2001–2002. Ministry of Health.

Ndeki, S.S.; Klepp, K.I (1994). Exposure to HIV/AIDS information, AIDS knowledge, perceived risk and attitudes toward people with … *AIDS Care*, Vol. 6, Issue 2, pp. 183–189

Prime Ministers Office (2001). National Policy on HIV/AIDS. Dar es Salaam.

Sudha, R. and Lakshmi, V. (2005). “Awareness, attitudes and beliefs of the general public towards HIV/AIDS in Hyderabad, a capital city from South India”. *Indian Journal of Medical Science* 59 (7\0 2005, pp. 307–316).

Tanzania Commission for HIV/AIDS. National multi-sectoral strategic framework on HIV/AIDS 2003–2007. TACAIDS, Dar es Salaam, 2002.

UNDP (2000). Tanzania human development report: the state of progress in human resource development 1999.

Wougnet (2005). A report on regional workshop on leadership challenges for African women in the campaign against HIV/AIDS. June 23–25 2005, Abuja, Nigeria. http://www.wougnet.org/HIVIADS/Abuja_Report_HIV-AIDS.doc

MAASAE RESOURCE CENTRE FOR INDIGENOUS KNOWLEDGE IN TANZANIA

Nathan Ole Lengisugi

ABSTRACT

The paper reviews definitions of the concept indigenous knowledge and proceed to narrate its role as the information base of the rural community's (pastoral groups – Maasae herders in particular) whereby, it facilitates communication and empowers as a technoculture tool of decision-making. It emphasizes the value of indigenous knowledge not only, for the cultural community from where it evolves, but also for scientists, librarians, information technologists, policy makers, planners and others. Furthermore the paper contends that, in order for development programmes to be successful and sustainable they need to build on the ethnic communities' indigenous knowledge and language.

The paper proceeds to give a detailed discussion on the account that, indigenous knowledge should be used as a starting point of a development process whereby, the indigenous knowledge and science can be merged into an effective development strategy. It further contends interventions that did not take into account indigenous knowledge systems have proved socially, economically and environmentally unsuccessful. It also makes reference a strong attraction the United Nations Conference on Environment (UNCED) has made by giving recognition issues of intellectual property rights in indigenous knowledge and innovations. The Convention on Biological Diversity (CBD) recognition of indigenous knowledge and the World Conference on Science for the 21st Century calling action for governments to formulate national policies that allow a wider use of application of indigenous forms of learning and knowledge.

Furthermore, it documents the United Nations organs emphasis on use and applications of IK. The Science Conference continued to urge concerned countries to strongly sustain indigenous knowledge systems of their local communities. Further reiterated that, this can be achieved through active support of the societies who are the keepers and developers of that knowledge, their way of life, and their social organizations. Give strong support protection and conservation of their environment, in which they live, and fully recognize the contribution of women as repositories of a large part of local communities' indigenous knowledge. The paper recommends use of indigenous knowledge in development interventions, bridged up and managed by the regional libraries in ECSA and professionals. It also highlight's an important link relationship between ethnobotany utilization in ethnoveterinary and ethnomedicine practices among the ecosystem herding pastoralists and others in Eastern, Central and Southern Africa. Then concludes by calling concerted action by professionals and academicians at higher schools of learning to create a thrust synergy on issues of knowledge management and indigenous knowledge for the development of Africa's information systems and services.

1 INTRODUCTION

It must be stated from the outset that knowledge management and indigenous knowledge for the development of Africa's information systems and service is the major concern of this paper. Indigenous knowledge of various rural ethnic communities is an area where few scholars in the named region have directed their attention to investigate the contribution of indigenous knowledge in the development of the society. This is because indigenous knowledge and indeed indigenous forms of scientific practices and knowing is one of the areas often neglected by predominant scholarship traditions. Most schools of higher learning are of the opinion that indigenous forms of knowledge and technologies are not important because their impact to the economy and development process is very minimal, and that such technologies are a dying out phenomenon and obsolete.

Regardless of such views, indigenous technologies and knowledge system are, and have throughout history been extremely important. Indigenous knowledge is important because it is indeed the cultural basis for further scientific and technological changes. If by knowledge we mean know-how, which, stands for a combination of applied science, accumulated experience and skill, it is then true that through indigenous knowledge systems, local communities and societies may be able to improve the old knowledge. In the process of adaptation may assimilate and adapt new and alien or modern scientific and technological changes in an approach often termed technoblending.

2 WHAT IS INDIGENOUS KNOWLEDGE

Indigenous knowledge systems have been various described as ethnoscience, traditional wisdom etc. but all fundamentally refer to a body of knowledge that evolves over time and is communicated orally from one generation to next. Riddles, proverbs, songs, and other oral forms of communication are means by which indigenous knowledge is transmitted (Warren, 1990).

In this light, indigenous knowledge systems refers to sets of concepts, beliefs, and perceptions comprising the stock of knowledge as well as the process by which it is acquired, augmented, stored and transmitted. Indigenous knowledge is the local knowledge that is unique to a given culture or society. It is the information base of the society, which facilitate communication and decision-making. Indigenous information systems are dynamic and are continually influenced by internal creativity and experimentation as well as by contact with external systems (Warren 1991; WB 2000). Indigenous knowledge therefore provides problem-solving strategies for local communities and help shape local visions and perceptions of environment and society. A better understanding of the local conditions, including indigenous knowledge systems and practices and therefore, help to better integrate global technologies to solve the problems facing local communities in the Eastern, Central and Southern African countries. Knowledge of local practices and the involvement of local communities can be a powerful tool for the effective adaptation by global knowledge of best international practices to the local setting.

3 WHY SHOULD SCIENTISTS/ACADEMICIANS BE CONCERNED WITH INDIGENOUS KNOWLEDGE

Many studies, Roling and Engel (1990, p.102) have shown that rural people living close to nature have intimate knowledge of their natural environment (plants, animals, soils, climate etc) and of environmental processes. They make rational resource use and management based on that knowledge. Such communities have well established systems and carefully developed techniques, which over many years allowed them to survive in disequilibrium environments. Building on that local knowledge to mount sound and Eco-friendly specific policy and supporting legislation will reduce the likely hood that such a development intervention will de-skill the local people (World Bank, 2000, Norgard, 1984). On the contrary, it will increase the local people self-reliance, confidence and capacity to utilize and manage their local natural resource and reproducing environments. Otherwise, local knowledge should be used as a starting point of a development process such as sustainable natural resource management, in which local knowledge and science can be merged into an effective development strategy. According to other researchers, Dommen (1988) assets that, the drive to achieve an intervention development without taking into account indigenous knowledge systems and sustainable practices have proved socially, economically and environmentally unsuccessful.

4 HERDING PASTORALISTS AND ECOLOGICAL DEVELOPMENT

Pastoralists herders (East Africa Maasae in reference) health care and that of their domestic animals genetic resources is environmentally depended. While moving their herds throughout the year to optimize utilization of rangeland resources for maximum meat and milk production, they gained profound and skills on environmental ecosystems. As a result of well-skirted livestock movement including identifying and classifying plants and accurately assessing the water holding capacity of distant pastures, they can name each plant and other forage species found in the rangelands. They can describe the palatability of different plant species, seasonality of growth, medicinal attribute, nutritiousness and toxicity. They know when to harvest drug plants for effective treatment of their sick animals, they know, when medicinal activity in a drug plant, in different seasons, is at the highest. They have learned how to estimate dosage to administer to various classes of animals they keep according to age and sex of species. In human healthcare or ethnomedicine applications, they know which plant bark, fibre, branch or root should be boiled with which particular part of the animal meat that will also act as a vehicle to transport the active material during the preparation of a healthy soup for boosting immunocompetance. With such profound knowledge of their ecological environment and accrued essential benefits, how would ecosystem people dire to harm any plant species in the range land ecosystems.

Chambers (1988) emphasized in those regards, if, we must depend on local people for such an important task, it requires that we have to understand them and therefore, utilize their knowledge which they have accumulated over a good number of years. All points out that indigenous knowledge is the key to local level development. In recognition of the importance of indigenous knowledge, the World Commission in Environment and Development (WCED) established in 1982 by the United Nations General Assembly, devoted attention to issues of indigenous peoples, particularly their knowledge in the sustainable development process. In another development, the United Nations Conference on Environment and Development (UNCED) held in 1992 addressed issues of intellectual property rights in indigenous knowledge and innovations. Agenda 21 adopted by more than 160 States at the UNCED, contained a whole chapter on indigenous peoples and their knowledge and makes a wide range of recommendations on how these people's rights should be protected. The Convention on Biological Diversity (CBD) signed during UNCED also explicitly recognized the rights of indigenous knowledge and innovations. The participants of the World Conference on Science for the 21st Century held in Budapest, Hungary from 26th June–1st July 1999 inspired by Science agenda framework for actions called for governments to formulate national policies that allow a wider use of the application of indigenous forms of learning and knowledge. The local knowledge systems, promotes better understanding and use of indigenous knowledge systems. They emphasized that African countries should sustain indigenous knowledge systems through active support, to the societies that are keepers and developers of this knowledge. Their way of life, their languages, their social organizations, and the environments in which they live. Also, called on full recognize, of the contributions of women as repositories of a large part of indigenous knowledge. Participants of the conference further urged governments, to support cooperation between holders of indigenous knowledge and scientists in order to explore the relationships between different knowledge systems and foster interlinkages of mutual benefit.

5 INDIGENOUS KNOWLEDGE AND DEVELPOMENT

Development activities that work with and through indigenous knowledge structures have several important advantages. Indigenous knowledge provides the basis for grassroots decision-making, much of which taking place at the community level, through indigenous organizations and associations where problems are identified and solutions to them are determined. Solutions-seeking behaviour is based on indigenous creativity, leading to experimentation and innovations as well as the appraisal of knowledge and technologies introduced from other societies (Warren, 1990).

Solutions offered by a project in one local community might fail in another because they do not fit in with that local knowledge. Indigenous knowledge specific to a certain culture though in the same altitude, may support alternatives.

Methods used effectively by one society could be used with minor adjustments to solve problems faced by another. A blend of indigenous and modern approaches may be most appropriate. However, capacity building is necessary and reasons for blending their know knowledge must be explained. Many successful innovations are based on indigenous knowledge. Both indigenous and scientific knowledge has intrinsic values and can reinforce each other.

6 INDIGENOUS KNOWLEDGE AND PASTORALISTS PRACTICES IN ETHNOBOTANY, ETHNOVETERINARY AND ETHNOMEDICINE

While ethnobotany is that part of ethnoecology that concerns plants, human and animals, ethnoveterinary is the pastoralist people's endogenous science dealing with ecosystems botanical knowledge, skills and innovations relating to health of animals. Ethnomedicine on the other hand concerns ways disease and illnesses are handled by human groups, which are products of indigenous cultural development.

Pastoralists peoples' ethnobotanical knowledge of medicinal plants was gained from empirical observation of nature interacting with domestic animals and from communication with other cultures. The therapeutic nature of a plant was recognized on the observation of what happened to the animal that ate a drug plant accidentally or instinctively. Through such keen observation, pastoralists came to recognize that, certain plants are effective against various animal and human diseases. Furthermore, the ecosystem pastoralists observed that, the therapeutic effects of plant extracts are a result of the mode of action of their active ingredients. In the same observations, pastoralists also learned that, the bioactive principle of plants fluctuates with seasons and time of the day, due to rainfall, soils, and temperature. Drug plant parts collected following the sunset have higher concentration of active material. Likewise, plants young leaves and bark have higher medicinal properties than matured. Tubers and roots are high in bioactive material too. Drug plants extracts concentrations are higher in the dry season than in the wet season. Seasonal concentrations of plant active ingredients are low (low in Flavonoids) from January to April. Between May and August drug plants extracts are generally high at 80% (high in Tannins). In the later part of the dry season between August to December extracts concentrations are at the highest at 81–92% (Martin, 1995).

The indigenous knowledge of the homogenous pastoralists living in a particular ethnographic region formed a techno-culture tool of animal and human health practices. Such knowledge is dynamic and adapts to new ideas and skills and interpreted in their technoculture language and practices. The drug plant parts used to cure illnesses and diseases in human include, whole plant, shrub, parasitic or epiphytic plants, roots, tubers or rhizomes, bulb or corms, bark of stem, woody or fruiting body, seeds, nuts or spores, pods, sap, latex or juice, shoots, buds or tips, serial parts, oil cake or residue and extract plant parts.

Pastoralists knowledge informs practitioners to boil the drug plant part for hours in order to optimize plant herb (active material) availability. On drug herb applications, the cultural indigenous knowledge informs that, the quickest way to get the prepared compound to the brain is to administer through a bleeding nose, a nasal mucosa, or as a rectal suppository, and/or as a vaginal suppository. In regards to ethnoveterinary applications, the ecosystem pastoralist gained knowledge and experience associating sick animals with medicinal plants on what drug plant part contains the active principle that inhibits vital processes of certain micro-organisms. What drug plant parts can inhibit the multiplication of bacteria. What plant parts acts as repellents to drive away ectoparasites and what plant parts acts as purgatives to expel endoparasites.

7 CONCLUSION AND RECOMMENDATIONS

Indigenous knowledge management and technologies are very important to the keepers and producers. The author has tried to establish areas of mutual relationship between indigenous knowledge and scientific knowledge. Approaches of blending the two knowledge systems for the development of Africa's information systems and services would be most appropriate. Finally, the paper recommends that libraries in East, Central and Southern Africa plays a key role as a bridge to knowledge management and indigenous knowledge applications and dissemination for the development of Africa's information systems and services.

Indigenous knowledge which is the cultural basis for further scientific and technological change, needs to be given strong support in it's applications world wide. The paper have tried to establish the vital role libraries can play to bridge up indigenous knowledge utilization in development and therefore, recommends institutions of higher learning to consider allocating more funds for research and development in this area.

Finally, the paper acknowledges the strong recognition local knowledge systems have received from the United Nations bodies such as; The Conference on Environment and Development (UNCED), the Convention on Biological Diversity (CBD), and the World Conference- on -Science Agenda.

REFERENCES

Agenda 21, Chapter 15: Conservation of biological diversity. As adopted in Rio de Janeiro, June 14, 1992.

Agenda 21, Chapter 26: Recognizing strengthening the role of indigenous people and their communities. As adopted in Rio de Janeiro, June 14, 1992.

Chambers, R. (1983) *Rural development putting the last first*. Harlow, UK: Longman.

Dommen, A.J. (1988). *Innovation in African agriculture*. Boulder: West View Press.

Earth Negotiations Bulletin: www.lisd.ca/linkages/vo/22/eub225/e.html

Norgard R. B. (1984) Traditional agricultural knowledge: performance, future prospects and institution implications. *American Journal of Agricultural Economics*, vol. 66, no. 5, pp. 874–878

Roling N. and Engel, P. (1990). "IKS and knowledge management: utilising indigenous knowledge", In: Warren, D. M. (Ed.) *Indigenous Knowledge System: Implications for Agricultural and International Development*. Ames: Iowa State University.

Warren D. M. (1991) Using indigenous knowledge in agricultural Development. World Bank Discussion Paper 127.

Warren D. M. (1990) *Indigenous knowledge systems and development: background paper for seminar series on sociology and natural resource management*. Washington, DC: The World Bank.

World Bank (2000): Website http://www.worldbank.org/html/afr/ik

WHAT CAN BE THE ROLE OF AFRICAN LIBRARIES IN COUNTERBALANCING THE "KNOWLEDGE POWER" OF THE WEST? CAN WE CREATE NEW KNOWLEDGE TOGETHER?

Thore Hem

ABSTRACT

Based on author's personal experience with working with the Norwegian development Agency (NORAD), this paper relates the useful work of NORAD with aspects of knowledge management. It shows how knowledge management is give value and practiced within NORAD. The use of tacit knowledge of the organisation and accumulation and management of knowledge are just a few examples narrated. The paper argues the need for development partners to enter into dialogue that would create true cultural understanding. The need to understanding the donation recipient, through open, free and sincere dialogue, is emphasised.

NORAD is a Norwegian directorate, subordinated to the Norwegian Ministry of Foreign Affairs.

We aim to be the centre of expertise for evaluation, quality assurance and dissemination of the results of Norwegian development cooperation, jointly with partners in Norway, developing countries and the international community and ensure that the goals of Norway's development policy are achieved by providing advice and support to the Ministry of Foreign Affairs and Norwegian Foreign Service missions. It also administer grant schemes so that development assistance provided through Norwegian and international partners contributes effectively to poverty reduction

Like with many similar organisations, we have come to understand our role as that of a "knowledge organisation." Our main activity should be to supply advices to others. It was in this context that we also realised that such responsibilities raised a certain demand for more conscious reflections regarding the creation and use of knowledge among ourselves. When we began our systematic work in knowledge management, the first steps we undertook, were to familiarise ourselves with the current thoughts and discourses regarding knowledge management and knowledge sharing. We learned that these disciplines had their roots in the private sector and business administration– and more particularly in the information communication technology (ICT) environments. The new technologies main advantage was that it made possible storage of huge masses of information – and fast recovery and searches in the information basis.

However, quite early in the age of ICT, one could hear the voice of protesters – arguing that ICT should only be considered as one of several tools available to improve quality and quantities of work processes. As the introduction of the conveyor belt in industrial production had lead to a counter-movement arguing in favour of more labour–managed processes, more team-work based processes etc, the emphasis in the knowledge disciplines was soon changed to give more priority to methods involving direct encounters and discussions between peers. It was realised that only in meetings and interaction could one have some hopes of sharing and at the same time also ensure production of knowledge. What became the themes of the day were: per assists, peer reviews, storytelling, after action reviews and communities of practice. All of them techniques where there is little technology and a lot of humans and human interaction involved!

In NORAD, we started out with a strongly introverted approach. Limiting our knowledge management (KM) concerns to our internal activities. How do we mobilize the tacit knowledge of the organisation? How do we ensure that tasks are given to the most relevant and capable workers? How do we accumulate knowledge? How does the organisation learn? Do we need more and better training programmes? E-learning? Seminars? Groups? Thematic groups? Databases? Knowledge banks? A better library in NORAD? Better Intranet?

Many of our sister organisations in the development business, have emphasised knowledge as an asset by itself in the development co-operation, arguing that to supply financing, expertise and material was not sufficient to trigger the development. One believes that the so called recipient partner needs access to "knowledge" as well. So the World Bank, from the late 1990s, started to call itself a "knowledge bank". And thus an impressing work was embarked upon to make available research-and-experience-based-knowledge to the "clients". Despite statements made from time to time that it was important to take into consideration that also the "loaner" did have some knowledge – often called "indigenous knowledge" – it remains after all the knowledge of the West that is *"the real thing"*! At least in the eyes of the Bank. It appears to be a discrepancy between what is stated from time to time – and what is actually expressed through daily practises.

For 10 years I worked as head of NORAD's Division for Cultural Cooperation. We had a strategy for our work, outlining that cultural was important in the development process because nobody would find the right way to the future without knowing from where he/she comes from! Or in other words: Cultural identity is necessary for the development of all people and peoples! We further stated: Cultural workers do not only reflect the word and times they live in – they also create the visions and the alternatives for the future. As they did in all liberation movements. As they have done and do all over the world, at all times. Furthermore, all cooperation and understanding will improve the more the parties get to know each other. And to get to know each other is also to get to know each others values, aesthetics, beliefs, music. Colours, shapes, materials, and stories. And we saw that by facilitating interaction in the various cultural fields, we also facilitated the creation of new cultural expressions. Something that the world had not seen or listened to before. But even more, not only were new expressions created. The parties were each one enriched. And the participatory experience stimulated their own work To the extent that for many the cross-cultural experience forever changed their professional lives.

Now the question is: Where are the differences between culture and knowledge? We all know that knowledge has its time and place. Much of the knowledge relevant for King Lobenguela of the Ndebele in Zimbabwe is not relevant for us today. And much of the knowledge possessed by the Masai of East Africa of today is not relevant at Greenland. Nor at Manhattan. But some could be? If we accept that there is a strong relationship between culture and knowledge, possibly we could approach co-operation in the field of knowledge with similar methods as we did with cultural co-operation? By facilitating knowledge interaction as we have facilitated musical interaction? However, this is not an easy task.

One of the characteristics of the so called development co-operation that has worried me for the last 30 years is the lack of real dialogue between the parties and stakeholders. It is as if it is all a game. The so called recipient party will know or think that he/she knows the donor party and her priorities. At the same time, the so-called donor will have his/her opinions about and experiences as well with the other party. In addition, the very relationship the parties have to each other – as a recipient and as a donor will influence the way they see themselves and the other. A donor will often emphasis everything negative on the recipient side. It is as if she seeks the justification for her own existence in the miserable situation of the recipient. We tend to see poverty, corruption, hunger, war – and no beauty, peace and wealth. Because it is the hunger, poverty, corruption and wars that makes us necessary – we want to believe.

So strong can be the impact of this imagination that it also influences the perception, values and understanding of history among the partners in the developing world themselves. Like when I some time ago sat with Mozambican colleagues in Maputo, trying to tell them about corruption in Norway often linked to our public sectors and local governments. My friends from Mozambique would not believe me. And as I went into details, they argued: "But this is not corruption!" Or some months ago when a musician from Mozambique visited me in Norway. We drove passed a women's prison in the outskirts of Oslo, our capital. Huhigo, my musician friend did not believe that Norwegian women could be criminals! Thus he did not accept that we had a prison for female prisoners! These are contemporary stories. 40 years after Franz Fanon, after Walter Rodney – and after the collapse of classical colonialism.

If you are trying to promote an open, free and sincere dialogue between two parties where one believes and claims that she stands for science, knowledge, modernity, wealth – and the other for superstition, ignorance, poverty and illiteracy – it is not difficult to understand that there will be no real balanced dialogue – but rather a monologue. As my late friend, Professor Dumisani Maraire from Zimbabwe often said to me: "Nobody realises that she is beautiful if she is never told that she is." And who can argue against knowledge? Against truth? Against science? Against modernity? Against development?

It was during the years that I served as a regional cultural adviser to NORAD and the Ministry of Foreign Affairs, covering the southern Africa region, that I really was confronted with this. Because as I travelled around in the region, I always visited the Norwegian Embassies. I took part in their internal meetings. The staff will always be composed of both Norwegians and so called local staff. I noted that about 80 % of the issues discussed in the internal meetings were related to negative aspects of the host country. Suspicions, complaints about delayed reports, accounts, imports, procedures, local politics etc. When I asked, after some time, my friend working at the Norwegian Embassy in Maputo, about how he reacted to all these expressions about his own country and his own culture, he explained me: "First, I have a good, well-paid job here. I want to keep it. Second: I know something about colonialists from the past, and about Europeans. I know what you guys are like. I can not change that, so I just keep my moth and ears shut!"

Where do the libraries of Africa fit into my story? Except for the old libraries of Alexandria and possibly of Timbuktu, libraries have not been the main media for storing African knowledge. As were museums, so also modern libraries were in a way invented by the west. To store written/printed material. Which is so important in a European culture where knowledge is – and since the days of Mr. Gutenberg, mainly has been stored and shared through books. Do other media for transmission of knowledge in space and time exist? Are other forms of expressing and sharing knowledge more frequently used in Africa? Is there something that we can do in order to ease and facilitate the exchange of knowledge between the "asomi" and the "non-asomi"? Much of Africa has for several hundred years been exposed to Western values and knowledge. With positive as well as negative impacts. Only rarely has the West taken African values and knowledge seriously. If we search for in which disciplines this has happened, we will find that it has been in the fields of culture: Music, stories, architecture, textile production. These areas have caught the emotional as well as the intellectual attention of many westerners. And hidden in them are the expressions of knowledge and wisdom – sometimes difficult for westerners to see – but it is there.

Preparing this paper, I sat some time ago in the cafeteria in NORAD discussing with a friend and colleague. He said that the mistake was about to make, was that I assumed that Africa has knowledge of worth to the West. He disputed that. I know he was wrong. In 1798 a huge army, under the command of Napoleon Bonaparte, set out on their voyage with 400 ships – from Toulon in France. It was on of the largest colonialising armies Europe had ever mobilised. And it was different from all other European military expeditions – to the extent that it included a great number of scientists and artists. Napoleon was indeed himself an intellectual with a sincere interest in philosophy and science. Thus, there were 21 mathematicians, 3 astronomers, 15 natural scientists, 4 architects, 17 engineers 15 geographers, 2 musicians, 10 writers, 1 plastic artist, and 10 visual artists. Napoleon himself brought a library of 300 books with him – one of them was particular important for him: Amongst them the Holy Book of Islam – Al Quran. In Arab, as well as in French translation. The reason for taking along all these civilians was indeed the search for knowledge. An understanding that the knowledge to be found in North Africa was precious. Had a value also for Europeans! Unfortunately, this knowledge encounter as it was took place in a context of occupation and uneven power distribution. Could it be called an exchange of knowledge – or was it actually Europe raping the knowledge of Africa? I would say that it was both. And I would say to my friend:" Look, even Napoleon, 200 years ago, realised the importance of African knowledge"

In the West, there is a growing understanding that we in our process of social, political, cultural and economical development have lost some important qualities or dimensions of life on our way. Western culture is based on plans, orders, and analysis of consequences, the power of the market, reading, discipline, law and order. Western mathematics is the midwife for the concept of the perfect circle, the straight line, or the 90 degrees angle – are all theoretical constructions that do not exist in the real world. And there is no way around it! You can not avoid western sciences or computer technology if you want to be a participant in today's societies – being it local, national or international societies! But it must be possible for the libraries, despite the fact that they are born of western thoughts and thinking, also to become tools to strengthen the self-knowledge about the societies' own values and wisdom?

Thinking of the history of the so called development aid brings to my mind our army of knowledge of more modern times. It was clear that the understanding of lack of knowledge as the main explanation of poverty and so called underdevelopment had been widely subscribed to. Thus it was only natural that the reply to this was: *Technical co-operation.* Often organised as a kind of military-like operations; young women and men were recruited to go to Africa, Asia and South America as Peace Corps participants. In the modern "army of knowledge" – bringing knowledge to the ignorant! Few were the voices in Europe that disputed this strongly Eurocentric apprehension. Few were those in Europe who dared to articulate that poverty could have other explanations as well. And that the supply of western knowledge was often not only irrelevant – but also a manoeuvre of diversion to cover for other motives.

It is as if knowledge is transmitted and the transmission happens on very different frequencies. As if the sender and receiver are not tuned or calibrated. Could the libraries play a role here? As tuners and as translators. As arenas for western and African knowledge to meet. And to enrich each other. As melting pots where new knowledge possibly will appear and grow in the interaction. And could the libraries also contribute to the "education" of westerners – give them insight and understanding for the phenomenon that all knowledge after all is local knowledge – being it European or African.

Only with knowledge can one dispute or change knowledge. If we in the West are allowed to pursue our own knowledge system to the very ultimate end, many fear that we might end up as machines, not humans. That is actually why, more than ever the world needs the knowledge of Africa. It is most likely a question of life or death for us all.

REFERENCES

Fanon, Frantz (1963). *The wretched of the earth*. London: Penguin Books.

Rodney, Walter (1972). *How Europe underdeveloped Africa*. Dar es Salaam: Tanzania Publishing House.

WORKING IN PARTNERSHIP TO BUILD KNOWLEDGE SOCIETIES

Sara Harrity

ABSTRACT

This paper puts forward the view that libraries, and the information professionals that staff them, have an important role to play in achieving change through education, skills development, and contributing to poverty alleviation. Librarians play an essential role in creating information societies. They supply and promote information resources within local communities, enable sharing of local knowledge and languages and maintain awareness of community information needs. They target disadvantaged groups and ensure access for all. Book Aid International has supported these efforts for many years through book provision and grants for book purchase for African public library partners. This paper explores the impact that these resources have had on readers, whilst also highlighting the need for changes to enable librarians to respond more effectively to community needs. Adopting a knowledge management approach entails developing a culture of shared learning. Book Aid International's experiences of working with African library partners through workshops, training and information exchange are illustrative of the willingness among librarians to take on new ideas and to apply them in the improvement of library services. Finally, we note the need for far greater investment in libraries' infrastructure, and in training for librarians, to equip the sector to promote significant change within the communities it serves.

1 INTRODUCTION

In its World Development Report 1998/99 the World Bank focused on knowledge for development and reported that *'knowledge gives people greater control over their destinies'* (World Bank 1999). With that in mind, I plan to conduct my own exercise in knowledge management, with the aim of sharing with you a little of the knowledge that I have acquired over my many years of working at Book Aid International.

Book Aid International has been in existence for over 50 years and in that time it has worked with a huge variety of library and book sector partners. We have engaged in capacity building work with libraries, both by helping to ensure that they are well-stocked and by offering training and learning opportunities for library staff. We are a registered charity based in the UK, which supplies around half a million books each year, together with training and advocacy programmes, and works with partner libraries in eighteen countries, seventeen of which are in sub Saharan Africa and 7 of which are SCECSAL countries.

Much of the learning I will be sharing with you has come from the practical experience of partnerships and the inspirational people I have met in African libraries, both librarians and service users. Book Aid International programmes are led by our library service partners, and ultimately, we hope, by the communities that we seek to serve, particularly the poorest and most disadvantaged in African societies. The challenges involved in discovering what the needs of these communities are and how best we can serve them are some of the biggest challenges facing African librarians today. I shall return to this point later in the presentation.

For now I will seek to define the role I believe that libraries can have in creating knowledge societies and promoting sustainable development. Libraries are able to bridge knowledge gaps, promote informal learning and support formal education. In doing so they contribute to poverty alleviation. To illustrate this point I have listed below a few examples that show the sheer variety of opportunity available to people using libraries. Library users can: maintain and develop literacy skills learnt in the classroom; access knowledge that will equip them to improve their lives and livelihoods; learn about health issues and be better able to protect their families from sickness; understand their democratic rights; and acquire skills that will help them gain paid employment.

At the heart of any library is the librarian, the information professional, who is able to use his or her training to make information accessible and to ensure that it is shared and promoted widely within the community that he or she serves. Not only this, but the most effective librarians are also able to be responsive and adaptive; they can use knowledge gathered through their work to continually enhance and improve the services they provide. This knowledge might be gathered from the immediate community, or imparted by managers, or gleaned from the broader environment of policy and practice in the book and library sector. In short, librarians need to categorise and render useful the knowledge they store on library shelves and must also have one ear to the ground to pick up on new developments and capitalise on them.

One of the ways in which Book Aid International seeks to help librarians in this task is to share what we have seen and heard from partners throughout our network. I shall begin this sharing exercise with a quotation from a Nigerian librarian, Mr Sanussi Nassarawa, which poses a challenge to librarians about how best we can ensure library services are as relevant, appropriate and useful as they can be, within the context of African development. Nassarawa advises 'Librarians must start seeing themselves as agents of change in terms of educational, information and cultural pursuits of the society in which they serve' (Book Aid International, 2004).

To some extent this is already happening and we hope that the examples we have gathered here in this paper will serve to illustrate the very positive activities taking place in many African libraries. We also hope to act as a spur to SCECSAL member libraries and all others attending the conference to engage more deeply with the agenda for change and ensure that libraries position themselves centrally with regard to education, information and culture in each of the countries where you work. We hope you will be able to prioritise reaching the most disadvantaged members of society, whether directly through community resources, or indirectly through professional training for those nurses, teachers, lawyers and extension workers who also have an immensely important role to play in facilitating Africa's development.

Our vision is of community libraries that offer knowledge beyond the book shelf. They need to create welcoming and attractive environments that are child-friendly and accessible to new literates and even non-literate users. We need to work towards achieving exemplary libraries which offer the widest possible range of services, from books, radio, talks, ICT and videos, to games, science and art. Programmes of events need to make the link with local literacy groups and schools, whilst also encouraging people to come along to activities such as reading groups, storytelling sessions, discussion forums and community meetings. All the services mentioned above are already being offered in some African libraries. The challenge now is to galvanise the continent's professionals so that all public libraries can fulfil this role. Book Aid International favours reform of library and information curricula to equip librarians with the skills to create libraries of this nature.

2 SHARING INFORMATION RESOURCES

The first section of this paper looks at the experience Book Aid International has gained through many years of supplying information and knowledge to Africa's libraries through our book provision work. Book Aid International's main activity has always been to supply books to support readers and learners. Each year around half a million books are distributed from our London warehouse and every one is chosen in response to an identified need expressed by a partner organisation. They in turn make their selections on behalf of the communities they serve and we are proud to be able to offer them a very wide range of subject areas and specialist material. Our selections encompass all stages of learning and development, starting with books for babies and young children, to support early childhood development and promote a culture of reading, right through to specialist teacher training or medical material to support higher education and ongoing professional development.

We seek to serve all these needs and many more besides. Our work is also driven by a desire to supplement local knowledge and we are conscious that our efforts are only one part in a much larger process of generating and sharing information through libraries. For instance, we strongly believe that the supply of books from the North should supplement information generated by communities and nationally, and materials in local and national languages.

We focus on the poorest and most disadvantaged and this explains why the vast majority of our support goes to sub Saharan Africa, where there is very little book purchasing power amongst the local population and a very great need for investment in the expansion of education provision, improved educational quality and the creation of literate environments that can sustain and promote a culture of lifelong learning. Community access to information is essential to this process of improving and expanding educational opportunities. We believe that public libraries are the essential knowledge management tools that will enable free and universal access to information. This in turn is one of the essential building blocks of a literate educated society.

One organisation we have been able to support is the Dadaab Refugee Camp in Kenya. I have chosen this example because it dramatically illustrates the power of the written word in transforming lives. On a visit to the camp in 2004 Book Aid International staff saw that the response to our books was universally enthusiastic. African writers' material and teaching methodology books were especially well received and felt to have a great impact on refugee teachers who need to read widely to embed their improving language skills. More recently we've heard how the education opportunities in the camp are seen as among the best in the district, all thanks to the impact of the camp's library on the learning of both pupils and teachers who have accessed its books to improve and extend on the lessons learnt in class. In fact one Dadaab student recently gained second place in the whole of Kenya in his Primary Leaving Certificate exams.

One of the benefits of Book Aid International's long history is that we've been able to build up a strong understanding of the subject areas and titles our partners need and we've developed systems that allow them the maximum amount of choice in the process. Indeed, just as we work hard to match up partners' requests with books from Book Aid International's stock our partner librarians are also playing their part in promoting choice and participation locally. They gauge local book needs and ensure that the material we send is appropriate. Community, school and higher education librarians all undertake to choose books that are useful and appropriate to the people they serve and to then display them in attractive and accessible ways that help those readers seeking to internalise the knowledge found within the books and other resources of the library.

Some of the chief ways that books are having an impact include the direct impacts on users. We have heard from a great many libraries reporting that more users are coming in to access their stock since a Book Aid International donation. Sometimes the effect is dramatic, as in the case of Adamawa State Library Board who had very few resources to offer readers prior to our support. They now have 200 users each day, which is a vast increase on previous numbers. We often find that our support for public libraries comes after years of low levels of resourcing from central government resulting in low stock levels and outdated collections of material.

Years of coping with resource shortages also frequently lead librarians to carefully guard the few resources they do have. Weeding of old and outdated stock may only be undertaken with great reluctance. It also leads libraries to accept inappropriate materials from aid agencies that are operating in a less than professional manner and engaging in what can only be described in 'book dumping'. Sadly there are still those people who sincerely believe that any book is better than no book, so irrelevant and unusable materials from the West are often shipped over, at no small cost. This is not a view that Book Aid International shares. We seek to bolster the position of librarians as professionals who understand and promote community information needs, not as passive recipients presiding over a jumble of irrelevant discards and unattractive material. It is the relevance of the knowledge inside books that counts and for this reason Book Aid International works to promote best practice in book donations.

Book Aid International has worked hard to be in a position where it is able to be hugely selective about the material it sends out, whilst at the same time supplying many thousands of books each year to our largest library service partners. Those who have national distribution networks have been able to utilise our book donations for a wide range of purposes. A typical example is the National Library of Uganda, which distributes Book Aid International books to public libraries, to schools and NGOs, and is also able to support the creation of new community libraries through books and training in the care and promotion of books.

One such library is Kitengesa community library in Uganda. The library is colourful and attractive, and runs a host of weekly activities including an open forum for teenagers called "Straight Talk", adult reading sessions, a reading club and writers club. Games are organised, particularly on Saturday nights. Literacy classes have attracted numerous local women and young people from all the neighbouring schools access books there. Book Aid International books are a vital part of the library's collection and are well used.

Another strong example is Chiwamba Information Centre in rural Malawi. All sources of information are incorporated into the centre's services, including a strong emphasis on using and sharing local knowledge. Newspapers and board games are available while television and video show a mixture of informative and entertainment films (Saturday night shows are very popular). A village newsletter for special events is also produced, which Malawi National Library Service staff type up and copy. Adult literacy classes are held at the centre, attended mostly by women. The centre is also used for meetings by extension workers. It offers a wide range of books for newly literate readers and there is a strong collection of agricultural information. In fact Book Aid International books have facilitated the expansion of library services through community libraries and public resource centres housed in schools, not only in Uganda and Malawi but also in Kenya, Namibia and Sierra Leone.

One other key component of Book Aid International's work has been our support for the local book chain of authors, publishers, booksellers and libraries. We are playing our part in supporting long term solutions to the overwhelming book shortages facing Africa. A strong book trade is central to this. We hope to strengthen businesses to provide locally affordable and culturally relevant material, which records and shares local knowledge. As part of this work we have for over a decade sought to place African published books in the hands of African readers, both through the purchase of books from all over the continent and grants for local and regional book purchase.

The first scheme was known as the Intra African Book Support Scheme (IABSS) and it enabled libraries to select African published titles from other nations, so enhancing intra-African trade, whilst at the same time creating or developing the stock of culturally appropriate material. An independent evaluation in 2005 revealed many positive benefits that the scheme had brought about. Readers who were interviewed frequently reported a preference for books which connected immediately or vividly with their lives or concerns. Rural Ugandan readers found that stories set in cities in Nigeria or South Africa appealed greatly and were not perceived as strange or exotic so long as they looked at issues faced by the readers themselves, such as family life, moral choices, love and relationships. One quotation from Namibia neatly illustrates the impact the project has had:

> 'The community library service has 48 constituent libraries and is in the process of opening more. The books help to build up starting collections, and increase the number of books in existing libraries. The libraries are in rural areas and the users love the books with an African background which they feel they can relate to.' (Community Library Service, 2005)

All this evidence demonstrates that our work is having an impact. We are changing people's lives, opening up opportunities to them and encouraging readers to keep returning again and again to make use of their local libraries. We always find that field visits offer important opportunities to interview readers and get a close analysis of the impact of our work on end users. We are primarily reliant on our partner organisations for close analysis of needs and impacts and we continue to work with them to overcome the resource constraints that limit their capacity to undertake this in sufficient frequency and detail. This is essential work as it is precisely this kind of information that we need if we are to reach non-users and ensure that library services are accessed by as many people as possible.

To maximise the impact we have on the lives of the poorest and most disadvantaged, needs analysis must take in not only what it is that current users need, but also actively seek out the 'invisible' and 'unheard' in communities. We must ask ourselves which groups in the community would benefit most from using the library and how we can ensure that they use it. Only through looking at the community as a whole can libraries assume their rightful place at the heart of the poverty reduction process. The poorest in society are those who most need accessible information to enhance their awareness of the options open to them, and to help them to improve their situations.

Each of us also needs to be armed with the right sort of knowledge when we approach funders and policy makers. We need the evidence that shows that what we are doing is having an impact, and proves that with the right resourcing we can achieve so much more. This is the vital next step to ensuring that our voices are heard and our contributions can be recognised.

To take this next step we need radical change – a move away from monitoring service delivery to active engagement with communities, to learn how best we can support and mobilise them to act in support of libraries and the greater cause of access to information and knowledge for all. This is a huge challenge and difficult to undertake alone. One of the ways in which Book Aid International seeks to make its contribution to this vital area is through our newer programme of work, which is based around shared learning.

3 SHARED LEARNING

A culture of shared learning is a key aspect of the knowledge management approach. Book Aid International is lucky to have a wide group of organisations within its network, each of whom brings a range of practical skills and experience. Partnerships, based on shared commitments to common goals, are at the heart of our approach. We ensure that we take the time to learn from organisations the positive and negative aspects of their experiences so that both inform our learning strategy and determine the types of training programmes we provide.

Our partner organisations have a great deal of knowledge that can be used and exchanged. They are also organisations that have frequently suffered resource cutbacks for years and training for staff is frequently a casualty of such cutbacks. Book Aid International's partners are often confronted by similar challenges to one another and this has helped us to draw an analysis of priority areas which now forms the focus of Book Aid International's training programme.

Before I go into detail with examples I should like to explain the ethos of our work to support building the capacity of public library services. We develop training with partners and work together on planning, delivery and follow-up. Needs are identified jointly, methods are always participatory and we are improving the relevance of our training by working increasingly with facilitators and resource people from within the local information sector. We have also always striven to ensure that any courses we run lay the foundations for ongoing learning and we believe there are two key elements to this. Firstly, there needs to be a commitment to enabling staff to contribute to changing and develop existing policy and practice. This allows a process of renewal and refinement in management and services, to ensure a library or library service is best placed to meet the needs of the community it serves. Secondly, establishing channels for information sharing, both within organisations and through partnerships with other organisations are a very good way of enabling the sharing of best practice and also of ensuring that in the context of a resource-poor environment access to learning and information resources can be maximised.

We are working with partners across a wide range of need areas. Priorities for many include the need to learn more about issues such as advocacy, monitoring, impact assessment and distribution and targeting of materials. In the last couple of years training has ranged from regional workshops, bringing together a wide range of stakeholders – such as our work with the East African Book Development Association (EABDA) – to work placements and systems development – such as our recent work on distribution and targeting with the Tanzania Library Service.

In East Africa, Book Aid International has been working with member organisations of EABDA and of Book Development Councils in Tanzania, Kenya and Uganda to build capacity in the delivery of their reading promotion work. Their programme incorporates national book weeks and outreach work in which reading tents are organised, books supplied to establish school libraries, teachers trained in the skills to care for and promote the books. It's a demanding approach that needs skilled personnel at all levels of project delivery. In 2005, for example, Book Aid International facilitated training for EABDA that combined reading promotion, 'training the trainer' skills and book collection management for teachers. All stakeholders within the Book Development Councils have a role to play in delivery of the project. Participants gained increased confidence in how to structure training which could enable teacher-librarians to manage and promote book stocks given to their newly established school libraries. Our investment consisted of devising a three day workshop and involving EABDA stakeholders drawn from all three countries.

The return on that investment is very positive and reports have been sent in illustrating how the newfound training skills have enabled shared learning with many new beneficiaries. For example, a workshop participant from Tanzania had held training for 50 new teacher-librarians during national book week, each of whom received a collection of Book Aid International books and locally purchased books to start off their new school libraries. Meanwhile, in Uganda teachers and pupils in Mbarara primary schools have taken part in a programme of work that has promoted reading and built up pupil and teacher support for library improvement within the school. Sessions within this programme included exploration of the books that pupils liked, producing pictures to improve the library environment, story telling sessions and training for teachers to enable them to organise reading clubs and to have library lessons incorporated in the curriculum.

A more internally-focused example of Book Aid International training consists in our work with Tanzania Library Service (TLS) to improve distribution and targeting of material and building on previous work to build the capacity of regional libraries within the context of decentralisation. Our overall aim was to ensure that the books distributed through the national library network were carefully matched with local needs. Much of the work was about improving systems and information flows, so that district and branch libraries could effectively feed in their needs and the headquarters library in Dar es Salaam could efficiently process books and be responsive to user needs throughout their distribution network. One of Book Aid International's librarians undertook a work placement in the headquarters library, working with TLS staff to solve problems and establish new ways of working for the future. One participant commented that he had gained *'knowledge which will help me work more efficiently and therefore meet our objectives of providing informal education for my region and Tanzania as a whole'* (Tanzania Library Service, 2004).

Creation of new partnerships to facilitate action and learning has also been a crucial aspect of our work and an example that illustrates this well is our book purchase grant scheme. Grants have been given to libraries to buy African-published materials, initially with a focus on local markets and local language books, more recently exploring cross-border trade and establishing new links, markets and mechanisms to enable greater intra-African trade. Workshops have been held at critical stages of these projects to enable sharing of the benefits, challenges and lessons learned. Workshop participants have then jointly planned and implemented the next phase of the project. The capability for shared learning has definitely been enhanced by broad participation from across the book chain. Booksellers, publishers and librarians joined together to build common ground and shared solutions to the challenges of book purchase in an African context. Exploration of both the differences and commonalities in perspectives from organisations representing participating countries. There is recognition that *'in the past the key players in the book industry used to operate separately when in fact their end target is the same user of books'* (Zambia Library Service, 2004).

In fact this new approach to learning and working together has also extended beyond the book chain groups that the project sought to link up. It has also enabled external linkages that have strengthened the position of participating organisations in ways that we could not have foreseen. Two particularly strong examples have emerged. Firstly, Zambia Library Service's links with literacy groups, some of whom were chosen by ZLS as project beneficiaries, whilst others heard about the book purchase project and sought closer collaboration and links with the library service in the future, thus helping ZLS to work more closely with new literates and ensuring they can make the best use of resources in public library services. Uganda's National Library then found that their participation in the project had resulted in greater recognition from the government of the important role that libraries can play in national development. As a result the NLU and public libraries have been included in the government's Social Development Investment Plan.

This is precisely the kind of policy recognition that many public library services desperately need. The challenge now will be to ensure that commitments to support libraries are realised in practice. Still there are others among our partner network who lack even the most basic government recognition of the importance of their work. For instance, the Zambia Library Service lacks the legal framework of a Libraries Act that could define the role and position of the organisation within the government's education, information and cultural development plans. Overall, it is fair to say that the infrastructure of public libraries that exists in sub-Saharan Africa has been largely neglected by governments and the international development community.

But with adequate support and a coherent policy framework, libraries can provide practical solutions. They offer a unique and cost-effective means of providing access to information for all, because resources are shared. In the context of great scarcity that exists in sub-Saharan Africa, libraries have a more important role than in the North – they are the 'universities of the people'. Those who benefit from communally-held resources include distance learners, such as teachers studying to gain qualifications, as well as the poor, people with disabilities, women and girls.

Libraries can be at the heart of personal and community development, encouraging and sustaining literacy, and supporting education for all. Libraries also support non-formal education, and give equality of access to information to women and girls.

In the UK, the library network extends to every community (there are 3,500 public libraries including mobile services). It is very different in sub-Saharan Africa. Kenya, with its population of 32 million, and large literate population of over 15 million, has only 36 public libraries. Namibia has 48, and Zambia 22.

Yet librarians have developed low-cost ways of extending the reach of their services, targeting rural and disadvantaged communities. In Kenya, 21 libraries were established when the local communities provided a building and equipment, and the library service provided training and books. In Malawi the library service has established 200 community library centres, as well as providing resources for 900 schools. A similar programme operates in Zambia. This example illustrates well the untapped potential that exists in Africa's libraries. Creative solutions to resource shortages are possible but government and donor support is essential to realising this process. Existing library structures in Africa need investment of resources and new initiatives, so that libraries respond to the information needs of urban and rural people in Africa.

It is therefore encouraging to note that policy discourse is increasingly taking account of the importance of libraries. One example of this recognition is UNESCO's *2006 Global Monitoring Report on Education For All.* The document emphasises the importance of creating literate environments, with a recommendation to support libraries, so that literacy for life can be realised (UNESCO, 2005). Libraries also need recognition of their contributions towards reaching each of the Millennium Development Goals (MDGs). Partner organisations of Book Aid International are requesting information across a very broad range of subject areas, from health information and environmental issues, to a broad range of formal and informal educational needs. Their contribution towards the health MDGs encompasses combating the stigma of HIV/AIDS through displays and information points in libraries, whilst also enabling health extension workers to access essential medical texts such as *Where Women Have No Doctor* (Burns et al, 1997) to help them in their work to address high levels of maternal mortality.

4 CONCLUSION

I'd like to conclude by returning to the World Development Report for 1998/99. Its authors may not have realised they were laying down a challenge to librarians with their emphasis on the importance of knowledge in combating poverty. They conclude with the following message, *'As people grasp the ways in which knowledge can improve their lives, they are encouraged to seek out new knowledge and become agents of change themselves'* (World Bank 1999). I believe there is a message in that for all of us attending the SCECSAL 2006 conference: librarians, funders, policymakers, NGOs and others. We all have a role to play, to act as agents of change through sharing and employing the knowledge that we gain. In particular, librarians, you are the professionals who manage knowledge and store information on behalf of communities and you are ideally placed to take up this challenge. You can enable people throughout Africa to access the knowledge they need to enable them to realise their potential and act as agents in their own development. I hope you will find ways of doing just that.

REFERENCES

Book Aid International (2004). *Telecentres in libraries* (Book Aid International email discussion)

Burns, A et al (1997). *Where women have no doctor* Macmillan: Oxford

Community Library Service (2005). Quoted in Bentham, G (2005) *Independent evaluation of IABSS Project 2001–2004* for Book Aid International

Tanzania Library Service (2004). Quoted in Steenson and Lang (2004) *Tanzania Field Trip Report* for Book Aid International

UNESCO (2005). *Education for all global: monitoring report 2006.* Paris: UNESCO Publishing

World Bank (1999). *World development report: knowledge for development.* Washington: World Bank.

Zambia Library Service (2004). *Local book purchase presentation* (made at Book Aid International Accra Workshop, November 2004)

KNOWLEDGE MANAGEMENT AND INDIGENOUS KNOWLEDGE FOR DEVELOPMENT OF AFRICA'S INFORMATION SYSTEMS AND SERVICES: SOME LEGAL ISSUES FOR INFORMATION SYSTEM EXPERTS

Paul Faustin Kihwelo

ABSTRACT

This paper gives an over view of the complex and controversial nature of the legal protection of indigenous knowledge systems. The article proceeds to examine indigenous knowledge and the arguments for recognizing and protecting it. It further examines the international protection provided by the Convention on Biological Diversity and the issue of biopiracy. Some selected few cases of biopiracy have been examined. Then after application of existing intellectual property rights to indigenous knowledge on the international and national level have been examined too in particular explaining the problems and benefits of protecting indigenous knowledge for the sake of knowledge management and development of Africa's information systems and services. An assimilation of indigenous knowledge to the current intellectual property laws have been briefly examined and evaluated. The article also seeks to examine some of the new sui generis systems for the protection of indigenous knowledge and addresses issues of indigenous knowledge in the WTO, examines the issues under the TRIPS Agreement and the present positions of WTO Members in connection with the revisions of the provisions of the TRIPS Agreement that have direct bearing to indigenous knowledge systems. Lastly the paper examines knowledge management system in the light of indigenous knowledge.

1 INTRODUCTION

The term indigenous knowledge (IK) or traditional knowledge as is interchangeably used does not command to a universally agreed definition. As such it has been defined and perceived differently by different groups of people and organization in different times and places. However, despite the existence of such disparities there seems to be certain acceptable definitions as per some scholars. For instance Hilde van Vlaenderen (1999) has attempted to provide a working definition of indigenous knowledge to be:

> "a collection of ideals and assumptions that which tends to emphasize the knowledge internal to a particular setting differing from local knowledge

which focuses on the locality in which the knowledge is used and embraces exogenous knowledge that has entered the local community overtime".

Stephen Brush (1999) has defined indigenous knowledge as 'the systematic information that remains in the informal sector, usually unwritten and preserved in oral tradition rather than texts ... [It] is culture specific, whereas formal knowledge is decultured.

According to Mugabe (1999) traditional knowledge is the totality of all knowledge and practices whether explicit or implicit which is used in the management of social-economic and ecological facets of life.

Lugeye (1994) defines indigenous knowledge as the sum of experiences and knowledge of a given ethnic group that forms the basis for decision making in the face of familiar problems solving. It is a mixture of knowledge created endogenously within the society and that from outside but then integrated within the society and this knowledge is continuously changing and has an inherent capacity for absorbing relevant new knowledge from outside.

The knowledge specific to Indigenous people can be very broadly defined as well as oral information that has been handed down from generation for hundreds and even thousands of years.

A more explicit definition of Indigenous knowledge was formulated by the Indigenous Knowledge and Development Monitor to mean the sum total of the knowledge and skills which people in a particular geographical area possess and which enables them to get the most out of their natural environment. Most of this knowledge and these skills have been passed down from earlier generations, but individual men and women in each new generation adapt and add to this body of knowledge in a constant adjustment to changing circumstances and environmental conditions. They in turn pass on the body of knowledge intact to the next generation, in an effort to provide them with survival strategies.

Indigenous knowledge, as far as we are concerned, is that knowledge that is held and used by people who identify themselves as indigenous of a place based on a combination of cultural distinctiveness, prior territorial occupancy relative to a more recently arrived population with its own distinct and subsequently dominant culture (Mugabe, 1999).

2 BETWEEN CONTRAST AND INTEGRATION

Traditional knowledge differs from formal knowledge in various aspects like ways of acquisition, storage and transmission. Whereas indigenous knowledge does not have a special institution to administer it, formal knowledge is administered through various institutions of learning and practices. Indigenous knowledge is holistic in character and is passed down through generations and comes from personal or collective innovations. The processes of modern development are either marginalizing or integrating indigenous communities, making them abandon or lose their vast traditional or indigenous knowledge acquired over years.

Indigenous knowledge is established on past experiences and observation. It is usually a collective property of society. Many members of the society contribute to it over time, and it is modified and enlarged as it is used overtime. This knowledge is transmitted from generation to generation. This information consists of organized bodies of knowledge, or, in other words, coherent systems of knowledge, which several authors have referred to as *Indigenous science.*

Formal knowledge is that type of knowledge that is produced and generated through formal institutions of learning such as schools, Colleges and Universities.

Disappointing is the fact that the education system that we have been schooled has succeeded in creating prejudices in our mindset against traditional knowledge. We have been schooled to believe and accept that knowledge is only that is produced in universities or colleges and by those who have gone to formal universities or institutions of higher learning. Short of that whatever is produced is not knowledge and those who produced it cannot be termed as scholars or intellectuals (Kabudi, 2003). This has raised matters of great concern between intellectuals and traditional doctors as some may refer them as witchdoctors. The debate at one point in time arose in the national assembly when the house called for restrictions in the use of the title Professor! Most members of parliament wanted the title to be used by intellectuals only schooled in formal universities.

Today this knowledge which previously was equated as heathenism, barbarism and witchcraft is sought by hooks and worms and stolen to be stored in the *citadel* of Western European institutions of higher learning and scientific research. Many researchers and scientists are going to Latin America, Asia and coming to Africa seeking to talk to traditional healers and wishing to collect samples of herbal flora and fauna and take them back to their countries (Kabudi, 2003).

Pharmaceutical firms mostly based in developed countries stand accused of plundering native lore, leaping benefits and making fortunes from natural remedies. For instance a western drug industry has painted a Hoodia cactus plant known to and used by the Kung Bushmen who lives around Kalahari dessert in South Africa for thousand years as herbal medicine.

Another area to which the prejudices of our mindset can be vividly reflected is in the media coverage where information on an innovation based on indigenous knowledge will attract scant attention from the reporters and editors. To the contrary a discovery emanating from an experiment conducted in a university will catch headlines and if possible in front page carrying a special prominence (Kabudi, 2003).

3 THE NEED FOR PROTECTION OF INDIGENOUS KNOWLEDGE

It is no wonder to say that one may be tempted to ask a couple of questions as to why do we protect indigenous knowledge.

Indigenous knowledge encompasses information and know how on a variety of matters including resources management, traditional medicines, crafts, artistic designs, cultural assets including folk tales, indigenous poetry, dances, theater, rituals that adopt artistic forms, drawings, paintings, sculptures, textiles, musical instruments and architect.

Lack of proper legal and policy frameworks for the protection of indigenous knowledge in the developing countries provides a vacuum for the industrialized nations to exploit the indigenous knowledge and resources of the indigenous people in the developing countries who are at least 300 million.

Protection of indigenous knowledge will stop the giant pharmaceutical companies from North (who purport to discover herbal medicine owned and used by the indigenous communities for thousands of years) from patenting the said plants at the expense of the indigenous communities like the case of Hoodia drug in South Africa which have been patented by Phytopharm which in turn licensed to Pfizer, the giant pharmaceutical company in USA for the price of US $21 million at the expense of the Bushmen's knowledge and ignorance of the invention protection procedures.

Protection of indigenous knowledge is essential so as to avoid or letting our indigenous knowledge to rack and ruin as an aspect of ascertainable comparative advantage across the rainbow spectrum of agricultural crops, medicine, the environment and cultural values. This is a cultural heritage property right which we must correspondingly protect, and share equitably in the interest of all human kind.

The need for protecting indigenous knowledge is more relevant now than ever before due to the fact that the present global legal situation is the result of a grim unlawful past. It is hard to see how to find a lasting settlement without resolving core problems, one of which is the lack of protection for the fundamental indigenous rights, such as indigenous knowledge. It has been revealed that commercial interests very often violate indigenous intellectual property rights. Although, such violations do not formally constitute a breach of written legal standards, as neither national legislation nor international standards acknowledge the rights of indigenous people, these enterprises are still accountable to indigenous customary law.

4 GLOBAL REGIME FOR THE PROTECTION OF INDIGENOUS KNOWLEDGE

The international community has realized the benefits that are and can be derived from indigenous knowledge and the risks that may occur to the communities that have produced such knowledge where a legal and institutional framework is lacking for their protection.

Over the past fifteen years or so, the subject of Indigenous knowledge more often referred to as traditional Indigenous knowledge or ecological knowledge has attracted growing interest. As Indigenous people have emerged as major players and partners on the national and international scene, this knowledge has come to represent a new sphere of cultural and political affirmation for them. The number of conferences and discussion workshops on indigenous knowledge is continuing to grow every year, and the legitimacy of this knowledge as relevant source of information to help protect ecosystems, increase our understanding of environmental phenomena, and manage natural resources has been recognized on countless occasions by the governments of many countries.

However it must be pointed out at the outset that in the sphere of international arena little effort have been made so far to secure adequate and effective protection of indigenous knowledge and this seems to be the outcome of the perceived prejudices of the developed world to regard indigenous knowledge as being primitive, barbarism, heathenism and associated directly to witchcraft. On the other hand, it may be argued that leaving aside indigenous knowledge out of the negotiating areas within the Uruguay Round and the framework of WTO was intentionally done so as to enable the rich North to keep on plundering and pirating indigenous knowledge from the poor South.

5 INTERNATIONAL PRINCIPLES AND CONVENTIONS ON INDIGENOUS KNOWLEDGE

Issues of indigenous knowledge have been extensively discussed in the global arena but as rightly pointed out little effort have been done to enable its secure protection despite the fact that the international communities underscore the contribution of indigenous knowledge to sustainable development. This can be seen in a number of resolutions and principles developed from various fora which are very explicit on indigenous knowledge. These principles also underscore the need for communities to have their due share from benefits accruing from the use of their indigenous knowledge and resources (Maembe, 2003).

5.1 The Rio Principles on Indigenous Knowledge

One of the Principles of Declaration on Development (1992) from the United Nations on Environment and Development (UNCED), which was held in Rio de Janeiro in 1992, is that local institutions through which indigenous and local people socialize and conduct their economic activities should be strengthened. Though it did not explicitly address the question of intellectual property protection of traditional knowledge, it created a political framework for addressing these issues within environmental circles (Mugabe, 1999).

The Rio conference at the recommendation of WCED, addressed issues of intellectual property rights in traditional knowledge and innovations. Agenda 21, adopted by more than 160 states at the UNCED, contains a whole chapter on indigenous peoples' concerns and makes a wide range of recommendations on how these people's rights should be protected (Mugabe, 1999).

Chapter 26 of Agenda 21 begins by noting that indigenous peoples and their communities, which represent a significant percentage of the global population, have developed a holistic relationship with the natural environment. Over many generations, they have developed a "holistic traditional scientific knowledge of their lands, natural resources, and environment" (United Nations, 1992). It also recommends that governments should adopt policies and/or legal instruments that will protect intellectual and cultural property of indigenous peoples. Tanzania is part to the Rio principles as it ratified the Rio Convention on 1st March, 1992.

5.2 The Convention on Biological Diversity

The Convention on Biological Diversity (CBD), which was signed by more than 150 states during UNCED, also explicitly recognizes the rights of indigenous and local peoples in traditional knowledge and innovations. Its preamble sates that "the close and traditional dependence of many indigenous and local communities embodying traditional lifestyles on biological resources, and the desirability of sharing equitably benefits arising from the use of traditional knowledge, innovations and practices relevant to the conservation of biological diversity and the sustainable use of its components" (UNEP, 1992)

Articles 8(j), 10(c) and 18(4) make reference to the rights of indigenous and local people. Article 10(c), for example, provides that each Contracting party "shall [p]rotect and encourage customary use of biological resources in accordance with traditional cultural practices that are compatible with conservation or sustainable use requirements." Article 18(4) defines technologies broadly to include "indigenous and traditional technologies" (UNEP, 1992).

Article 8(j), is perhaps the most authoritative provision dealing with traditional knowledge. It provides that each Contracting party shall, as far as possible and as appropriate, "subject to its national legislation, respect, preserve, and maintain knowledge, innovations and practices of indigenous and local communities embodying traditional lifestyles relevant to the conservation and sustainable use of biological diversity and promote their wider application with the approval and involvement of the holders of such knowledge, innovations and practices and encourage the equitable sharing of the benefits arising from the utilization of such knowledge, innovations and practices" (UNEP, 1992).

There are a number of limitations with Article 8(j) in so far as the question of intellectual property rights in traditional knowledge is concerned but however it is not the intention of this present text to delve much on this discussion.

6 TRADE RELATED ASPECTS OF INTELLECTUAL PROPERTY RIGHTS (TRIPS)

Intellectual property rights are a form of ownership of human creativity. They take various legal forms including patents, trademarks, copyright, trade secrets and plant variety rights (Stokes, 1998). They give the holder of a right a legally protected monopoly over commercial use of his intellectual property, usually for a specified period. Controversy arises mainly concerning patents. These are often justified as an incentive to invest in research and development (R & D) which may lead to commercially exploitable innovations (Phillips and Firth, 1990). This view has been the subject of much debate, which the UN conference on Transnational Corporations attributes to insufficient and contradictory empirical evidence on linkages between IPR protection and investment and technology flows.

The negotiation and adoption of the Agreement on Trade-Related Aspects of Intellectual Property Rights (TRIPS) as part of the Uruguay Round in 1994 have added new dimensions to the debate on intellectual property rights in traditional knowledge. Tanzania is among the founder members of the Trips Agreement as it signed the Uruguay Round for Multilateral Trade Negotiations that culminated to the formation of the WTO which also formed the Trips Agreement.

The TRIPS agreement sets minimum standards for countries to follow in protecting intellectual property. Its objective is stated in the preamble as "to reduce distortions and impediments to international trade, and taking into account the need to promote effective and adequate protection of intellectual property rights, and to ensure that measures and procedures to enforce intellectual property rights do not themselves become barriers to legitimate trade" (Goldstein, 1997). Countries that ratify the Agreement are expected to establish comprehensive intellectual property protection systems covering patents, copyright, geographical indications, industrial designs, trademarks, and trade secrets.

However, Article 1 of TRIPS (on the nature and scope of the obligations) provides some flexibility in the implementation of the provisions of the agreement. It states in paragraph 1 of that Article that "[m]embers may, but shall not be obliged to, implement in their domestic law more extensive protection than is required by [the] Agreement, provided that such protection does not contravene the provisions of [the] Agreement" (Goldstein, 1997). According to Dutfield (1997), parties to TRIPS can invoke this provision to enact legislation for protecting traditional knowledge. He asserts "[t]he absence of any mention of traditional … knowledge in the Agreement, does not prevent any member from enacting legislation to protect such category of knowledge".

After reviewing TRIPS, we consider that it is not possible to protect traditional knowledge under current patent law. The TRIPS Agreement requires member States to provide patent protection for any inventions, whether products or processes, in all fields of technology, provided that they are new, involve an inventive step and are capable of industrial application.

The "inventive step" and "capable of industrial application" requirements are deemed to be synonymous with the terms 'non-obvious' and 'useful respectively'. Traditional knowledge products fail the test for patenting on one, or all, of the "new" inventive step and industrial application standards. On the "new" standard they will probably fail because by its very nature traditional knowledge has been known for some length of time. One could try and argue that traditional knowledge has been known for some length of time it is new to the world outside of the community from which it came but this is unlikely to succeed.

Article 29(1) of TRIPS requires that a patent applicant disclose sufficient and clear information regarding the invention so that another person "skilled in the art" would be able to reproduce the product or complete the process. This is a standard patent law condition. Opponents of patenting have been quick to point out that this condition of information disclosure could erode the rights of indigenous and local people because it would make traditional knowledge easily available to commercial entities. Given the absence of financial and organizational competencies of indigenous and local peoples to monitor and enforce patents in modern economic space, their knowledge could easily be used without due compensation.

On the whole, in my view, the conditions set under TRIPS do not enable the patenting of traditional knowledge and/or traditional innovations.

7 THE INTERNATIONAL LABOUR ORGANIZATION

The International Labour Organization (ILO) was the first UN Organization to address issues of indigenous knowledge. A committee of experts established in 1926 examined and developed international standards for the protection of natural workers. This committee generated the basis for the adoption, in 1957, of the convention concerning the protection and integration of indigenous and other tribal and semi-tribal populations in independent countries. This convention is commonly referred to as Convention 107. It aimed essentially to integrate indigenous people into the modern production system.

The Convention was revised in June 1989 as Convention 169 concerning indigenous and Tribal Peoples in Independent Countries. The revised Convention schemes the approach of promoting the assimilation of indigenous and tribal peoples. It promotes the protection of indigenous peoples as distinct and separate peoples. Article 292(b) imposes responsibility upon the governments to develop measures to promote full realization of the social, economic and cultural rights of the indigenous peoples. Article 5(a) provides for the recognition and protection of the cultural, religious and spiritual values and practices of indigenous peoples. As rightly pointed out by Mugabe (1999) these provisions should be broadly read to include recognition and protection of traditional knowledge of these indigenous peoples. The recognition of collective species is a critical aspect of the convention and is important in intellectual property rights issues, since collectivity is fundamental to transmission, use and protection of traditional knowledge.

It is important to stress that ILO Convention 169 is the only United Nations convention that specifically deals with indigenous people. Although the Convention does not specify Intellectual Property Rights, its language is conducive to protection of these rights. Interestingly to note the convention is not even mentioned in the Secretary General's concise report on "Intellectual Property of Indigenous Peoples" (Sheldon, 1993). This to a great extent leaves much to be desired as one would expect under normal circumstance that such a crucial convention that touches on indigenous peoples would have formed part of the Secretary's General report.

8 INDIGENOUS KNOWLEDGE AS AN IMPORTANT HUMAN RIGHTS CATEGORY

The 1948 Universal Declaration of Human Rights (UDHR) and subsequent International Covenant on Economic, Social and Cultural Rights (ICESCR) of 1966 guarantee fundamental freedoms of personal integrity and action, political rights, social and economic rights of cultural rights. The principle problem with the "human rights approach" to cultural protection is that action (or inaction) is directed toward nation-states and does not easily provide a basis for claims against multinational companies or individuals who profit from traditional knowledge. Any remedies would be against either the state where the indigenous are located (for failure to protect them) or against the sate or the company profiting from the knowledge (if there are transnational obligations or if the state is partly owner of the enterprise).

Nonetheless, Intellectual Property Rights are consistently seen as basic human rights and are implicit in the Universal Declaration. For example, article 1 establishes the right of self-determination, including the right to dispose of natural wealth and resources, including intellectual property. Article 7 allows for equal protection under the law, whereby implying that intellectual property rights (IPR) protection should be available to indigenous peoples as well. Article 17 provides for the right to own collective property and not to arbitrarily be deprived of that property. Article 23 guarantees the right to just and favorable remuneration for work, which could undoubtedly be interpreted as work related to traditional knowledge.

It is clear that IPRs should be seen as manifestations of basic human rights. Further more, it is clear that human rights organizations should take up the cause of IPRs, and appropriate international legislation should be used to defend indigenous and traditional knowledge.

9 MANAGEMENT SYSTEM FOR INDIGEOUS KNOWLEDGE AND LEGAL ISSUES FOR INFORMATION SYSTEM MANAGERS

Since knowledge management system is a collection of interrelated components and consisting of hardware, software, applications and people involved in the process of finding, selecting, organizing, distilling and providing information in a way that improves the employment of comprehension in a specific area of interest and because knowledge management helps an organization to gather information and understanding.

Information system is an organized structure of interrelated components and consisting of hardware, software, applications and people that collect and process data into information for support decision making. Specific knowledge management activities helps an organization to gain insight and understanding from its own experience on acquiring, storing and utilizing knowledge for such things like solving, dynamic learning, strategic planning and decision making. It also protects intellectual assets from decay ads to firm intelligence and provides increased flexibility. We have seen before that unlike formal knowledge traditional knowledge is not produced and stored in libraries and universities and that presents a great challenge to knowledge management system in modern context.

The current laws do not protect indigenous knowledge either so is the laws that govern information systems for Africa.

There is one constraint of knowledge management system in the light of indigenous knowledge and that is knowledge management system is often defined in terms of inputs such data, information technology, best practices etc, that by themselves may be inadequate and inappropriate for effective indigenous knowledge. While 'plug-and-play' technologies could enable rapid adaptability of integrated technology infrastructures, success of the business. Designers of the next generation knowledge management systems would need to understand how to streamline indigenous knowledge with modern knowledge in the management system.

The next generation knowledge management system must be extended to cover indigenous knowledge despite the unprecedented and rapid pace of change. A key challenge for managers in the forthcoming turbulent environment will be cultivating commitment of traditional knowledge holders to share that knowledge for purposes of knowledge management systems. As it becomes increasingly difficult to specify long-term goats and objectives, such commitment would facilitate real-time strategizing in according to knowledge managers' organizational vision and their real time implementation on the frontline.

Despite the fact that national, regional and international laws do not seem to realize and recognize protection for indigenous knowledge systems and its management it is high time that information managers take the lead by recognizing storing it in modern libraries in terms of information and data relating to indigenous knowledge so that it can be freely shared upon between researchers and policy makers in Africa and else where. It is understood that more often than not there are more challenges in trying to pursue this and more especially taking into account that indigenous knowledge can not be easily gathered and stored.

10 ACKNOWLEDGEMENTS

The context, discussions and presentations in this article are based upon the author's original works including authored and in-print publications, working papers, keynote presentations and speeches.

REFERENCES

Vlaenderen, H. (1999) "Local knowledge: what is it, why and how do we capture it? In: Selected papers from the First National Workshop held in Morogoro", edited by A.A. Kauzeni, 22–23 June, 1999 Gender and Biodiversity and Local systems (LINKS) Report No. 2.

Brush, S.B. and Stabinskyed, A. (1999). *Valuing local knowledge; Indigenous peoples and intellectual property rights*. Covelo, USA; Island Press.

Mugabe, J. (1999) Intellectual property protection and traditional knowledge; An international policy discourse, *Biopolicy International*, vol. 21.

Lugeya, S. (1994). The role of farmers' indigenous knowledge in natural resources management in Sokoine University of Agriculture, Convocation Workshop.

Kabudi P.J (2003). Intellectual property rights: Tanzania experience with reference to indigenous knowledge". A paper presented to a sub-regional workshop on indigenous knowledge organized by the University of Dar es Salaam in collaboration with the Technikon Northern Guateny, South Africa at Courtyard Hotel, Dar es Salaam, 11th to 13th March, 2003.

Kihwelo P.F. (2005). Indigenous knowledge: what is it? Why and how do we protect it? The case study of Tanzania. *Journal of World Intellectual Property*, vol. 8, no. 2.

Maembe A.T. (2003). "Indigenous knowledge policy in Tanzania". A paper presented at the workshop on the Role of Indigenous knowledge in Socio-Economic Development in Eastern and Southern Africa: Human Health and Biodiversity at Courtyard Hotel, Dar es Salaam, 11th to 13th March, 2003.

Kathryn Stokes, (1998). Intellectual property rights and the transfer of biotechnology to Zimbabwe in managing biodiversity. National systems of conservation and innovation in Africa edited by John Mugabe and Norman Clarck.

Golstein, Petal, (1997). *Selected statutes and international Agreements on unfair competition, trademarks, copyright and patents*. New York; The Foundation Press.

Dutfield, G. (1997). Can the TRIPS agreement protect biological and cultural diversity? *Biopolicy International*, vol. 19.

Shelton, D. (1993). Legal approaches to obtaining compensation for the access to and use of traditional knowledge of indigenous people. Draft report to WWF, Gland, Switzerland Worldwide Fund for Nature-International.

Phillips, J. and Firth, A. (1990). *Introduction to intellectual property law.* London: Butterworths.

Vicente, S. and C. Juma (Eds.), (1994). Biodiplomacy, genetic resources and international relations, Nairobi, Acts, 1994.

CROSS-CULTURAL INFORMATION RETRIEVAL: SEARCHING FOR ENGLISH DOCUMENTS USING ZULU QUERIES

Erica Cosijn, Ari Pirkola, Theo Bothma and Kalervo Järvelin

ABSTRACT

South Africa is a multicultural nation – it possesses eleven official languages, nine of which are African. This implies that a large percentage of what is termed "indigenous knowledge" may not be available to large percentage of the population, due to the fact that it is written in a language that people do not understand. Thus, there is a need for research in Cross Language Information Retrieval (CLIR) systems in order to provide access to indigenous knowledge. CLIR may be contextually defined as automatic translation in order to accommodate other language queries into English language databases, and vice versa. We present the experimental results to determine the applicability of dictionary-based Cross-Language Information Retrieval (CLIR) from Zulu to English. Due to the lack of resources and tools for morphological analysis, novel approaches had to be found to deal with the processes of CLIR. Approximate string matching, combined with a monolingual Zulu word list was used. Most research in CLIR concentrates on languages with comparable vocabularies in terms of, for instance, technical and scientific terminology. Our research has shown that a set of new problems is encountered if the language pairs used contain disparate vocabularies, and this increases the complexity of CLIR, especially when one of the languages dealt with lacks resources for word form analysis. Techniques are proposed to deal with these problems.

1 INTRODUCTION

Definitions of Knowledge Management (KM) abound, yet in its simplest form, KM seeks to make the best use of available knowledge, and to create new knowledge in the process. Indigenous Knowledge (IK) is a unique and very valuable source of knowledge, and for this reason it is of prime importance that this knowledge has to be captured and made available. IK is typically captured in the original language, and for this knowledge to be shared in order to create new knowledge, it has to be accessible. South Africa has a very complex language situation due to the fact that there are eleven official languages, *viz*. English, Afrikaans and nine African languages, including Zulu which is the most commonly spoken language in South Africa. There is an increasing amount of unique full-text material available in these indigenous languages, and thus accessibility to this material has become crucial. It is often the case that the user is able to read a foreign language, but is not fluent enough to construct an appropriate query in that language. Then, even if the user cannot read the retrieved documents, the user has at least a relevant set of retrieved documents that may be translated manually.

The basic idea of Cross-Language Information Retrieval (CLIR) is to provide access in one language (the source language) to documents written in another language (the target language). This paper focuses on the use of a dictionary-based query translation (as opposed to document translation) approach, which is one technique that may be used to facilitate CLIR. The idea with this research is to make documents in Zulu accessible using English queries, but at this stage, we are still testing the reverse process, namely accessing English documents using Zulu queries.

The dictionary-based approaches use bilingual dictionaries for query translation. A very basic strategy for query translation is to process it word-by-word and, for each source language word, look up its target language equivalents and place them into the target language query.

Linguistic resources for South African indigenous languages are limited, with no bilingual dictionaries available in machine-readable form. For this project, an electronic dictionary had to be created, but due to various limitations, a monolingual Zulu word list was retyped from a published Zulu-English dictionary. Due to the lack of morphological analyzers, the challenge was to match the Zulu inflected forms to the Zulu base forms.

The CLEF 2001 English topic set was used and 50 query topics were translated into Zulu. The dictionary-based approach was followed and approximate matching of the inflected word forms in the topics to the base-form in the monolingual dictionary was made.

Approximate string matching gave relatively good results, but several types of problems were experienced, e.g. inflected word forms and paraphrased translations. The correct base-forms were not always top-ranked and this introduced ambiguity into the translation process. However, the process indicated another interesting problem *viz.* the impact of the lack of technical terminology in Zulu CLIR. The CLEF database and queries are very Eurocentric, and this gives rise to a novel concept of cross-cultural information retrieval (CCIR), which is broader than, but encompassing CLIR. This not only deals with different languages, but also different cultures.

For the query construction, the InQuery retrieval system was used and the original English queries were run as baseline queries. Undisambiguated, as well as two types of syn-structured queries were formulated.

The paper is organised as follows. In Section 2 we present an overview of the characteristics of the Zulu language. In Section 3 we discuss the methodology used and the problems experienced. Section 4 presents the empirical results. Section 5 discusses the processes followed and the significance of the results obtained, while Section 6 contains some concluding remarks.

2 THE ZULU LANGUAGE

Zulu is spoken by more than 8,8 million people in Southern Africa. Of all the languages (including Afrikaans and English) spoken in South Africa, Zulu has the largest number of speakers. The Bantu languages spoken in South Africa are divided into three distinct groups, *viz.* the Nguni languages, the Sotho languages and the Venda languages. The Nguni languages in turn consist of Zulu, Xhosa and Swazi.

Zulu is an agglutinative language, which means that grammatical information is conveyed by attaching prefixes and suffixes to roots and stems. Zulu nouns are divided into classes or sets, called grammatical genders. Each gender has two distinct prefixes, one for singular and one for plural nouns. The classes far exceed the familiar European classifications of masculine, feminine and neuter, and are roughly associated with semantic characteristics relating to, for instance, human beings, kinship terms, animals, plants, artifacts, abstract concepts and so on.

Verbs are complex – a system of affixes marks the different grammatical relations, such as subject, object, tense, aspect and mood. For example, suffixes on verbs (*e.g.* verb root *fund-* + verb ending *-a* = *funda*: *learn*) are used to derive passive (*fundwa*: *to be taught*), active (*funda: learn*), causative (*fundisa: to teach*), reciprocal (*fundisana: to teach one another*) and prepositional (*fundela: to learn for*) verb forms. There is a system of concordial agreement in which subject nouns, object nouns and other words must agree with the verb of the sentence in class and number. Adjectives, possessive nouns and demonstratives also agree with the noun that they modify in class and number [Doke et al., 1990; Doke, 1968; Taljaard & Bosch, 1988; UCLA 2002).

3 METHODOLOGY

The aim of the research is to test whether English search strings could be run against a Zulu database, and to see which technologies are possibly viable in this regard. Since no Zulu database was available, we had to reverse the process, i.e. to run Zulu queries, translated into English, against an English database. We therefore tested whether inflected Zulu words can be matched with a dictionary entry through approximate matching techniques.

3.1 Zulu topic collection

The corpus used was the CLEF English document collection with 50 topics (CLEF 2001). The title and description fields were translated from English into Zulu by independent translators, one of whom is a Zulu mother-tongue speaker. An independent reviewer confirmed that the translations were indeed close to Zulu conversational language.

The process of translation highlighted an interesting problem that should be investigated in its own right, *viz.* the lack of technical terminology in Zulu and the impact thereof on CLIR. The CLEF database and queries are very Eurocentric, and many of the search terms could not be translated directly into Zulu, as Zulu does not have single word translation equivalents for many technical and scientific terms. This is solved either by paraphrasing to explain concepts or by borrowing words from other languages. This approach in turn causes problems for CLIR, as conceptual matching becomes quite difficult. The examples of paraphrasing and borrowed words given below illustrate these problems.

3.1.1 Paraphrasing

Paraphrasing is very commonly used to describe words or phrases in technical or scientific terminology. The following is a complete example and illustrates the complexity of paraphrased translations:

CLEF 2001 topic C068 contains the following query description:
Find documents that describe acts of terrorism or vandalism against European synagogues since the end of the Second World War.
The Zulu translation of the same text reads:
Thola imibhalo echaza izenzo zokuphekulazikhuni noma izinto ngobudlova elwa nezindlu zesonto zamaJuda ase-Europe kusukela ekupheleni kwezimpi zesibili zomhlaba.

The word-for-word translation back into English is as follows:
Find scriptures that describe acts of terror and the breaking of things with violent force that fight the houses of Sunday of the Jews of Europe from the end of the war of second of the world. (Nel, 2003)

Mechanically, n-grams match most of the individual words, even in inflected form, quite well to the dictionary entries. On a conceptual level however, it appears that the result may not always be very good.

3.1.2 Borrowed words

In modern times, Zulu has borrowed extensively from English and Afrikaans. These borrowed words may take one of two forms – the word is either kept as in the original language, but prefixed as if it is a Zulu noun, or adopted into the Zulu language. Some of these adoptives are of acceptable use and are included in the dictionaries. However, some are new additions, and the modern concepts are very often not entered in dictionaries (which are not updated on a regular basis). An example in the CLEF topic set is *amakhemikheli* (consisting of the prefix *ama-* (indicating that it is an adoptive) and stem *-khemikheli* which is borrowed from the English word *chemicals*) which was not found in the dictionary (Nel, 2003).

Some of the words are not assimilated into the language, but stay in the original language from which it was borrowed, with a Zulu class-prefix added. Examples which occurred in the translated CLEF topic set are, *inter alia, ama"computer mouse", i"film festival"*, and *i"mad cow disease".*

3.2 The monolingual Zulu word list

As there were no Zulu-English bilingual translation dictionaries available in electronic format, part of a printed dictionary had to be retyped manually in a word-processing program. Due to various restraints and restrictions, it was decided to only create a monolingual word list (Zulu entries only) in electronic format. The dictionary used was the 1990 edition of the Zulu dictionary by Doke *et al.* (1990). A distinctive feature of dictionaries in the Nguni languages (of which Zulu is one) is the fact that entries of all Zulu words which include a stem in their construction, for instance nouns and verbs, are entered in the dictionary under the first letter of the stem. Noun stems are preceded by a hyphen and the stem is then followed by the singular (singular prefix + stem) and plural (plural prefix + stem) forms. The entry for *gift*, for example, is listed as *-khungo* *umkhungo imikhungo*. Verbs, however, are listed only as base forms, e.g. *ngena* for *enter*.

In the writing of the history of Zulu, particular during the second half of the nineteenth century, attention was focused on improvements in the orthographical representations of the Zulu sound system, *i.e.* the Zulu alphabet. The result is that there are spelling variants not only between different dictionaries and different editions of the same dictionary, but also differences in spelling between dictionaries and the writings of mother-tongue speakers. The latest changes to Zulu orthography and spelling conventions were made as recently as 1993 (Nel, 2003).

For CLIR purposes this problem is not insurmountable because orthographical variation, like morphological variation, can be handled using approximate matching techniques.

3.3 Approximate string matching used in the study

We tested the following approximate matching techniques to match the individual Zulu words in the topics against the words in the monolingual Zulu word list: (1) digrams, (2) trigrams, (3) classified s-grams, (4) edit distance, and (5) LCS.

The first three of these are *n-gram matching* techniques, a *non-metric* approximate matching technique. In n-gram matching query keys and index entries are decomposed into n-grams, *i.e.*, into the sub-strings of length *n* (Pfeifer et al., 1996; Robertson & Willet, 1998; Salton, 1989; Zobel & Dart, 1995). In cases 1 and 2 above, n-grams were formed of the adjacent characters of words. The *classified s-gram (skipgram) matching* technique refers to a novel n-gram matching technique described in detail in Pirkola et al (2002a).

The last two, namely *edit distance* and *LCS,* are *metric* similarity measures,. Edit distance is defined as the minimum cost required to convert one string into another. Conversion includes character insertions, deletions and substitutions. For two words, their LCS is the longest character sequence of the sequences that occur in both words.

Five of the CLEF 2001 topics, containing a total of 75 Zulu source words were used as a trial to establish which of the procedures described above would give the best results. Ten of these were proper nouns, which were not matched, and therefore not used in the calculations. The results were thus based on 65 source words. For each procedure the six approximate best matches were listed for each of these source words. It was then manually established which one of these six words was the correct match for the source word.

Based on the five trial topics, skipgrams yielded the best results. It was calculated that the stem identification rate would be 78% within the first 3 matches and 82% within the first 4. Saturation occurs around the third match. This means that the correct Zulu word should be identified within a set of three words about 80% of the time.

3.4 Identifying Zulu base-forms

Each word in the Zulu translations of the query topics was matched, using skipgrams to the base-forms in the monolingual Zulu word list. For each source word, the three best matches form the triple to be translated and these are to be treated as synonyms. It was found that inflected word forms do have a significant influence on accuracy of matching.

Below is an example of the approximate matching of an inflected noun. The Zulu monolingual dictionary entries for nouns are of the format:
stem, singular (prefix + stem), plural (prefix + stem)
The entry for *danger* thus is: *-ngozi ingozi izingozi.*

In one of the translated CLEF topics the inflected form is *ezinengozi.* This inflected form was matched as follows by the five different matching techniques: Trigram: n=3, LCS: n=1, Edit: n=7 (no match), Skipgram: n=4 and Digram: n=2

3.5 Zulu to English Translation

As there was no bilingual translation dictionary, the base-forms were identified from the monolingual word list, and then had to be manually translated back to English. Strict rules were followed and stopwords were removed manually according to a list. The stopword list used was a typical list containing prepositions, pronouns and other non-informative function words.

For all CLIR queries (undisambiguated, syn1, and syn2; see Section 3.6.) proper names were handled differently. Borrowed proper names in Zulu usually are prefixed, with the stems being in their source language forms, e.g., *eSiberia*. The capital letters are kept in the middle of the proper names. This simplifies proper name identification and handling in CLIR: the prefixes were removed from the Zulu proper names (single and hyphenated words having a capital letter in the middle of words), and the unprefixed forms (e.g., *Siberia*), were used in the final queries. In Zulu, borrowed phrases (common nouns) are indicated using inverted commas, e.g., "computer virus". Both unprefixed proper names and borrowed phrases were passed to the final queries as such. The number of queries containing these two expression types was 34 and 6 respectively (some queries contained both). The number of queries which did not contain either one of these was 13.

3.6 The retrieval system and test queries

The *InQuery retrieval system* (Allan et al., 2000; Broglio et al., 1994) was used in this study. The InQuery query language provides a set of operators to specify relations between query keys (Sperer & Oard, 2000). To show the performance level of the test queries we ran *the original English queries as baseline queries.* They contained as query keys the title and description words of the CLEF topics (the test queries were formed on the basis of the same words).

The original English queries and *undisambiguated CLIR (test) queries* were flat sum-queries, where query keys (a, b, c, …) were combined with the sum-operator: #sum (a b c …).

In many CLIR studies the *Pirkola method,* i.e. treating translation equivalents as synonyms and combining them by the InQuery syn-operator, has been demonstrated to perform well (Ballesteros & Croft, 1998; Gollins, 2000; Meng et al., 2000; Pirkola, 1998; Pirkola et al., 2002b; Oard & Wang, 2001; Sperer & Oard, 2000). We therefore formulated two types of syn-structured queries.

In *syn1 CLIR queries* all the translations of the three best matches of a Zulu topic word were combined with the syn-operator. For example, the three best matches and their translations for the Zulu word *esesabekayo* are the following:
esabeka: *capable, feared, fearful, terrible, awe, inspiring, prodigious, wonderful*
sabeka: *fearful, terrible, wonderful*
esabela: *respond.*

The syn-statement thus is as follows:

#syn(capable feared fearful terrible awe inspiring prodigious wonderful fearful terrible wonderful respond).

In *syn2 CLIR queries* the translations of each three match of a Zulu topic word were combined with the syn-operator. For example, for the word *esesabekayo,* the syn-statements are the following:

#syn(capable feared fearful terrible awe inspiring prodigious wonderful) #syn(fearful terrible wonderful) #syn(respond).

In both cases (syn1 and syn2) the syn-statements were combined with the sum-operator.

4 RESULTS

The effectiveness of the test queries was evaluated as precision at 10% recall (Pr. at 10% R) and interpolated average precision over 10%–100% recall levels (Avg. Pr.). These are commonly used evaluation measures (see, for example, Pirkola et al (2002b) and Xu & Croft (1998). Statistical significance of the difference between the performance of the test queries and that of baseline queries was tested using *Wilcoxon signed ranks test.* The Wilcoxon test uses both the direction and the relative magnitude of the difference of comparable samples. The statistical program that was used is based on Conover (1980).

The results are presented in Table 1. As shown, the average precision of baseline queries is 34.3%, while that of undisambiguated CLIR queries is only 4.0%. Syn1 queries perform substantially better than undisambiguated queries. Performance difference between syn2 and undisambiguated queries is also clear.

Table 1 also presents the relative performance of CLIR queries, i.e., with respect to baseline queries. For syn1 queries it is 58.6%–62.7%, for undisambiguated CLIR queries only 10.8%–11.7%.

As described above, we removed prefixes from the Zulu proper names. The stems that were English words were passed unchanged to CLIR queries. It was obvious that unprefixed proper names contributed to the good retrieval performance of the syn1 queries. Also, the phrases indicated by inverted commas probably had positive effects. To test the effects of these untranslated English words, we divided both the test and baseline query sets into two subsets: (1) proper name queries – queries which had either at least one proper name or an 'inverted comma key' (the latter ones were infrequent), and (2) non-proper name queries – queries which only contained Zulu-English translations. The results of these runs are shown in Table 2. As can be seen, proper name CLIR queries perform quite well in relation to proper name baseline queries, while the performance of non-proper name CLIR queries is very poor, that is, 3.5% (Pr. at 10% R) and 1.4% (Avg. Pr.) respectively.

The performance of all CLIR queries differed statistically at the levels of p = 0.01 and 0.001 from that of the baseline queries for both evaluation measures, i.e. precision at 10% recall and average precision.

Table 1. The performance of CLIR queries

Query type	**Pr. at 10% R**	**Avg. Pr.**
N=50		
Eng – Original English	54.8	34.3
Undisambiguated	5.9	4.0
% Undisambiguated /Eng	10.8	11.7
Statistical sign. level	0.001	0.001
Syn1	32.1	21.5
% Syn1/Eng	58.6	62.7
Statistical sign. level	0.001	0.001
Syn2	17.2	11.7
% Syn2/Eng	31.4	34.1
Statistical sign. level	0.001	0.001

Table 2. The effects of untranslated English words on the performance of the best test queries (syn1)

Query type	**Pr. at 10% R**	**Avg. Pr.**
Proper name queries, N=37		
Eng – Original English	59.7	39.7
Syn1	42.2	28.6
% Syn1/Eng	70.7	72.0
Statistical sign. level	0.01	0.01
Non- proper name queries, N=13		
Eng – Original English	41.3	19.2
Syn1	3.5	1.4
% Syn1/Eng	8.5	7.3
Statistical sign. level	0.01	0.01

5 DISCUSSION

Essentially, this paper summarizes the findings of our research towards finding unique and specialized solutions to the problems of CLIR when the target (or the source) language is an indigenous language lacking linguistic resources and exhibiting strong inflectional morphology.

Zulu queries, translated into English, were run against an English database and we tested whether inflected Zulu words can be matched with a dictionary entry through approximate matching techniques.

Some of the most important empirical findings were:

- An abundance of mistranslated query keys occur in Zulu-English CLIR.
- The removal of Zulu prefixes from proper names resulted in quite good retrieval performance of the syn-queries, due to identical proper names in their English form.

- Proper name queries contained many mistranslated keys, but owing to the syn-structure, performed quite well.
- The fact that borrowed words (common nouns) may be marked using quotation marks probably contributed to good retrieval performance.
- Paraphrasing may give some good keys but the syn-structure does not help in these cases. The disambiguation effect of the syn-structure is based on the fact that important keys occur as single keys (outside the syn-statements), thus resulting in more weight being assigned to the latter than to mismatched keys.

Regarding CLIR techniques, we outlined the process of translating queries from Zulu to English. Matching the inflected word forms in Zulu topics to the Zulu base form dictionary was a novel challenge, due to the lack of morphological analyzers. We used monolingual approximate string matching in Zulu to do this. A monolingual Zulu word list was used, since no electronic bilingual translation dictionaries are available. Translating matched Zulu base form words into English was done manually but simulating a mechanical process based on a translation dictionary.

The first step of identifying correct base-forms for Zulu was already problematic. Although relatively good results were obtained from approximate string matching, they were far from perfect. Typical problems encountered at this stage were mainly related to incorrect ranking of base-forms, incomplete translation and matching, and paraphrasing of translations. This introduced ambiguity into the translation process, partly ascribable to the disparate vocabularies of English and Zulu.

6 CONCLUSION

Present research in CLIR concentrates on languages with comparable vocabularies in terms of, *inter alia*, technical and scientific terminology. This paper has shown that a set of new problems will be encountered if the language pairs used contain disparate vocabularies. Lack of technical vocabulary leads to paraphrasing and descriptive translations. The complexity of CLIR is increased even more when one of the languages dealt with lacks resources for word form analysis. These problems need further investigation, and specialized techniques will have to be found to deal with this. On the other hand, queries formed from paraphrased translations may yield many relevant keys. We therefore believe that interactive CLIR, which enables a user to select the best translated keys and may add his/her own keys, might be well-suited to Cross-Cultural IR. This may present unique opportunities for research in CLIR.

ACKNOWLEDGEMENTS

The *InQuery* search engine was provided by the Center for Intelligent Information Retrieval at the University of Massachusetts.

REFERENCES

Allan, J., Connell, M.E., Croft, W.B., Feng, F.-F, Fisher, D. and Li, X. (2000) InQuery and TREC-9. *The Ninth Text Retrieval Conference (TREC-9)*, Gaithesburg, MD. Available at: http://trec.nist.gov/pubs/trec9/t9_proceedings.html.

Ballesteros, L. and Croft, W.B. (1998) Resolving ambiguity for cross-language retrieval. *Proceedings of the 21st Annual International ACM SIGIR Conference on Research and Development in Information Retrieval*, Melbourne, Australia, pp. 64–71.

Broglio, J., Callan, J. and Croft, W.B. (1994) InQuery system overview. *Proceedings of the TIPSTER Text Program (Phase I)*, pp. 47–67.

Conover, W.J. (1980) *Practical non-parametric statistics*. New York: John Wiley & Sons.

Doke, C.M., Malcolm, D.M., Sikakana, J.M.A. (1990), *English-Zulu Dictionary*, Johannesburg: Witwatersrand University Press.

Doke, C.M., 1968, *Textbook of Zulu grammar*, 6th Ed. Johannesburg: Longmans Southern Africa.

Gollins, T.J. (2000) *Dictionary based transitive cross-language information retrieval using lexical triangulation*. University of Sheffield. Master of Science Thesis.

Meng, H., Chen, B., Grams, E., Khudanpur, S., Lo, W-K., Levow, G-A., Oard, D., Schone, B., Tang, K., Wang, H-M. and Wang, J.Q. (2000) Mandarin-English Information (MEI): Investigating Translingual Speech Retrieval. *HLT 2001, Human Language Technology Conference*, March 18–21, 2001, San Diego, California.

Nel, J.G. (2003) *Zulu-English Cross Language Information retrieval: an analysis of errors*. Unpublished M.A. Thesis, University of Pretoria.

Oard, D. and Wang, J. (2001) NTCIR-2 experiments at Maryland: comparing structured queries and balanced translation. *The Second NTCIR Workshop*, March 7–9, Tokyo, Japan.

Pfeifer, U., Poersch, T. and Fuhr, N. (1996) Retrieval effectiveness of proper name search methods. *Information Processing & Management,* vol. 32, no. 6, pp. 667–679.

Pirkola, A. (1998) The effects of query structure and dictionary setups in dictionary-based cross-language information retrieval. *Proceedings of the 21st Annual International ACM SIGIR Conference on Research and Development in Information Retrieval*, Melbourne, Australia, pp. 55–63.

Pirkola, A., Keskustalo, H., Leppänen, E., Känsälä, H. and Järvelin, K. (2002a) Targeted s-gram matching: a novel n-gram matching technique for cross- and monolingual word form variants. *Information Research,* 7(2). Available at: http://informationr.net/ir/7-2/infres72.html.

Pirkola, A, Leppänen, E. and Järvelin, K. (2002b) The RATF formula (Kwok's formula): exploiting average term frequency in cross-language retrieval. *Information Research*, 7(2). Available at: http://informationr.net/ir/7-2/infres72.html.

Robertson, A.M. and Willett, P. (1998) Applications of n-grams in textual information systems. *Journal of Documentation,* vol. 54, no.1, pp. 48–69.

Salton, G. (1989) *Automatic text processing: the transformation analysis and retrieval of information by computer*. Addison-Wesley.

Sperer, R. and Oard, D. (2000) Structured translation for cross-language IR. *Proceedings of the 23rd Annual International ACM SIGIR Conference on Research and Development in Information Retrieval*, Athens, Greece, pp. 120–127.

Taljaard, P.C. and Bosch, S.E. (1988) *Handbook of IsiZulu*, Pretoria: Van Schaik.

UCLA Language Materials Project. (2002) *Zulu Profile*. Retrieved January, 9, 2002 from: http://www.lmp.ucla.edu/profiles/profz01.htm.

Xu, J., and Croft W.B. (1998). Corpus-based stemming using co-occurrence of word variants. *ACM Transactions on Information Systems,* vol. 16, no. 1, pp. 61–81.

Zobel, J. and Dart, P. (1995) Finding approximate matches in large lexicons. *Software – practice and experience, vol.* 25, no. 3, pp. 331–345.

KNOWLEDGE MANAGEMENT: ISSUES FOR AFRICA'S LIBRARY AND INFORMATION PROFESSIONALS

Alli A.S. Mcharazo

ABSTRACT

Based on documentary and library research, this paper highlights some of the issues that are necessary in creating a conducive environment for addressing and tackling knowledge management issues in Africa. The paper argues the need for African library and information professionals who are entrusted with handing information and knowledge to understand all the issues and aspects that surround KM. In this way they can better articulate the way forward for managing knowledge for the betterment of their professional practices and communities. The issues in this paper include knowledge as key to national competitiveness, the need to understand knowledge management, the role of libraries in knowledge management, the need to include indigenous knowledge, knowledge management education, and possible ways forward.

1 BACKGROUND

The significance of knowledge and knowledge management (KM) to the modern world we are living in cannot be overemphasized. The idea behind the formation of a globalised world is well-rooted in having a strong knowledge base that is driving the knowledge economy. Some writers on globalisation, such as Nayyer (2006) and others have maintained that the growth of digital information both draws from and contributes to globalisation. Cate (1998) observes that "digital information is the ultimate example, and significant cause, of globalisation." This means librarians and information professionals have new roles in ensuring that the new knowledge demands are satisfied. This calls for new practices and strategies that would ensure that the available knowledge is well managed for the betterment of the communities served by libraries and information units that handle knowledge.

It is of paramount importance, therefore, that professionals who are entrusted in handing information and knowledge understand all the issues and aspects that surround KM. In this way they can better articulate the way forward for managing knowledge for the betterment of their practices and communities. This essay, based on theoretical and library research, highlights and discusses some of the issues that are necessary in creating a conducive environment for addressing and tackling KM issues.

2 KNOWLEDGE AS KEY TO NATIONAL COMPETITIVENESS

Library and information professionals need to be aware that progress of society is determined to a large extent by the extent of use and application of information and knowledge. The application of knowledge will be the main instrument for communities, companies, and nations in Africa, to compete in today's knowledge driven world. The Prime Minister of Singapore (Goh Chok Tong) had this to say about the importance of information and knowledge:

> "The future belongs to countries whose people make the most productive use of information, knowledge and technology. These are now the key factors for economic success, not natural resources ..." (Singapore Ministry of Information and the Arts, 1994:33)

That knowledge and information have become the most important economic resource and the engine that drives the global economy in the 21st Century is now widely recognized. The World Bank report of 1998/99 was wholly devoted to knowledge for development (World Bank, 1999). The reported noted that because knowledge matters in development, "understanding how people and societies acquire and use knowledge – and sometimes fail to do so, is essential in improving peoples lives especially the lives of the poorest."

A big challenge for African countries is that information and knowledge is being produced at a frenetic pace creating an information overload, but both are becoming obsolete at a quicker rate. A key paradox to all this is that many communities in developing countries suffer from acute information poverty. Lacking essential information in key areas such as: health, education, community development, appropriate technology, employment creation and income generation to mention a few. It is thus a case of starvation in the midst of plenty. On the other hand, many such communities are rich in their own indigenous knowledge which goes to waste because it is unappreciated, disorganized, and de-linked from the inward flow of modern scientific information and knowledge.

At the heart of all these information and knowledge issues is the need to master communication technologies to acquire, manage and exchange speedily the required information and knowledge by a country. Ultimately the utilization of information for competitiveness is dependent upon capacity building for the population to learn faster and apply the knowledge better than other nations, thus creating learning communities, institutions, companies, and nations. Developing countries have been called upon to put in place a policy framework for reducing knowledge gaps, acquiring knowledge by adapting knowledge available elsewhere in the world as well as creating knowledge locally. Such policies should also lead to speedy absorbing and application of knowledge for development. In addition, the area of effective communication and dissemination of knowledge within respective countries also need urgent attention to ensure that knowledge reaches all parts and sectors of the country, to serve as an engine of development.

3 THE NEED TO UNDERSTAND KNOWLEDGE MANAGEMENT

The library and information scene has seen a lot of recent literature on various aspects and practices of KM. The explosion of this information has, sometimes, sent a wrong signal to some library personnel that KM is a new concept. Knowledge is not new, and KM is as old as knowledge itself, and one of the main reasons why KM is spoken about a lot and given emphasis and prominence is some countries is the advent of ICT as a tool to manage knowledge and a pillar of globalisation. Al-Hawamdeh (2002) summarises the situation thus:

> "... with KM as a concept is looking so attractive, many organisations are jumping on the bandwagon ... it is also important to note that for many organisations, KM is something trendy and has a positive impact on the organisation image ... for many IT vendors and management consultants KM is a business opportunity that enables them to take advantage of the current interest in KM."

Library and information professionals need to be clear on the definition of knowledge and KM. Although knowledge is often not distinguishable from information and data, it is more often taken to refer to a state of being aware or of understanding a particular subject under discussion. This focus on knowledge follows Spender's (1996) idea that knowledge is the basis of a dynamic theory of a firm or institution. It is believed that an institution that is less knowledgeable stands to make less rational decisions than a knowledgeable institution. Kanter (1999) says knowledge can be acquired through two different ways, i.e. through personal experience, insight and intuition, or through learning from others. He defines the former knowledge as tacit knowledge (i.e. the knowledge that is carried in an individual's mind and not presented in databases), and the latter as implicit knowledge (i.e. knowledge acquired through learning). Davenport and Prusak (1998, p.5), on the other hand, define knowledge as a fluid mix of framed experiences, values, contextual information, and expert insight that provides a framework for evaluating and incorporating new experiences and information. The authors maintain that "knowledge originates from the mind of knowledgeable people. In organisations however knowledge is often embedded in documents or repositories, organizational routines, processes and norms". Nonaka et al (2005) sum up the distinction as follows:

> "There are two types of knowledge: explicit knowledge and tacit knowledge ... explicit knowledge can be expressed in formal and systematic language and shared in the form of data, scientific formulae, specifications, manuals and suchlike ... tacit knowledge is highly personal and hard to formalize ... subjective insights, intuitions and hunches fall into this category ... tacit is deeply rooted in action, procedures, routines, commitments, ideals, values and emotions"

It is a common knowledge that tacit knowledge, unlike explicit knowledge, is difficult to communicate to others, since it is an analogue process that requires simultaneous processing. Knowledge is also the essence of KM without which this new endeavour is a mere recycling of management topics.

KM, on the other hand, can be viewed as the process of turning data (raw material) into information (finished goods) and from there into knowledge (actionable finished goods) (Kanter, 1999).

On KM, Alavi and Leidner (1999) give a more elaborate definition of KM as a systematic and organisationally specified process of acquiring, organising and communicating both tacit and explicit knowledge of employees so that others may make use of it to be more effective and productive. On the evolutionary nature of knowledge, Corrall sums up the issue as follows:

> "KM involves taking a more holistic view of information, not only combining internal and external information – previously practiced by in some corporate libraries, relatively rarely in other sectors – but also co-ordinating planning and control (monitoring) information, and consolidating informal (soft) and formal (hard) information."

As for the relationship existing between information management and KM, Davenport (2005) states that:

> "KM is related to information management, but is not the same thing simply because knowledge and information are not identical. Information is atomic and static, but knowledge is associative, rich, multilayered, multi-faceted, contextual, accessible and dynamic."

It should be borne in mind that ICT, *per se*, is not KM but facilitates the management of knowledge.

4 ROLE OF LIBRARIES IN KM AND FORMATION OF AN INFORMATION AND KNOWLEDGE SOCIETY

In supporting information and knowledge acquisition, dissemination of information, and management of information resources, access to ICTs, libraries and information centres play a role that is second to none. There is thus a high potential in facilitating the transition process taking place in the nations of the subregion to move towards a knowledge society and knowledge economy. It is time for the library and information profession in Africa to assess and debate how African libraries and information centres can support the creation of knowledge and information society in their respective member states.

The professionals and para-professionals who manage these libraries and information centres, and the funding agencies and sponsors who support them, however, require to build on their considerable awareness and understanding of the leading concepts and innovations which are guiding the emergence of knowledge and information societies, including the policies and programmes of their own countries and leading continental and international bodies. A key part of the re-tooling and empowering staff of information centres and libraries is a clear understanding of what KM is or is not given that there are a variety of meanings attached to this hot topic today. Equally important is familiarization with programmes such as NEPAD (The New Partnership for Africa's Development), the African Renaissance, the role of the civil society in the transition to knowledge and information society, indigenous knowledge, ICT for development, and the role of knowledge and information in addressing the scourge of HIV/AIDS.

Changing the mind-set of library and information centre staff is a key part of the empowering and en-skilling process. For example, the repositioning of libraries/information centres to play a broader role and stimulate social learning and knowledge sharing by providing opportunities to users to gather knowledge through events held in libraries such as talks, exhibitions, lectures and debates, and forums to supplement the published sources of information traditionally found in libraries.

5 INCLUSION OF INDIGENOUS KNOWLEDGE

It has been shown earlier that KM involves the process of managing both explicit and tacit knowledge. This, according to many practices in Africa, is a big move. It is a move away from practices characterised by the belief that information or knowledge was that which was coded and documented in a formal manner. The importance of capturing personal knowledge, insight and intuition is now recognized. Africa is rich in tacit knowledge – indigenous knowledge. Ikoja-Odongo (2006) maintains that most of African knowledge is tacit-based and characterizes the richness as follows:

> "African peoples use story telling as a means of sharing information … other ways are group activities such as ceremonies (marriage, birth, burial festive sessions), fables, riddles, proverbs, parables, poetry, folklore. Music, dance and drama to educate themselves and disseminate and thread knowledge among different age groups and chaining their knowledge and practices from one generation to the next."

Unfortunately the richness of indigenous knowledge, which is mainly based on oral traditions, has not been fully exploited to the advantage of all the people. This is due to, amongst other things, failure to manage it accordingly. Failure to classify and catalogue ingenious knowledge has resulted in failure to locate and utilize it. Efforts to properly manage this information and be part and parcel of the KM systems would revolutionize African KM systems for the betterment of existing and future generations.

6 KM AND EDUCATION

As for the education sector, although KM is gradually gaining acceptance in the field of higher education, institutions of higher learning in the world are still "on the very first steps of what appears to be a long ladder", to use the words of von Krogh and Roos (1996). In fact, academic institutions have not yet adequately addressed and evaluated the advantages offered by KM tools to enhance teaching, learning, scholarship and research, and innovation. Research has shown that KM is a viable means in which higher education institutions may build and exploit intellectual and social capital effectively and gainfully. The application of KM principles may improve performance at institutions of higher learning and foster a culture of excellence. In that regard, institutions of higher learning in Africa should embrace KM practices and principles in order to address the challenges they are facing in a society that is increasingly becoming knowledge-based.

The second level of KM education is for library and information professionals. Because KM activities involve, amongst other things, knowledge creation, validation, presentation, distribution and application (Bhatt, 2001), and a greater part of these are in the form of data, information and knowledge, it is of paramount importance that librarians and other information providers are well equipped with all the necessary skills. Firestone (2001) has observed that "KM cannot be successful if the field avoids philosophical and in-depth scientific analysis and theorizing about the nature of knowledge." The logical place to provide this kind of education would be in programmes for trainee library and information professionals. The schools would then be responsible for research, development of knowledge on KM, suggesting the best practice for handling and organising knowledge and producing an army of experts on KM. This calls for library schools to include KM in their syllabi and curricula.

7 THE WAY FORWARD FOR AFRICAN LIBRARIANS AND INFORMATION SPECIALISTS

The most pressing challenge facing the region is capacity building in KM for both practicing librarians as well as newly recruited information workers. The fact that KM is a relatively new innovation needs to be understood and internalized by the people in the continent.

We have noted the important role that KM plays in human development, and further recognized the important roles, which libraries play in the development process of the different African nations. To conclude, an outline of key aspects that characterize the way forward for Africa's library and information units is provided. Against this background, it is worth noting the recent effort of library and information professionals who assembled in Dar es Salaam to deliberate on the way forward in terms of KM practices in the continent. The recommendations that came out of the SCECSAL XVII (2006) conference on *"Libraries as Bridge to an Information and Knowledge Society in Eastern, Central and Southern Africa"* have direct relevance to the above analysis. The delegates noted the important role KM plays in human development, and that libraries are a bridge to an information and knowledge society. Delegates of SCECSAL XVII after deliberating and reflecting on the conference theme made the following recommendations:

a) Schools of library and information science must incorporate KM as an important ingredient to be studied in their curriculums.

b) Library associations should also work very closely with schools of library and information science and other partners to run refresher courses for practicing librarians and information workers on KM at national level.

c) Library associations must adopt KM tools to strengthen their own performance and role.

It is clear that the benefits of knowledge sharing and networking among librarians and information workers in Africa, and the opportunities that electronic communication can provide, are many. It is therefore recommended that:

a) African governments should facilitate the creation of an interactive website in their respective nations, to allow knowledge sharing through discussion forums, networking, and effective communication.

b) Each member state must come up with effective strategies on the management and operation of the national website.

Similarly, African librarians and information specialists should create KM partnerships. It should be noted that KM is multi-disciplinary in nature, and that effective action can only happen through partnership and networking arrangements. In this way,

a) Library associations and libraries should seek to create working partnerships with other agencies involved in the dissemination of information and sharing of knowledge, including but not limited to: extension workers, public health, ICT practitioners, teachers, and development agencies.

b) Library associations and libraries should work with other stakeholders to conduct advocacy and to lobby policy makers to ensure that policies are in place to ensure appropriate structures are created, resources and set aside, ensuring there is adequate flow of information to support development processes in a country.

A need to strengthen local library associations and libraries, so as to shoulder more effectively the role of non-government organisations in promoting use of knowledge as a factor of production and application of knowledge for development, should also be given more priority by undertaking the following:

a) Library and information workers must consider integrating millennium development goals into the library development agenda.

b) Library associations and libraries should develop a vision statement, long and short term strategic plans to guide them in their activities with special reference to KM.

c) Library associations and libraries should work closely with the mass media to create effective communication channels with the general public, opinion makers, and policy makers at national level to promote library and information use for development.

Other issues such as funding, personnel, ICT, research, have been discussed in great depth, in the context of information and KM, in various many literatures. These issues together with ones discussed in this paper, if well addressed, can pave the way and create a suitable environment for creation and running of KM programmes and activities to the advantage of the profession and the end users.

REFERENCES

Alavi, M. and Leidner, D. (1999). "Knowledge management systems: Issues, challenges and benefits", *Communications of the Association for Information Systems (AIS) Journal*, vol. 1, article 7. AIS, Atlanta.

Al-Hawamdeh, Suliman (2002). "Knowledge management: rethinking information management and facing the challenge managing tacit knowledge". *Information Research*. Vol. 8, no. 1, at http://informationr.net/ir/8-1/paper143.html

Bhatt, G.D. (2001). "Knowledge management in organisations: examining the interaction between technologies, techniques and people". *Journal of KM*, vol. 5, no. 1, p. 58–68.

Cate, F.H. (1998). Introduction: sovereignty and globalisation of intellectual property. *Indian Journal of Global Legal Studies*, vol. 6, no.1, at http://ijgls.indiana.edu/archive/06/01/crews.shtml

Corral, Sheila (2006). "Knowledge management: Are we in the knowledge management business?" *KM* no. 8, at http://www.ariadne.ac.uk/issue18/knowledge-mgt/

Davenport, T.H. (2005). What is knowledge management? At http://www.mccombs.utexas.edu

Davenport, T.H. and Prusak, L. (1998). Working knowledge: how organisations manage what they know." Boston: Harvard Business School Press.

Drucker, P.E. (1995): "The post capitalistic executive" in P.E. Drucker (Ed.) *Management in a time of great change*. New York: Penguin.

Firestone, Joseph M. (2001). "Key issues in knowledge management". *Knowledge and Innovation: Journal of the KMCI*, vol.1, no.3, p.8–38, at http://www.dkmas.com/papers/firestoneissuesklv1n3.pdf

Ikoja-Odongo, J.R. (2006). "Quest for knowledge and knowledge management in rural societies in Africa". In: *SCECSAL XXII: Librarianship as a bridge to an information and knowledge society in Eastern, Central and Southern Africa,* Ed. Kingo Mchombu *et. Al*. Dar es Salaam: Tanzania Library Association, p. 196–218.

Israel, Spiegler (2000): "Knowledge management: A new idea or recycled concept?" *Communications of the Association for Information Systems (AIS) Journal*, vol. 3, article 14. AIS, Atlanta.

Kanter, J. (1999). "Knowledge management, practically speaking" *Information Systems Management*, Fall issue, p. 7–15.

Nayyer, Kim (2006). Globalisation of information: intellectual property and law implications, at http://firstmonday.oeg/issue/issue7_1/nayyer/

Nonaka, I., Toyama, R and Konno, N. (2005). "SECI, Ba and leadership: A unified model of dynamic knowledge creation". In: *Managing knowledge: An essential reader*, ed. Stephen Little and Tim Ray, 2nd ed. London: Sage.

SCECSAL XXII (2006). *Librarianship as a bridge to an information and knowledge society in Eastern, Central and Southern Africa*. Dar es Salaam: Tanzania Library Association.

Singapore Ministry of Information and the Arts (1994) *Library 2000: Investing in a learning nation (Report of the Library 2000 Review Committee)*. Singapore: Singapore National Printers Ltd.

World Bank (1999). World Bank development report: knowledge for development. Washington: World Bank.

Kolibri 360 GmbH
Ferdinand-Jühlke-Straße 7
99095 Erfurt, Deutschland
produktsicherheit@kolibri360.de